CONTEMPORARY MAYA SPIRITUALITY

Contemporary MAYA Spirituality

THE ANCIENT WAYS
ARE NOT LOST

JEAN MOLESKY-POZ

University of Texas Press, Austin

The illustration at the beginning of the preface is by Patricia Amlin, and the
illustrations at the beginning of Chapters 1–7 are by René Humberto López Cotí.
The illustration at the beginning of the introduction is by Jean Molesky-Poz.

The photograph in Figure 1.1 was taken by Martín Poz Pérez and that in
Figure 7.1 was taken by Joanna Poz Molesky; with the exception of the photograph
in Figure 1.3, which was given to the author by Norma Quixtán de Chojoj, and
the photograph in Figure 4.7, which was given to the author by a former student,
all other photographs were taken by Jean Molesky-Poz.

Requests for permission to reproduce material from this work should be sent to:
Permissions
University of Texas Press
P.O. Box 7819
Austin, TX 78713-7819
www.utexas.edu/utpress/about/bpermission.html

♾ The paper used in this book meets the minimum requirements of
ANSI/NISO Z39.48-1992 (R1997) (Permanence of Paper).

LIBRARY OF CONGRESS CATALOGING-IN-PUBLICATION DATA

Molesky-Poz, Jean, 1947–
Contemporary Maya spirituality : the ancient ways are not lost /
Jean Molesky-Poz. — 1st ed.
p.   cm.
Includes bibliographical references and index.
ISBN-13: 978-0-292-71315-4
ISBN-10: 0-292-71309-6 (cloth : alk. paper)
1. Mayas—Religion.   2. Mayas—Guatemala—Social life and customs.
3. Maya calendar—Guatemala.   4. Rites and ceremonies—Guatemala.
5. Guatemala—Social life and customs.   I. Title.
F1435.3.R3M64   2006
299.7′842—dc22
2006001969

To Roberto Poz

To women and men Ajq'ijab' *of Guatemala*
whose enduring faith
manifests itself in a great productive love . . .

To Martín Poz

And to Joanna and Joseph, our children

Contents

Foreword

In seven chapters that reveal the ancestral and contemporary shape of the sacred geography of the Maya soul, Jean Molesky-Poz has elegantly interwoven the cosmic identity of our Maya culture. This culture that originated some fifteen or twenty thousand years ago believes and understands that humans and all that exists are part of an indivisible whole.

Jean Molesky-Poz' spirit and literary talent, which illuminates contemporary ancestral Maya spiritual beliefs and practices through ethnographic work with today's Ajq'ijab' in dialogue with archaeology, anthropology, political history, mythology, philosophy, and recent science, suggests a mythic-historical dance very much in keeping with the aesthetic foundations of space-time-movement of the life ways of a people directly related to Mother Earth, the stars, and the galaxies.

The significance of this literary work, which is concerned with an ancient spiritual tradition, contributes in essence, or better yet, calls to a return, to the harmony of being human within the cosmic cycles, which constantly reaffirms life. To return to this daily re-creation simply refers to the experience of incorporating ancestral and millenary knowledge into the ways a society conducts itself in order to discover the mystery of life. This approach allows us to infer that integrating a comprehensive and cosmic vision to solve problems of development can enrich not only sociology, law, politics, and culture, but also universal understanding. It is above all critical in these times, when new concepts for the configuration of a new kind of society—a sustainable one—are under construction.

Basic ideas about relationships, the earth, the circularity of time, ceremonial ritual, the unforeseen and the uncertain, the magical and the sacred, for example, can bring to light new perspectives about life born of experience from a vibrant and profound historical background. Surely, living like this will make us healthy, quick, and wise in our personal lives and will support the conception and implementation of policies and strategies that can resolve problems derived from the incoherence of struggling to dominate nature and to submit the lives of all humans to the plans of small groups that promote the logic of instrumental reasoning.

To be more precise, the welcoming of Maya thought and the unfolding of Maya identity in the jade reliefs crafted by Jean Molesky-Poz' plume of maize reflects a model that can forge unheard-of paths toward substantially modifying obsolete sociopolitical concepts and opening a new channel for broad and frank participation in humanity's crucial decision making about its identities and cosmovisions.

The pulse that one perceives in the reflected light throughout sister Jean Molesky-Poz' entire work allows us to appreciate objectively the fact that the millenarian peoples of the Americas constitute at their root part of the substance and future of the continent.

Jean Molesky-Poz' narrative also allows for reflection in the sense that paying attention to those who have lived in America for thousands of years can initiate and unfold an alternative—a deep, profound and long-lasting sustainable proposal for development. Among the Maya population today there is a great conviction of this. It is beginning to be seen among a large number of non-indigenous populations as well, especially now that our spirituality has risen in the national public agenda and consciousness.

The Maya people, in the context of the Peace Accords, signed in Guatemala on December 29, 1996, legitimately demand—and these demands are being recognized—more and better social, political, cultural, and economic relationships through which they can express their ideas about how to achieve the highest good for humanity. One of these proposals, perhaps the most important, asserts that rationalist approaches have not been the best ones for solving the Earth's problems in cultures that recognize and feel themselves to be part of the Earth herself.

Which brings me to the significance of Jean Molesky-Poz' work—beyond a simple, material, and historical description. In every instance, she keeps in mind that the essence of a people is rooted in their traditions, in their concepts of life, in their artistic representations, in their civil structures (e.g., their justice and conflict resolution mechanisms), in their language, in their convictions, and in their values.

It is gratifying to open the pages of the work of my friend-sister Jean Molesky-Poz, who at the dawn of this awakening envisions the new cycle of light, which for the Maya is already brightening the horizon of the planet, in order to bring to life new and ancient conceptions of the world. This awakening of life is based on the freedom for all creative activity, for all forms of self-expression and self-knowledge. This consciousness respects the autonomy of others, the principles of new science, and of intuition.

DANIEL MATUL MORALES
Quetzaltenango, Guatemala, July 2005

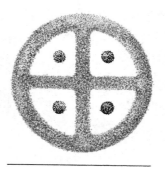

Portal
At the Dawn

At dawn on June 12, 1988, my husband, Martín, with our infant daughter on his back, and I, pregnant with our second child, pilgrimaged single-file with seventy people toward a Maya altar. Fifteen Ajq'ijab' (spiritual guides), family members, people from Zunil and from the outskirts of the village, and several friends from the United States, had joined us for the ceremony. We filed across the red-brown river, called Samala' Shikekel, which threads through Zunil in the northwestern highlands of Guatemala, and pours miles later into the Pacific. We trudged up a dirt path that wove through green cornfields, wet with morning dew. Roosters crowed, dogs barked, and children giggled, peeping over low fences as we passed their adobe homes, which dotted the hillside. Tender bean plants wound round and up the knee-high cornstalks, seeded together in groups of three, each trio planted in a little mound of earth. We threaded higher into verdant hills, the wind murmuring in the pines, until we arrived at the cave, Xe' kega ab'aj (under the red rock), near a spring of fresh water on the eastern edge of Zunil. We were presenting our child, performing a "giving thanks to the mountain" ceremony for our firstborn, Joanna, eight months old.

Several days earlier, Martín, or Atín as he was addressed in K'iche', and I had visited his ninety-four-year-old maternal grandmother in an *aldea*, a small village on the western side of the volcano, Santa María. In the dark adobe room, Doña Rosa lay in bed, her body twisted from polio, her eyes clouded from cataracts.

FIGURE 00.1. The ceremonial base is constructed with sugar, *ensarte* (pine resin discs), and other aromatic materials.

"Atín," she asked, "what took you so long to get here?"

"What do you mean, Grandma?" he asked, bending closer to her.

"I saw you walking down the road for three days."

I was stunned. No human courier, no phone message, no telegram had communicated our arrival in Guatemala to her, much less our plans to visit her. I looked at Martín. Did she have another way of seeing?

As she touched her gnarled fingers along her great granddaughter Joanna's face, we explained the upcoming ceremony. She smiled through her blindness, and said, "Oh, the 'giving thanks to the mountain' ceremony. We haven't done this for a generation. This is good. This is good. This is good for your child!"

I remembered Doña Rosa's words as we entered the cave, its walls darkened with soot. I watched Don Tino and the young Ajq'ijab' kneel before the crosses, pray in audible voices, kiss the earth, then begin to clean the large earthen hearth area. Under the direction of Don Tino, who was garbed in a self-fashioned, bright red jaguar cape, the young Ajq'ijab' prepared the ceremonial site. They poured white granules of sugar from a plastic bag in a twenty-inch diameter circle on the earth, then streamed a line of sugar from East to West, from North to South, dividing the circle in equal quarters (Figure 00.1).

"Red flowers in the East, purple flowers in the West," Don Tino directed the younger Ajq'ijab', as he pointed to the corners of the cavern, "yellow flowers in the South, white flowers in the North. Do it very well, very well."

They scattered handfuls of green pine needles around the circle of sugar, softening the ground and freshening the cave. Kneeling around the hearth, Don Tino directed the Ajq'ijab' to spiral the small *ensarte* discs (pine resin), round and round sunwise, until they filled the circle. Don Tino planted a thin green candle and then a blue one in the center of the hearth, circled the candle couplet with laurel leaves, then *ocote* (pine kindling), still glistening with sap.

Addressing the crowd of family, friends, and villagers, he directed, "It's good if you push back a little bit from the circle," indicating we were ready to begin.

Don Tino wrapped a scarf-like cloth over his head, picked up his *vara* (ritual bundle), kissed it, raised it toward the sky, then began to speak in K'iche'. I leaned closer to my husband, listening as he translated in English.

"Good morning to everyone who comes from everywhere, from far away or not too far away. And I'm going to say good morning to the people who come from the other side of the water. Some people are coming from faraway places to be with us in our tradition, which our grandparents celebrated.

"This is our religious tradition. These aliens have also come to know, to learn, to see our old customs from our grandparents. And I say, see here is Atín who comes with others from that far place to bring this little one, his little flower, and to ask to present her to the mountain, to show her to the mountain and to the face of the earth.

"That's why the parents are bringing her here to the Owner of us because we give thanks for this child. She has started crawling, walking, moving, urinating, and defecating on the face of the earth. So for all of this we have to present her to the Creator. One of the things we are going to talk to our Owner about is that the Owner pardons this child if she ever kills a bird, kills a tree, or yells at her parents. So we have to mention this lack of respect to the Creator. This child will grow up and we let her have her wisdom, her development. So we need to present her to the mountain, the Owner, the Creator. Each child is born and has a very big, wide wisdom. The child has an eye in the mind, in the heart, which we shouldn't kill."

He sprinkled sugar on the kindling, then motioned to Martín and me, "Come here, mother and father of this little one. I will tell them to make it clear what I'm going to say.

"In the name of the Heart of the Creator of the Wind, in the name of the Heart of the Creator of the Fire, in the name of the Heart of the Creator of the Water, in the name of the Heart of the Creator of the Earth, we give thanks to you that you work with us. You, Creator, you planted us, raised us, and you make us, work us. So, we give thanks to you, Creator. Thank you for all of this, all you did, all you do. Thanks for all your work. You, the one who made the road, made the mountain, who created the trees. You, the one who created all the animals in the world. You made the road for the rivers, the ones who live in the house, the ones who live in the mountains. You create all the trees, all the weeds, all the animals who take care of the mountains. You create the air, the clouds, the wind. You make the farther and the closer. You worked on it; you put your seeds on it. You created it; you worked on it. And we remember those who never give thanks to what you made. For all of your children, who never remember you, we wish that you wouldn't place any sickness on them. Don't abandon them."

Then calling names of Maya heroines/heroes, he continued, "Ixmucane, Xpiyacoc, Junajpu, Xb'alanke, B'atz'. We're here. Those who call you, these really pray, really beg you in the night of the darkness, in the day, in the sun, in front of the stars, in the wind, in the drizzle, in the mists, in the thunder, in the rocks, for all those in this sacred cave. These are the words that our ancestors gave us. And that's how it started when the light hadn't yet come, when it was not clear.

"In the name of the Heart of the Creator of the Wind, in the name of the Heart of the Creator of the Fire, in the name of the Heart of the Creator of the Water, in the name of the Heart of the Creator of the Earth," he continued, as we signed ourselves again on our forehead, our stomach, our left shoulder, then right, the Catholic sign of the cross.

Don Tino knelt and kissed the earth; we followed his directions. As I kissed the earth, tenderness welled up and passed from my lips to the damp soil under the pine needles.

"Everyone, stand up and we'll begin."

He lit the blue and green candles centered in the altar. "Heart of Heaven, this is how our ancestors talked with the people. This is what the *Pop Wuj* says, "You are the Creator, Former. Don't leave us. Give us ancestors forever. Give us peace, good descendants. B'alam K'iche', they said all the prayers." The candle couplet caught fire, flames raced across the aromatic ceremonial materials, and burst into tongues of fire, sending up clouds of incense. As a young Ajq'ij stirred the fire, the flames brightened, blazed, and danced.

Don Tino picked up Joanna and cradled her close to his breast.

"We've come to the mountain. Father, Mother, talk to us. Look at us. We've come to present to you, one Ajmaq, two Ajmaq, three Ajmaq . . . thirteen Ajmaq. They that made them, worked them. Our ancestors, people who planted, cultivated corn, the house maker who worked night and day."

Don Tino held our daughter several feet above the fire and then circled her sunwise over the fire four times.

Offerings—hundreds of tossed tallow candles, chocolate, alcohol, sesame seeds, *copal* (incense) and *cuilco* (tokens/discs of pressed, dried resin)—sizzled in the fire as Don Tino called out and honored each of the 260 days of the Chol Q'ij, the sacred calendar. A rooster and hen, one after another, were presented to the fire. Each head was snapped off, each heart torn out. Don Tino rubbed the heart on the soles of our daughter's feet, then pressed the throbbing hearts into the right palm of our hands: Martín received the hen's, I the rooster's. Don Tino directed us to offer the hearts to the fire, then toss them in.

"Accept this Father, Mother. We're giving this to you in the air, in the wind, in the darkness with stars, in the day, with the moon, in the day of sun. Take it in the fire. Take it in the clouds. We're giving this to you. This is what we bring. This is our gift, our payment to you, to your face, to your lips, to your eyes, to your nose, to your hands, to your feet."

Don Tino dismembered the remainder of the fowls' flailing bodies and tossed them into the blaze.

"These are the words, Creator," continued Don Tino, "give her knowledge, goodness, favor, wisdom."

The fire leapt. "We give this as a present to you. You give us wisdom and knowledge. Thank you so much."

The fire was fed, flames leapt high. The fire would talk. Utterances, oriented toward a transcendent consciousness, undertaken in a spirit of "aesthetic love," asked forgiveness, pardon, trusting that the Owner of us all would "accept our offering, but also give back to us."

At one point, Don Tino poured a clear liquid from a dark bottle into a transparent cup, and instructed the godparents, Roberto and Lesbia, to give it to Joanna (Figure 00.2).

Don Tino explained, "The water is virgin, collected from the leaves of the trees this morning before dawn. So, it's very special water."

They gave a small sip to Joanna, but she started coughing and choking.

"Don't let her choke! Don't let her choke!" Don Tino yelled. "Help her drink it!"

FIGURE 00.2. At the "giving thanks to the mountain" ceremony for the birth of a child, the infant is given dew that has been collected at dawn.

"Pay attention to what I'm saying," he said, realizing the crowd was distracted. "These are the words of our grandparents. The day comes, and we all have to go back, they say. And they went back where the day ends. We are going back and we'll be saying bye, bye. We'll have to say good-bye to our houses, to our land. We're going back to where we came from. These are the words that our grandparents left, that we're remembering and mentioning now."

For two hours, the fire was fed, stirred, and addressed; flames leapt, twisted, spiraled within the circle, until the simmering embers gradually dimmed. Don Tino picked up the stick, stirred the coals, spread them out, studying the small traces of rising white smoke, waiting until every last ember was burnt, until the last bit of incense had been set free. The Ajq'i-jab', their faces blackened, seared from close attention to the fire, gazed intently at the smoke.

This event recalled the ritual narrated in *Popol Wuj*, when the first people, fashioned of white and yellow corn, "givers of praise, givers of respect," lifted their faces, made their fasts and prayers, just watching intently, waiting for the dawn. They saw the sun carrier, the morning star, Venus. They unwrapped their *copal*, burned their incense. When the first sun, the moon, and the stars appeared, they rejoiced.

They were overjoyed when it dawned . . . Their dawning was there and they burned *copal* there, incensing the direction of the rising sun. They came from there; it is their own mountain, their own plain. Those named Jaguar Quitze, Jaguar Night, Not Right Now, and Dark Jaguar came from there, and they began their increase on that mountain. (D. Tedlock 1985, 182)

That dawn the ceremony initiated not only our daughter, but also me. Little did I know what was before me.

In years of sustained work, I would travel in and out of Maya and Western storehouses, linger over and grasp to an extent the logic of Maya cosmovision and its recent public emergence, to conceive an aesthetic whole. In attending to the distinctiveness of Maya spiritual practices, I would learn to take seriously and even lovingly the particularity of this tradition. I would engage in dialogues and conversations, which would unfold in depth, in *creative activity*. I did not on that morning imagine myself seeking conversations with scientists whose job is to describe "the mysteries of physical existence as far as possible and sincerely show the edges of such knowledge," as well as with religious studies partners "who deal with our personal consciousness and . . . how we establish our stance toward the mysteries of both the physical and the personal" (E. Carlson 1995, 88). I did not know I would engage with theologians who investigate and interpret the human experience of Mystery through the field of theological anthropology, nor with cultural studies technicians who posit theories of time and space, of knowledge and power, of discursive practices, of thinking and acting in images. Nor that I would examine the genealogy of the long, tyrannical, silencing shadow, a creeping, violent hegemony of terror, which spread from Spain to reach the remote corners of the Maya highlands, driving religious practices underground. The quest would lead me to a dialogic *live entering* with contemporary Maya conversation partners about the very valid and significant Maya spiritual practices and beliefs, which provide a localized meaning and assertion of agency, nurturing strength, hope, and community identity. I now release this understanding into its own time and space, from my horizon.

That morning, pregnant with our second child, I stood in a cave, which the Maya understand as a portal between the world of humans—specifically, the invisible world of their ancestors—and the Great Mystery. Little did I know that I was about to begin going backward and forward in time, that I was entering "a world whose obligation [the Ajq'ijab'] know to be older than Christianity, obligations to the mountains and places where they continue to live and to all those who have ever lived there before them" (D. Tedlock 1985, 62). Little did I know that morning, that the Maya, because of an entry of historical forces, were on the brink of emerging and unfolding from a cycle of darkness, into a new dawning on the face of the earth.

The ceremony was over. Joanna, enfolded in the bright woven striped cloth of Zunil, now lay asleep and tranquil in Martín's arms. Roberto turned to us and said, "This ceremony is very, very good. The child will have a good future."

Shortly after, as we walked down the mountain, I called to Martín, following behind. "Martín, there is so much I don't understand about all this."

"There's a lot I don't understand either," he called out. "But I respect Roberto and the ways of my ancestors. We will learn what we need for our journeys and for the lives of our children. My ancestors used to say 'as we do good, it will come back to us. Nothing is lost.'"

We zigzagged back down through the cornfields, and I watched the leaves of the corn plants slap and wave in the wind, their yellow tassels, the daughters of the plants, tossing their limbs in the morning air. Doña Rosa had prophesized, "This is good. This is good. This is good for your child." Perhaps as the "grandmother of day, grandmother of light" she had seen from her position of age and experience that "this is the sign" of dawn for the new generation.

This ceremony coincided with the emergence of a new spatial sphere of historical existence among the indigenous, a generative time marked in part by an overt reclamation of ancestral spiritual traditions. This book documents, contextualizes, and illuminates the distinctiveness of Maya spiritual traditions through diverse interdisciplinary lenses.

Acknowledgments

I owe profound gratitude to many persons without whose support this book could not have become a reality. My first debt of gratitude is twofold: to Roberto Poz Pérez, my brother-in-law, and to Calixta Gabriel, without whom this work would not have been begun. I want to acknowledge María del Carmen Tuy, who has generously helped me over the years to clarify and deepen in understanding Maya spirituality. I am indebted to the women and men of Komun Tohil, particularly Doña Marta Chávez, Vilma Poz, Berta Quiej Tamayac, Catarina Kiej, Faustina Chay Poz, Catarina Wix, Edgar Rolando Ixcot, Juan Quiej Wix, and Ixquic Poz, each of whom has generously shared ceremonies, rituals, their life stories, and friendships with me. In Quetzaltenango, many have contributed to this ethnographic work: the city's mayor, Rigoberto Keme Chay, María Antonieta Cofulum, Aura María Cotí, Audelino Sac Coy, Carlos Escalante, Jorge Hernández, Victor Lem Masc, Norma Quixtán, and Cayetano Rosales. I thank also Professor Victor Ruben Ovando for his generous sharings on Maya cosmovision and visits to ritual sites. I want to especially recognize Tom Hart, an Irish national and Ajq'ij who has contributed extensively to this search. Further, conversations in Quetzaltenango with Tom Hart and Lena Knutsson, an Ajq'ij from Sweden, have greatly assisted me in understanding the profound attraction of Maya spirituality to non-Guatemalans as well as the complexities of carrying on the spiritual responsibilities in transnational contexts, material I was unable to incorporate within the boundaries of this book. I want to recognize René Humberto López Cotí, an emerging K'iche' artist in Quetzaltenango, for his complementary illustrations. Finally, I thank Daniel Matul Morales for extensive conversations over the years and for a generous foreword.

In the greater highlands, conversations with many individuals have influenced this work profoundly. They include Anastasia Mejia Tiriquic, María Can Sahony and Pablo Pérez, Jesús Jutzuy and Tomás Lucás Morales, Miguel Matías Miguel, Ajq'ijab'; Martín Chacach, sociolinguist; José Mucía Batz Lem, writer. In Guatemala City, Professors Narciso Cotjí and Father Antonio Gallo, S. J., provided sociological contexts for understanding Maya identity and the contemporary emergence of spirituality; Sam Colop assisted in careful rendering of terms. To the Catholic priests—Victoriano Castillo González, S.J., of Santa María Chiquimula, and Bascilio Chacach Tzoy and Tomás García, of Quetzaltenango diocese—goes my profound gratitude for conversations on the emerging theological issues and social processes of Catholicism and Maya spirituality.

In the United States, I have been influenced and assisted by many people along the way. From the beginning, Judith Thorn set me on track with Mikhail Bakhtin's theoretical contributions. This work would not have its particular shape without her bold moral concern and complex comprehension of ethical responsibility and its potentiality. Patricia Amlin, producer of the award-winning animated film *Popol Vuh*, provided inspiration and friendship which has encouraged me throughout; her creative vision shaped the aesthetic presentation. To other friends who have supported and illuminated this venture, I owe thanks to Clare Fischer and Judith Berling of the Graduate Theological Union; and to Rosemary Joyce and Martha Macri at the University of California. I am grateful for the inspired and inspiring support of Diana Wear, whose intelligence, patience, and attention to editorial details helped bring this to completion, and to Virginia Bouvier for translation of Matul's foreword. I am grateful to Leonie Neuhaus for making valuable comments; to Bonnie Hardwick at the Graduate Theological Union library, who provided the quiet carrel to complete this work. I am grateful to the Hayes-Fulbright, which allowed six months of valuable time for concentrated research in Guatemala. Finally, I express my sincere gratitude to editors at the University of Texas Press: Theresa May, Allison Faust, Lynne Chapman, Nancy Bryan, Sue Carter; and to the two reviewers for invaluable comments.

Most of all, I am indebted to my husband, Martín Poz Pérez, who has walked with me along the whole process with patient endurance. In fieldwork and many conversations, he has selected, extended, and clarified K'iche' Maya ways, contributing a fine honing of cultural and linguistic details. Finally, to our children, Joanna and Joseph, I offer thanks for their patience, understanding, and good humor as they waited for me to finish this work.

CONTEMPORARY MAYA SPIRITUALITY

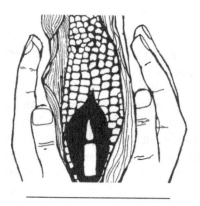

Introduction

The highlands of Guatemala and of southern Mexico, a predominately indigenous region, are unique in terms of relationships between religion and indigenous populations. These communities, with legacies of traditional Maya[1] beliefs and practices for tens of thousands of years, have been the objects of many religious projects in the past five centuries: the long tyrannical shadow which passed from the north in Pedro de Alvarado's invasion in 1524; the imposition of Spanish Catholicism during the colonial period; the introduction of Protestantism during the anticlerical liberal years of 1870–1926; projects of Catholic Action in the 1950s; and the more recent U.S.-exported missions, which have ushered in an expansive growth of evangelical Protestantism since the 1970s. The political and religious trajectory of each endeavor has attempted to inscribe its own construction of knowledge and power on indigenous people. Religious discrimination and conflict have marked the history in distinct, and sometimes extreme, ways. The responses of indigenous communities to these projects have been varied, and deeply complex.

Over the centuries, ancestral practices, often masked or shrouded in secrecy, have continued to sustain highland people. Due to their geographical remoteness and high altitudes, they were relatively inaccessible to colonial Spaniards, the liberal reforms of the 1870s, and pastoral visits from Catholic priests. The highland communities developed religious teachings and rituals relatively free from control of the Catholic hierarchy (Earle 1995; Falla 2001; Lovell 1992; Oss 1986). Compared to areas of intense Spanish activity, such as the eastern lowlands, where the process of syncretism may better explain religious developments, Maya in these relatively neglected zones were able to construct and maintain distinct theological systems and spiritual practices. The Maya strategy of resistance was to appropriate when necessary Catholic icons, rituals, and social organizations as well as to maintain a religious-based civil authority system in order to ensure at least some cultural autonomy (Earle 1995). Today, indigenous communities, cultural workers, ethnographers, and educators, as well as Western scholars, recognize that elements of Maya belief and their public expressions in the form of ritual dances, calendar keeping, prayers, and ceremonialism have never been completely suppressed (Oakes 1951; Gossen 1974: Bricker 1981; B. Tedlock 1982; Farris 1984; D. Tedlock 1985; Freidel et al. 1993; La Farge 1994; Alvarado 1997; Earle 1995; Carlsen 1997a; Cook 2000; Christenson 2001).

Maya spiritual leaders say that 40–50% of the indigenous population practice some form of indigenous ritual, but only 10% do so openly. Observance varies. In some highland communities, 45–80% of the people follow traditional practices; in other communities only 5–10% have conserved Maya practices (Molesky-Poz 1999, 2004). And, while there are uniform underpinnings of belief, upon a closer look, there is much diversity in the particular beliefs, with distinct genealogies and practices in which religious inscriptions are embedded. That is, there are differences between villages as well as within the same village in the maintenance of traditional beliefs and practices. Further, there have been periods in history when communities have concealed or publicly practiced their ancestral worship.

This work, which examines the contemporary public emergence of Maya spirituality, is situated in the western highlands of Guatemala, a country of 12 million inhabitants, approximately 60% of whom are Maya of twenty-two distinct language groups. From its inception, this ethnographic project sought through dialogues with Ajq'ijab' (keepers of the 260-day calendar) to comprehend contemporary praxis, perceptions, and theological underpinnings of contemporary Maya ancestral beliefs and practices. The inquiry grew to an investigation of archaeology, anthropology, political history, mythology, and hieroglyphics. Coincidentally, this study concurred with Guatemala's burgeoning pan-Maya movement, in which some indigenous women and men are reclaiming ancestral spirituality and worldview as the basis of their cultural and political renaissance. This chronotope, then, opened a venue to examine its distinct theological system and praxis, but also how Maya are reappropriating, generating, and shaping contemporary forms of Maya spirituality.

In addition, creative dialogues with scientists, philosophers, and theologians regarding the surfacing paradigm of Emergence[2] have influenced me to view this faith practice as a variation of human experience which over generations has developed a specific sentient, ecological, religious consciousness with its own distinct spiritual, aesthetic, and ethical activity. This work intends to contribute visibility, understanding, and respect for these indigenous religious traditions, to contribute to efforts for legal recognition in Guatemala, and to encourage interreligious dialogue.

GENEALOGY OF THIS WORK

In a sense this ethnographic work has been "the start of a different journey." Calixta, a young Kaqchikel woman who assumed the name "Eugenia" in exile in the United States, first introduced me to Mayan thoughts, worldviews, and ceremony in 1980 (see Chapter 3). A year later, in San Francisco, she introduced me to Martín, a K'iche' from Zunil, to whom I am now married.

On my first trip to Guatemala in the mid-'80s, I was particularly anxious to meet Martín's brother, Roberto, as Martín had spoken of him so often. I knew of his attempted arrest and murder by village rivals in 1980, and that he had gone into hiding for two years. I knew that he was married to Lesbia, a woman from the neighboring village of Cantel; that they were parents of two daughters and one son. What I came to know on that first visit was that after recurring dreams, illnesses, and problems from 1980 to 1983, Roberto had decided to become an Ajq'ij (calendar keeper). When I first met him in 1985, he was deeply devoted to understanding the 260-day sacred calendar.

One evening on that first visit, I sat across the wooden table from Roberto in the soot-walled kitchen. Lesbia, attentive and listening, stirred the *atole* (corn drink) over the wood-burning stove, one child on her back, another tugging at her *corte* (woven skirt) while gray kittens scampered underfoot. What attracted my attention to Roberto was his open, intense, yet calm countenance. When he spoke, he guarded his broken teeth with his thick right hand, his dark brown eyes reflected his openness and kindness, and his words resonated a deep reserve of wisdom. I asked him about Maya spirituality. Roberto was at first silent and meditative. He cleared his throat, then said, "Among the Maya, there is no theological doctrine, just an encounter with the cosmos." For long hours into the night, and on many other evenings, we conversed. He mapped the Maya calendar, unlocking meanings and complexities of specific days and illustrating their interrelationships. Our discourse traced his decision to become an Ajq'ij and went on to explanations of circuits of energies from his increasing perception of the motions that ran through his body. In sharing, we were traversing similar inner geographies; yet our words, maps, calendars, rituals, myths, and icons were different. I was situated in Catholicism, formed in particular by ten years in a Franciscan religious community, he within a Maya paradigm.

This story, then, begins through specific relationships with Calixta, Martín, and Roberto. It extends primarily to women and men in Komon Tohil, an informal group of thirty Ajq'ijab' founded by Roberto in Zunil, to a wider circle of contacts in Quetzaltenango as well as to multilocal ethnographies in the greater highlands. I have talked with Guatemalan scholars and cultural workers as well as several Catholic priests in whose parishes members are actively working to reconcile historical fractures and hatreds. These friendships initiated and deepened as we returned to the Guatemalan highlands for summers between 1988 and 2003 and for seven months in 1997.

I have come to understand that Maya spirituality is not a conservative, static survival of the past nor a syncretic Catholic development. I understand and interpret it as theologically distinct, with its own logic and processes. Maya women and men establish a relationship to the world, unique in time, space, and culture. Those who embrace Maya cosmovision and their obligation as Ajq'ijab' are living aesthetic and ethical lives, shaped by their own "field of vision" or "horizon of being." Again, this ancestral practice is but one of many faith expressions undertaken in Guatemala today; the religious diversity is very visible.

Of course, the "I" who writes here must also be thought of as itself "enunciated." We all write and speak from a particular place and time, from a history and a culture, which is specific. What we say is always "in context," *positioned.* I came to the Maya as an insider/outsider: insider through marriage and friendship and outsider as a non-indigenous North American woman, attentive to religion, culture, and spirituality in its various expressions. Many aspects of Maya cosmovision and spirituality are attractive to me, particularly situating and engaging ourselves as persons within the physical universe.

My position as an ethnographer, then, is unique to this project. Through friendship, marriage, and thus family ties, I have been brought into the Maya community. Over seventeen years, I have developed relationships through which I have cultivated a unique perspective and voice. Further, as mother to our children, Joanna and Joseph, I have a stake in understanding the religious heritage from which they, in part, will understand their capacities and potentials and thus navigate their lives.

At a foundational level, the aim of intrareligious dialogue is to understand. When seen against a wider and common horizon, divergences and common perspectives appear. Russian philosopher Mikhail Bakhtin writes that dialogue is a matter of "communication between simultaneous differences." His notion of the "dialogic imagination" holds that discourse or conversation—the enlargement of consciousness through the dialogic engagement with alterity—provides a most appropriate model of human experience. What issues from dialogue, he says, is creative understanding, which explores the *surplus of seeing,* in terms of both interpersonal and intercultural relationships (Morson and Emerson, 1990, 52–56). In this work, I hope to provide what Bakhtin calls *the excess of seeing* and *sympathetic understanding* (1990, 25).

When I write from my experience, I am engaging in what Bakhtin calls "live entering." He writes that if one's relationship with another is to be rendered meaningful—ethically, cognitively, or aesthetically—it requires "live entering," a simultaneous experience of empathy and "outsideness" (1990, 25–27). He writes that if one is to help or understand a particular person one must first "empathize or project myself into this other human being, see his world axiologically from within him as he sees this world." As one does so, "a whole series of features accessible to me from my own place will turn out to be absent from within this other's horizon." There must also be "a return to one's own place," because only from this place will one be able to "render" the other ethically, cognitively, or aesthetically.

What comes into view in *Contemporary Maya Spirituality* is "not a mirroring or duplication," but a fundamentally and essentially new valuation, what Bakhtin calls *sympathetic understanding* (1990, 102). The form, rhythm, language, and concepts of time and space of Maya spiritual practices are distinct from mine; I have found that entering into the Maya worldview has been deeply transformative and generative. As Bakhtin writes, *sympathetic understanding* "recreates the whole inner person in aesthetically loving categories for a new existence in a new dimension of the world" (103).

In one of my recent interviews with Roberto Poz, he turned off his tape recorder; I turned off mine. He looked at me and said,

Juana, with open arms, come what comes. What is very important is our dialogue, so that every time we speak, we increase, with more aesthetics and ethics. Aesthetics because you can amplify; ethics because we learn to live. Like *Pop Wuj,* our conversation is poetic, mystical, and historical.

As translator and interpreter of this work, I have attempted to attune myself as accurately as possible to the speech and textures of meaning manifested in dialogues with Ajq'ijab'. I understand that in this interpretive
translation, the quality and texture of Maya religious experiences are not
similar to mine. All experience is processed through, organized by, and
makes itself available to us epistemologically (Katz 1978, 26). Here
Steven T. Katz's work on cross-cultural interpretations of mysticism is
helpful. He writes, "In order to understand mysticism it is not just a question of studying the reports of the mystic after the experiential event but
of acknowledging that the experience itself as well as the form in which it
is reported is shaped by concepts which the mystic brings to, and which
shape, his experience" (26). The issue is not the experience, but its consciousness:

> The respective "generating" problems at the heart of each tradition sug-
> gest their respective alternative answers involving differing mental and
> epistemological constructs, ontological commitments, and metaphysical
> superstructures which order experience in differing ways. (62)

This interpretation of ancestral spirituality is further a translation
passed through a continuum of transformations in the interplay of
K'iche', Spanish, and English. We conversed in Spanish, the language we
hold in common; yet Spanish was the second language for nearly all. Conversations required occasional "halts" to dialogue with one another in order to capture the cultural context, the accumulated meaning of a word.
In conversations where participants spoke K'iche', Martín, my husband,
facilitated the translation between K'iche' and Spanish or English, often
stopping to encircle or "fill out" the word or experience with cultural qualities. This helped me to attune to the layers and textures of meaning. Even
finer tuning has taken place as Martín, Roberto, and I have dialogued with
one another over a kitchen table or in long-distance phone calls between
Zunil and Berkeley.

With permission of participants, most interviews were audiotaped and
ceremonies were videotaped. I transcribed and translated these oral accounts into written English; Martín translated the ceremonies which were
in K'iche' and I transcribed them from Spanish into English. In these tran-
scriptions, I noted that a K'iche' speaker or Spanish speaker of K'iche' de-
scent would refer to him/herself as "we" or as "one," not directly engaging in the personal pronoun "I." I have maintained this grammatical
pattern in my English translation as I feel it conveys the sense of their

identity, of being "of a people," part of an "event of being." In the case of translation from a text written in Spanish to English, I am responsible for its interpretation. Further, I recognize that this ethnographic text, written in English, takes place within relations of "weak" and "strong languages" that govern the international flow of knowledge (Asad 1986, 141–146). Finally, I suspect the metaphoric, relational, and multidimensional texture of the K'iche' language is flattened and objectified in English.

The primary goal of this book is to illuminate ancestral Maya spiritual beliefs and practices that have significance for individual, collective, and historical lives. This work is concerned with a viable spiritual tradition, the theology of which has woven itself into the fabric of Mayan life. It investigates this tradition's underpinning order and its theological constructs and processes while recognizing its distinct diversity in practical forms and methods. Marcus and Fischer write that ethnography should "continue to provide a convincing access to diversity in the world at a time when the perception, if not the reality, of this diversity is threatened by modern consciousness" (1986, 167). This ethnographic work intends to examine this "valid and significant" spirituality and treat it as seriously as we do other religious forms.

More specifically, illuminated through the narratives of Ajq'ijab', this work documents, contextualizes, and interprets the meaning of Maya spiritual practices and their public emergence since the mid-1980s. It further looks at the ways women and men are reappropriating ancestral cosmovision and logic, sacred time and place, and myth and ritual in the process of reconstructing viable identities and "practicing [their] own inventive loyalty toward self" (Minh-Ha 1991, 17).

It is my intention to create a polyphonic text, "to foreground dialogue as opposed to monologue, and emphasize the cooperative and collaborative nature of the ethnographic situation" (Tyler 1986, 126). The statements we hear come to us already dialogized, already thought and spoken about, already evaluated. Consequently each individual perspective is unique; words and forms exist in the speakers as they exist in their social world, as "living impulse," with a memory and an activity (Morson and Emerson 1990, 145). Each utterance embodies a worldview, a perspective shaped by his/her position. For clarification, I do not intend in any way to present the narratives as *the* Maya position nor to collapse their diverse standpoints for this emergence into one Maya view. Instead of interpreting what Bakhtin warns us is a false tendency toward reducing everything to a single consciousness (60), a unity of a world emerges that is essentially one of multiple voices and polyphonic. In this polyphony, we can hear the "living impulse" of a public emergence. This, then, is a cooperative story, one that is shaped by reflective dialogic activity. To accomplish these goals, the book is organized in the following manner:

In Part 1, *The Florescence of Maya Spirituality*, Chapter 1, "A New Cycle of Light," engages the public emergence of Maya spiritual practices, discussing the cultural and political context of this emergence and addressing the question of why this florescence is happening at this particular historical juncture. Chapter 2, "Maya Cosmovision and Spirituality," identifies the foundational principles and distinct marks of Maya cosmovision, the basis of Maya spirituality. In Part 2, *A Cultural Inheritance*, Chapter 3, "Ajq'ijab'," focuses on the role, capacity, and responsibility of the Ajq'ijab' as a key cultural inheritance, and is in many ways the heart of this research. Here, contemporary Ajq'ijab' interpret their lives and work. This chapter explores the activity of Maya Ajq'ijab' from the perspective of the philosophical anthropology of Mikhail M. Bakhtin, who states that "the problem of the soul from a methodological standpoint, is a problem in aesthetics" (1990, xl). I draw on Bakhtin because it is clear that he was interested in religion in terms of its immanent meaning for human consciousness as one of the categories through which the self is constructed.

Part 3, *The Aesthetics of Space, Time, and Movement*, provides the conceptual blueprint for understanding distinct images of sacred space, time, and ritual practice, built up over time. This section investigates ethnography, archaeology, political history, mythology, and hieroglyphs to illuminate root meanings and transformed continuities in contemporary understandings and practices. Chapter 4, "Sacred Geography," addresses the reciprocity between humans and the earth, the mappings of sacred geography, and quatrefoil cartography as inscribed in ancient and contemporary landscapes. Chapter 5, "The Calendar," presents the Chol Q'ij, the 260-day sacred calendar, as the central matrix of a culture. Chapter 6, "Ceremony," investigates one form of spiritual practice, the ceremonial fire. It identifies the centrality of fire, its legacy in Mesoamerica, and how contemporary Ajq'ijab' understand the fire as a conduit between humans and the sacred. Attention is given to the reading of the fire as a form of discernment, as one way of knowing, in this spiritual praxis. Finally, Part 4, *Thinking, Contemplating, and Acting into the Future*, contains Chapter 7, "The Ancient Things Received from Our Parents Are Not Lost," which raises issues, questions, and potentialities regarding the public reclamation of Maya spirituality.

Part 1

THE FLORESCENCE OF MAYA SPIRITUALITY

CHAPTER 1

A New Cycle of Light
The Public Emergence of Maya Spirituality

I was waiting outside the popular Doña Luisa restaurant in Antigua at 7:00 a.m. when I saw the energetic figure approaching down the cobblestone street lined with adobe and Spanish tiled-roof shops. From his deliberate, quick gait, I recognized Martín Chacach, a Kaqchikel-Maya linguist from the University of Rafael Landívar whom I had met a month before in Quetzaltenango. He had delivered a lecture to a group of young Maya bilingual educators on the resurgence of Maya culture. We exchanged greetings, and then he motioned for us to enter the colonial courtyard. We took seats at one of the tables along the patio wall and each ordered a cup of coffee. Small groups of middle-aged tourists and young students were beginning their day over breakfast in the open-air courtyard, bright and warm with morning light.

"Don Martín, thank you for meeting with me this morning," I began. "As I mentioned to you, I want to talk with you about the rebirth of Maya spirituality."

"Yes, recently Maya have been public, drawing their spirituality out into the light," he commenced. "It's evident at the initiation of cultural and national events. Groups are using the services of the Ajq'ijab' so that their activities are successful, asking God that all should go well. There is a rebirth, a new dawning of Maya spirituality, philosophy, and cultural pride in Guatemala. In fact, it is a movement that can not be stopped."

"And what is the root of this emergence?" I asked, pressing to understand.

Don Martín paused, took a sip of coffee, and set the cup on the table. "It's about understanding our own philosophy, how our world is in relation to

God, to nature, to humanity. We lost much, we did not lose ourselves, but we lost much that is a dynamic form of life over five hundred years. It was an attitude. Colonized, we were not able to speak. But now, we look around us and reassess our lives. We begin to make comparisons to establish and maintain a cosmic equilibrium."

"What do you mean, you make comparisons?" I asked, puzzled.

"We see one single plant, one human being, one fruit, yet we recognize that we all share in the life of one another. If we take care of the plants, they will take care of us. In our way of understanding, we wake up in the morning, greet the four points, Señor Tat, the sun. We greet adults in the house, in the street. We greet one another with the same respect.

"You and I understand that every child is conceived at a particular time and place, so there is no doubt that this person has a distinct cultural root. But if one considers, as we Maya do, that all this is bound up with what happens in the cosmos, it is not simply a cultural question. It is beyond culture, into a cosmological reality. It would be good to have a conference with Hindus, with Buddhists, to see that it is part of a larger feeling, a larger ecological reality.

"This rebirth of Maya culture, spirituality, and intellectuality," he continued, redirecting the conversation, "is bound to the will of the people. It is a dynamic process and has a life, like the life of a people. It ebbs and flows. We have to use Maya resources, resources of the people and of the world. The life of all people emerges and dissipates. For example, the United States has the power now, but for how long will it have this power?

"In my case, my parents were very Catholic. I grew up in the country, but was not exposed to Maya spiritual ways. It was not affirmed, so now I am reclaiming it."

"Do you think that there are more Maya Ajq'ijab' now?" I inquired.

"Yes. I also think Ajq'ijab' have to be more public. Now, most practice their spirituality privately. Catholics have their masses on television; fundamentalists broadcast their predictions on television. Why don't we have Maya ceremonies on television? Maya spirituality must have public light. People need to know our spirituality, not as folklore, nor as a tourist event, but as an integral part of our cultural lives."

"What are the obstacles to this reemergence?" I asked.

"I see with good eyes," he continued, nodding, then looking into the distance. "We have some obstacles. Our people are poor. We need teachers, curricular guides, and schools. Poverty doesn't allow it to happen. We need economic support from other countries. At this historical moment, we have to heal. We have our own existence; but also others, too, have to support our existence. This is the process of peace. Each culture has a right to be. This is the *balance that we look for. We have to look at our spirituality because there we find our philosophy, our dialogues, our rituals."*

He glanced at his watch. Knowing he had to catch a bus soon, I thanked him. We bid one another farewell. Don Chacach picked up his briefcase and headed to Guatemala City.

THE PUBLIC EMERGENCE OF MAYA SPIRITUALITY

At dawn at a selected altar in the Guatemalan highlands, a gathering of people, led by Ajq'ijab', encircle a fire and in prayer remember the names of ancestors, recalling their suffering, silence, persistent patience, and endurance. They lift up their hearts and voices in thanksgiving to petition and procure strength before the rising flames and incense. Nearby in the city of Quetzaltenango, on 4 K'anil, the day of the 260-day sacred calendar on which the new proprietors decided to open their small cafe, the invited Ajq'ij directs the owners to place red, black, white, and yellow candles and flowers in designated four corners and set the blue and green ones in the center, as family and friends gather for a ceremony of initiation. In Patzun, an embroiderer raises a silver needle, the yellow thread catching the light, and pierces the red-and-white striped woven cloth; she brocades the next glyph of the twenty-day signs circling the neckline of a *huipil* (woven and embroidered blouse). In Sololá, an Ajq'ij runs her hands across the *tz'ite'* beans, and in counting the days and attending to the movements in her body, advises the troubled client. In Salcaja, an Ajq'ij is invited to explain Maya spirituality to Presbyterian seminarians; the next week, he addresses students on the Maya calendar at the University of Rafael Landívar in Guatemala City. In recent years Ajq'ijab' have prayed publicly with widows and children before their husbands and sons' assassinated bodies are exhumed from mass graves. Thousands of miles to the north, in Mission Dolores Park in San Francisco, California, eighty people gather at dawn around the fire as the transnational Ajq'ij explains the significance of the Maya New Year ceremony. In every instance, indigenous cosmovision is being brought to a new, liberating expression. Maya who interpret their lives in cycles of time, in folds of darkness and light, speak of a new cycle of light, a florescence of Maya identity, culture, and spirituality. "For the Maya, things are hidden, revealed, hidden, revealed," explains Miguel Matías, a Kanjobal Ajq'ij. "This is a time of manifestation." (See Figures 1.1, 1.2, and 1.3.)

What marks this public emergence of Maya spiritual practices since the mid-1980s in Guatemala? To appreciate fully the significance of these now

FIGURE 1.1. A community gathers at Chuwi pek for a Wajxaqib' B'atz ceremony in Zunil.

open acts requires us to situate the recent historical context, to examine the social and political processes for this current emergence, and to ask the question: Why is it happening at this historical juncture?

Emergence, the coming out from a hidden realm to the light above, echoes the activity of the ancient Mesoamerican ball game, where the ball symbolizes the disappearance of the sun into the underworld and its rising after a nightly journey through the darkness. The planted kernel of corn also replicates emergence as it germinates in the dark, moist soil, surfaces into light, and sprouts stalk, leaves, ears, and tassels. Emergence is the exploration and expression of all potentialities for life.

Philosophers and scientists in the West labor to interpret the increased complexity emerging in the universe over 14.5 billion years. From matter, life, mind, and consciousness, spirit emerges in slow progressions. Process theologians and scientists explain that disorder is a condition for the emergence of new forms of order, further extending the concept. Michel Foucault wrote that emergence designates the moment of an arising, and "is always produced through a particular stage of forces" (1985, 83).

I will borrow a framework from Dr. George Ellis,[1] who discusses the activity of emergence in his Five Levels of Emergence within the universe, to show this development.

His paradigm understands human community as a group of complex and comprehensive systems which have finally become selves. These selves are conscious, knowing, loving, free, volitional, and responsible agents. For Ellis, in the process of emergence, existence is a feedback control system which assumes or requires reflective humanity interacting in an ecological environment, while *striving toward* explicit goals. These goals, which are related to memory, are influenced by specific events in individual history. For humans—as distinct from other living organisms—these goals have been explicitly experienced through language systems, and are determined by a symbolic understanding of complex modeling of the physical and social environment. Therefore, we can say that culture, informed by language and symbol making, shapes the neurology as well as the neurological development, of individuals.

FIGURE 1.2. Maya educators held the First Congress of Maya Education in Xelajú (Quetzaltenango), Guatemala, August 8–11, 1994. The banner announces, "The time has arrived. We reinitiate the cycle of the light . . ."

FIGURE 1.3. Norma Quixtán de Chojoj was elected governor of Quetzaltenango (Xelajú) in 2003; in April 2005 she was appointed Secretary of Peace, a national position created in 1997 to oversee the Peace Accords. She is founder and director of Centro de la Mujer Belejeb' B'atz, an association of indigenous women in Quetzaltenango area whose goal is to gain cultural, economic, and political rights. Photo courtesy of Norma Quixtán de Chojoj.

I understand the contemporary reclamation of Maya cosmovision to be a specific example of Ellis' formulation.

People develop forms of consciousness, which are distinct as they relate to a particular geography and community. As we shall see, at this historical juncture, some Maya have begun to reexamine their ancestral ways and spirituality in order to clarify their distinct cosmovision (worldview). This human consciousness, which is knowing, loving, and willed, is a consciousness that wants to survive, to carry on.

This emergence is linked to the question of identity, a people's insistence to understand what it is *to be human* within a particular history, geography, and memory. On the heels of a civil war marked by ethnocide of the Maya, in the midst of a national shift from the dominant religious ideology of Roman Catholicism to a growing Protestant Pentecostal population and of the country's deeper involvement in transnational hemispheric processes, individuals and communities are articulating their difference and constructing new political and social space. Maya are taking into account the experience of themselves as sentient subjects in the natural world. They have developed a relatedness to creation and in turn engendered profound attunement, respect, and gratitude. Secure in their embodied relational consciousness, they want this perception to survive, be brought into light, amplified, and passed on.

This rejuvenation and public visibility of ancestral spirituality is marked by an increase of private and public communal ceremonies; the recuperation, reclamation, and daily use of the Chol Q'ij, the 260-day sacred calendar; and the commitment of more women and men, of diverse ages and professions, backgrounds, from rural and urban areas, to undertaking lives as Ajq'ijab'. It is no longer strange to see Maya rituals or interviews with Ajq'ijab' on front pages of national newspapers or broadcast on national television networks. Alvaro Colom, second runner-up for the 2003 Guatemalan national presidential elections, was publicly recognized as an Ajq'ij. Ajq'ijab', invited by various Maya communities in diaspora, indigenous, university, or religious groups in the Americas or in Western Europe, cross geographical boundaries to support, pray with, and advise Maya in exile, or to lecture, share ceremonies, and help those who seek their counsel.

The historical context of this emergence is noteworthy.[2] Under Spanish colonialism, the Church, charged by the Crown with converting the Maya and protecting them from colonists, imposed hegemonic political, economic, and religious forms and controls for purposes of tribute, production, and labor over indigenous communities, which mirrored secular colonization (see Ricard 1966; MacLeod 1973, 120–122; Farris 1984; Lovell 1992, 72–73; Oss 1986, 14–17; Meyer 1989; Watanabe 1992, 42–58; R. Carlsen 1997b, 71–100). From 1871 to 1926, anticlerical Liberals took a number of steps to undermine the Catholic Church. In the 1870s, Catholic religious orders were expelled, Jesuit landholdings were nationalized, and monasteries were abolished. Liberals encouraged Protestants from North America and northern Europe to immigrate and establish their projects in Guatemala (Garrard-Burnett 1988, 1–46; Steigenga 1999, 152–153). The anti-Catholic rhetoric of the Protestant missionaries did not win them large numbers of converts, but did create divisions between traditional Maya leaders and those associated with Protestant missionaries. After the 1870s, highland Maya religious leaders and laypersons directed religious activities, with clergy appearing annually to baptize and marry people.

The hegemony of the Catholic Church, as it neglected many highland towns, ebbed and fractured during the late nineteenth and early twentieth century (Watanabe 1992, 185). Mid-twentieth century, the institutional Church reemerged due to two processes. The Church, now viewed by state and ecclesiastical authorities as less radical, even as anticommunist, developed ties with the government and elite interests of the country. Second, due to the paucity of Guatemalan priests, the Church invited priests from Europe and the United States to reconstitute local congregations through social and spiritual programs (186). Handy writes that "by the late 1960s, only slightly over 15 percent of the [415] Guatemalan clergy were native born. The most important foreign sources of priests were Spanish Jesuits and American Maryknoll fathers" (1984, 239).

By the time of the U.S.-backed coup in 1954, when progressive Jacobo Arbenz was Guatemala's president, the conservative national Catholic hierarchy had initiated Acción Católica (Catholic Action), a reform movement that could not be easily stopped. Its original intent was to bring Maya back to observance as defined in Rome and to stem the tide of radical peasant politics that were gaining popularity in the countryside. To bring popular religion closer to the orthodoxy of Roman Catholicism, Catholic Action was launched as a large-scale catechist movement in the highlands, "comparable" writes Wilson, "to the first evangelization of the 1530s. . . . By becoming catechists, indigenous lay Christians played a role they had not enjoyed since the 1530s" (1995, 174).

Catechists not only challenged the traditional community religious practices and civil-religious order, but the entire village power structure. Catechists gained access to village authority and prestige, monopolized relations between the parish and the community, and marginalized elders and practices of *costumbre* (ancestral beliefs), often in extremely zealous actions. Catholic Action attacked native religious organizations. Zealots destroyed Maya altars; followers of *costumbre* were ridiculed and punished in public (Watanabe 1992, 204). Catholic priests attacked Ajq'ijab' as agents of the devil. In some villages, catechists destroyed images, and elders were prohibited from higher positions of responsibility.

Don Pedro Calel, keeper of the calendar in Santa María Chiquimula, related to me the effect of Catholic Action in Santa María when a new priest arrived in 1952. "The priest didn't appreciate Maya. He threw the candles away. He even went to the municipal court; then we couldn't practice our religion anymore. He stayed six to eight years." Don Pedro continues:

> After Catholic Action in 1952 when the priest threw out all the candles and went to court so it was illegal to practice our religion, we were all tied up. We were so sick. Many people got sick because the Church authorities took away our religion, our lives. We people of *costumbre* would just sneak around the outside of the church, but we could never go in. We were too afraid. People began to go to other religions. You see, when you have a *barre* [sacred bundle], it is your destiny. It is like you were selling something, not just selling merchandise, but as if this selling is your whole way of living. Someone comes and throws it away. How are you going to eat? How are you going to live? Our religion is our way of surviving.

During this period, conversion to Catholicism in Quiché and Huehuetenango led to social reorganization (Falla 2001) as well as to violent and permanent splits within the indigenous communities. In some villages, two churches were built to cope with the divided groups. Some priests administering villages in the highlands had to give two masses, one for the *cofrades* (members of a religious society) and one for the catechists. Evidence indicates, as we shall see later, that due to intersecting international and regional processes over two decades, Catholic Action also became the basis of a fairly strong ethnic revitalization and rural modernization movement (Carmack 1988; Falla 2001; Davis 1988; Warren 1978; Wilson 1995).

Mid-century, Vatican II (1962–65) established the Roman Catholic Church as a community (not a hierarchy) of believers, firmly set within contemporary society, engaging all peoples, but identifying especially with the poor. The Latin American bishops' conference of Medellín (1968) went beyond Vatican II by introducing the concepts of "structural sin" and "institutional violence." In the early '70s the Guatemalan Catholic Church, polarized between maintaining the status quo and responding to the Church's new "option for the poor," found herself challenged to respond to the economic poverty and marginalization of its nation. It undertook projects of education, cooperatives, and mass communication; during the period of the civil war, these developments were often targeted in areas of violent conflict between the army and guerrillas. It became safer to be a Protestant than a Catholic. In the late 1980s, the Church engaged in progressive projects to reconcile and heal the nation after the civil war and extensive genocide, to address the growing fundamentalist Protestantism, and to build a theology of inculturation, that is, interactions of the Gospel with distinct cultures. At present, it is estimated 50–60% of Guatemalans are Catholic.

Since the 1970s global religious evangelical processes, with economic and political implications, have competed for converts (R. Carlsen 1997b; Garrard-Burnett 1998; Goldin and Metz 1997; Steigenga 1999). The dramatic expansion of evangelical Protestantism constitutes a new and increasingly visible presence in the social, economic, and political life of Guatemala. Steigenga (1994) writes that the decision to convert to Protestantism is "both an economic necessity and part of a larger change in value systems for most Guatemalan converts" (155). Reliable estimates place the current Protestant population in Guatemala, mostly evangelical, between 25 and 30%, the highest percentage in Central America. The largest Protestant denomination is the Assembly of God, followed by the Church of God of the Complete Gospel, and the Prince of Peace Church; Presbyterians, Baptists, Lutherans, and Episcopalians are also strongly present. Other religious groups include the Mormons, Jehovah's Witnesses, the Mennonites, and small communities of Jewish and Islamic faith.

Since the 1970s, indigenous individuals, families, and communities have found themselves reconsidering, realigning, and shifting loyalties among Catholic, mainline Protestant, neo-Evangelical, and ancestral groups. Watanabe, who examined the interplay of identity, history, and experience in the Mam-speaking town Santiago Chimaltenango in 1978–1980, 1981, and 1988, renders the process in Chimaltenango slightly differently, arguing that the "abandonment of former religious conventions has not necessarily prompted wholesale conversion to new ideologies and practices but has left many Chimaltecos in limbo, *sin religión*—without (formal) religion" (1992, 187). In this context of disorder, religious pluralism, and respect for religious freedom, I see the public emergence of ancestral spirituality as a distinct and significant form of spiritual expression among other diverse forms within Guatemala.

Roberto Poz assesses the situation:

Yes, there is a resurgence of Maya Ajq'ijab' and the practice of our Maya ways in the past ten years. The Catholics said, "Believe our way, it is the true way." Then in the late 1970s, the evangelists came down from the States and said, "No, believe our way." We see that neither way is our way. Look at the destruction the Spanish have done to us. Look at the division the evangelists are doing to our villages, separating us in every way. So we are returning to the ways of our ancestors.

Embedded in his words, we hear the praxis of inquiry, the reassessment of history, and reclamation of Maya subjectivity and agency—a process of individuation. Critical of religious processes throughout history which have purported to save the Maya but instead have usurped their autonomy, these words echo a living impulse of persons who are reexamining spiritual practices which are more resonant with their cultural lives.

"LIVING IMPULSE" HEARD IN MULTIPLE VOICES

Maya women and men say of their ancestral practice, "It was hidden for a long time, but in the last years it has emerged publicly." For example, Rolando Ixcot, journalist for *El Regional* and Ajq'ij from Quetzaltenango, says,

Due to fear and insults from the community around us, Maya have hidden our spiritual practices from the public, and even often from our children and grandchildren. People no longer hide their ceremonial materials under a mantel or pray in a concealed location in the middle of the night. In the past ten years, Maya have become more public with our religious practices.

An attendant at the Chapel of El San Pascual, in San Juan Olintepeq, concurs: "Yes, in the last five years here, there are more people of *costumbre*. Before we were persecuted; we were forbidden to use *copal* (incense). But now the government has given an opening for us to practice our ways." In Zunil, Faustina, who has been an Ajq'ij for fourteen years, explains, "I think Maya spirituality is becoming more public. A lot of people talk about their time now." (Here "about their time" refers to their day of birth on the 260-day Maya calendar.) In another example, María del Carmen, of Sololá, says, "Ten or twenty years ago, there were only a few women Ajq'ijab', and very old. There is a progressive development, and today, there are many women Ajq'ijab' who are preparing to be our spiritual guides." Fr. Victoriano Castillo González, S.J., explained to me that in Santa María Chiquimula,

> it all began in 1992, on the 500th anniversary of the invasion of Columbus in the Americas. Before October 12th, I had asked, "Well, what are we going to do here in Santa María Chiquimula?" And out of it came an act of reconciliation between the catechists and the people of *costumbre*. The catechists went door-to-door, calling on each of the *Chuchqajaw* [keepers of the calendar], saying that on October 12th they wanted to have an act of reconciliation.
>
> During the ceremony, we recounted the story of conflicts of Catholics with people of *costumbre*. People even of opposite sides, like a son whose parents had been very active in Catholic Action in the parish, asked pardon from the *Chuchqajaw* for all Catholics for their actions and attitudes. During the ceremony, hugs and reconciliations were exchanged. People rediscovered and reaffirmed traditional values.
>
> Before 1992, the theme of *costumbre* was taboo. Now the people of *costumbre* have a *cofradía* in the parish. In the 2000 census, over sixty percent of the people in the village stated that they practice *costumbre*. (Conversation with author, July 31, 2003)

While each individual perspective and contribution here is distinct, reflecting the speaker's social world, each narrative resonates a "living impulse" of a new time.

Professor Victor Ruben Ovando explains, "To survive the last five hundred years, Maya have developed a great secretiveness." Yet, stories now emerge which demonstrate the repressive period and what ensued as a period of private space fraught with memories kept secret by the colonized, those who have been excluded from the writing of history. The story of Anastasia, a young woman who fled to Costa Rica during the civil war, but returned later, is an example of an unofficial history that had been buried for a long time in people's memories.

> The truth is that from the time I was very young we had our own *costumbres* within our own family. Then from one moment to another, it was cut because of many attacks. During my grandparents' generation (1950s), the bishop sent people to come and drag the Ajq'ijab' out of their houses, and in front of the Church in Chichicastenango, they hit

them. They persecuted them until they converted. So my parents were Catholic, but they had all this Maya richness within themselves. The form changed, other things within them were the same.

I want to make a clarification here. As I have learned from listening to many Maya, this emergence is not a revitalization movement. Revitalization suggests the return of a faith that has declined. Maya practice did not disappear; rather, there is a new openness. Due to a series of historical and political forces, its public expression has become possible. Roberto Poz, who reassessed his earlier statement on its rebirth, says, "Jean, let me clarify our conversation of last night. It really is not a resurgence at all. It's just that in the last few years, we've had the freedom to act on this call."

Census data from two highland Catholic parishes support this position. In the first survey, taken in 1990 in both Santa Lucía de la Reforma and Santa María Chiquimula, no one admitted to following ancestral practices. Six years later, after each parish facilitated processes for historical reconciliation and cultural recuperation in each village, 45% of the Santa Lucía de la Reforma and 60% of the Santa María Chiquimula communities disclosed that they practiced Maya belief and ritual (Molesky-Poz 2004).

As Calixta Gabriel said in an interview with Victor Perera in response to the question of whether she was part of a religious revival:

"Oh, no," she said. "You don't revive something that has never died. We have practiced our religion and observed our calendar without interruption since the time of the conquest. But we have kept it hidden from outsiders. Now, after the destruction of many of our communities and the scattering of thousands of our people across the face of the earth, the time for secrecy has passed." (1993, 333)

In highland regions, ancestral religious features were often disguised, masked in Christian saints, rituals, and calendars, and blended into Spanish custom. In adopting Western images, which had been imposed on them, Maya have selected, integrated, and interpreted them from their own unique worldviews. In this way, the Maya have been able to keep the underpinnings of their faith. Here are a few examples.

Catarina, an Ajq'ij of Zunil, invited me to see her altar (Figure 1.4). In a small adobe room, she points to the framed painting set on a woven cloth on a table, and says, "That's lightning, that's the Plumed Serpent, that's the energy." My eyes saw the Catholic icon of St. James on horseback, brandishing the red and white flag, the famed saint still honored in Santiago de Compostela and to whose honor millions still pilgrimage each year in northwestern Spain. During

FIGURE 1.4. Catarina refers to the image of St. James as the lightning and the Plumed Serpent as the energy.

the centuries-long war with the Moors, the Spanish had named him "Slayer of the Moors." This was the first saint image many Maya saw when the colonial Spanish carried the cult of the saints into Guatemala. But Catarina sees "the spirit of Santiago," the electric energy connecting sky and earth.

Visits to Ajq'ijab' María and Pablo in Panajachel also helped me understand. "My house is for ceremonies," explains María, as she and Pablo lead me into a spacious room, vacant of furniture. "Here, we help people to live, and to live is to go forward." Against one wall was a large three-tiered altar, constructed in steps, painted bright red, with a large poster of Jesus in prayer centered at the top (Figure 1.5). "This room is for meetings," María says. "Here we invoke the spirit, the spirit of the altars, of the mountains. We ask them, the spirits of the temples, the volcanoes, the caves, to come with us to help us. We call the spirits of all—the owners of the air, the sun, the clouds."

Later in conversation, María explains, "My parents believed in the altars, the caves. My father did, too. He said, 'Be careful. Don't put yourself in other religions. Put yourself in this space, on this road, or it will take you in a wrong direction.'"

I refer to the poster of Jesus praying at Gethsemane at the apex of her altar, and ask, "María, then, why do you have the large picture of Jesus above your altar?"

FIGURE 1.5. María and Pablo of Panajachel constructed their large three-tiered altar, as informed in María's dream, like a Mayan pyramid. She explains, "People feel more comfortable with Christian images, so I do most of my work here, but for my other real work, I have another altar where my rocks are."

She nods and responds. "Ajaw is first. Not to abandon Jesus, nor to leave him behind. We cannot leave him behind. We cannot leave him aside. He suffered much; he taught us to be humble. He cured people, and he translated the message of Ajaw. He showed us how to be human. He showed us to be humble, to cure people, and to speak God's word. He reminds me what I have to do. But Ajaw is first".

Upon a return visit to María in 1999, I notice her altar is now painted a celestial blue, rather than the red I remembered from several years before. Four twelve-inch wood-carved angels guard the altar; the poster of Jesus is still in the central position. When I comment on her new altar, she smiles and says, "These are the four corners, the four guardians of the earth: St. Michael, St. Gabriel, St. Raphael, and St. Seraphim; you know, the angels, the four corners." Then María explains that many people come to her, but are frightened to see just Maya images; they are more comfortable with Christian images. "So when people come, I do most of my work here, before this altar. But for my other real work, I have another altar in another room where my rocks are."

On another occasion, Audelino Soc Coy explains, "At the Church of Esquipulas, you see a person lighting thirteen or twenty candles. It's not just an accident, but a way that the Maya calendar still informs people's spiritual practices."

These narratives not only show that Maya religion persists, but they also demonstrate the incorporation of Western symbols into a Maya cultural paradigm. I am inclined to agree that contemporary practices are grounded in ancestral Maya worldviews. As Robert S. Carlsen notes, "Despite Spanish efforts, Mayan culture has been far more resilient and self-directed than many scholars have believed," and while there have been some changes due to Western influences, it remains "distinctively and identifiably Mayan" (1997b, 48–49).

This supports my understanding that the mid-1980s were but an opening for the public practice of Maya spirituality. This open space allowed for individuals and groups to investigate, reclaim, and elaborate on ancestral beliefs and practices, which they found culturally consonant, useful, and comprehensive to navigate their personal and communal lives.

THE CONSTRUCTION OF NEW SPATIAL SPHERES OF HISTORICAL EXISTENCE

In the *Crónica* cover story entitled "The Maya Renaissance" (July 1996), leading Maya social scientist Demetrio Cojtí Cuxil stated, "For the first time, Mayas are speaking for themselves about themselves. It is not that someone is speaking on our behalf, defending us, but that we ourselves are developing visions of our own identity and questioning everything, from a colonist church to our relationship with the state."

The conferring of value upon indigenous spirituality concurs with a cultural movement of reaffirmation of identity among the Maya. In this new spatial sphere of historical existence, Maya are articulating their difference, their "otherness"—not as the Spanish or Ladinos have defined it, but as they themselves define it (Cojtí Cuxil 1997b). In *The Maya Movement Today*, Choy and Borrell note that these changes constitute a true "sociological awakening" of the indigenous population or the birth of a "new indigenous consciousness" (1997, 27–28). They identify two basic characteristics: (1) the role of Maya leaders; and (2) a change in the perception of 'being Indian' vs. the Ladino. This change focuses on a positive reassessment: "being Mayan as a source of pride, a re-encounter with one's roots, . . . and above all, a consciousness of identity based on their own specificity, and not only in terms of the differences with regard to the ladino world" (35). Fischer and McKenna Brown, in Maya Cultural Activism in Guatemala, broaden the context. They write that since 1985 Maya activism has sought a culture-based solution to Guatemala's many problems. "The approach is two-pronged: to work for the conservation and resurrection of elements of Maya culture while promoting governmental reform within the framework of the current (1985) Guatemalan constitution and international law" (1996, 13).

For many Maya, the reconstruction of identity, history, knowledge, and power consists in recuperating features of the Maya world. They say that the reconstruction of their worldview is foundationally linked to their ancestors' teachings. That is why Maya reassessment of identity, moral resources, and agency is rooted in the reclamation and rejuvenation of Maya beliefs and spiritual practices. Robert S. Carlsen, too, found in his ethnographic work in the Guatemala highlands that "Mayas conceive of a sacred past which sustains, is replicated in, and symbolically informs the present and the future" (1997b, 63). The recuperation of knowledge and power, the construction of meaning and identity are foundationally linked to ancestral beliefs, values, and spiritual practices, flamed by a hope and responsibility for present and future generations. We can trace recent efforts toward this reclamation back to the 1960s in the western highlands.

"In the 1960s in Quetzaltenango, we felt the necessity to move beyond thinking, reflecting, and talking about Maya spirituality within our private circles; it was time to do it more publicly. But we felt it wasn't the moment," explains Norma Quixtán, former governor of Quetzaltenango and now Secretary of Peace in Guatemala (Figure 1.3), at the Second National Mayan Congress at Rafael Landivar. "First, we had to initiate a process of sensitizing the population to the theme of Maya culture." The first trilingual (K'iche', Mam, and Spanish) radio program, Aj Itz del Pueblo, was founded and directed by her father, Mauricio Quixtán, one of the first two Mayan congressmen. The program first aired in August 1969, offering pieces on Maya agriculture, family, music, and community.

The early 1970s saw the development of political, cultural, and linguistic activism centered in the K'iche' region. Adrián Inés Chávez (1904–1987), K'iche' educator, scholar, and promoter of Maya self-expression in language and culture, first clearly expounded the importance of the tripartite relationship between language, culture, and politics. He became the intellectual father of current ideas of pan-Mayanism (Fischer 1996, 57). Between 1970 and 1972 the Asociación Indígena Pro Cultural Maya-Quiché, the Asociación de Forjadores de Ideales Quichelenses, and the Asociación de Escritores Mayances de Guatemala (AEMG) were all established in Quetzaltenango to promote Maya culture (Arias 1990; Fischer 1996, 59). The first international congress on *Popol Wuj*[3] was held in 1979 in Santa Cruz del K'iche'; the second was not held until June 1999 in Quetzaltenango (TIMACH 2002). We see here the seeds of a revitalization movement, which Wallace defines as "a deliberate, organized, conscious effort by members of a society to construct a more satisfying culture" (1956, 265).

These processes were precipitated in part by progressive activities of the Catholic Action program (Handy 1984, 103–147; Warren 1978; Carmack 1988, 41; Davis 1988, 16; Watanabe 1992, 204; Wilson 1995, 174). Vatican II (1962–65) and the Medellín Conference of Latin American Bishops, both of which embraced "the Gospel's preferential option for the poor," influenced the work of a new church in Guatemala. The training of catechists was at the heart of this movement. I earlier discussed the destructive aspects of Catholic Action, but there were also relationships and processes, generative ones that would affect future Maya developments in unexpected ways. First, Maya catechists established new relations of power between themselves and *ladinos*. Second, educational training workshops took them beyond their villages, and, as Kay Warren writes, Catholic Action not only "began to forge a more active Indian population" but also inspired an increased sense of connection with other neighboring villages and their common problems (1978, 89). At the same time, secondary and vocational educational institutes, run as boarding schools by religious orders, were established for Mayan women and men. "This migration of young Maya to cities for economic and educational purposes," writes Montejo, "put them in contact with people from other Mayan linguistic communities, broadening their views of themselves, their people, and their country" (2002, 136–137). Third, in some villages, efforts of priests to promote Catholic Action were coupled with the establishment of cooperatives, health centers, bilingual educational ventures, rural development programs, and radio programs to address economic, cultural, and political injustices and promote Catholic teaching in various indigenous languages. In time, lay activists emerged at the forefront of what Sheldon Davis calls a "generalized social and political mobilization . . . in the Guatemalan highlands" (20). Further, through Catholic Action and the

University of Rafael Landívar, the Church initiated programs for young Maya to cultivate leadership qualities; these young people developed skills and later became community leaders and activists in the Maya movement (Fischer 1996, 59).

"Continuing the thread of history," Norma says, "in the 1970s, Kaqchikel, Kekchi, Q'anjob'al, and K'iche' students at the University of San Carlos and the University of Rafael Landívar initiated the idea of the First Indigenous Seminar as a way to deepen and widen the discussion of Mayan spirituality and worldview." This First Indigenous Seminar, which began to facilitate national contact between local Maya leaders, took place in Quetzaltenango in 1973. Norma explains:

> During the seminar there was a momentum that moved all to find a response to the questions: "Where do we come from?" "What are we doing?" "Where are we going?" Another way to say it is that these are the three moments of a people: the past, the present, the future.

Participants recommended organizing a Second Indigenous Seminar in Tecpán in 1974. "But this thread of history was cut short," continued Norma, "because it coincided with the most difficult epoch in the recent social and political life of Guatemala."

The wave of state-sponsored terror in the highlands began in the late 1970s. First it focused on destroying grassroots movements, eliminating unions and labor leaders, as well as organizations of urban residents, high school, and university student associations. Soon the government counterinsurgency was carrying out extensive massacres and projects of repression, torture, and internal and external displacement, which continued into the early 1980s. Approximately two hundred thousand Maya were forced to migrate across borders as political refugees, over 1 million were internally dislocated, and tens of thousands were murdered. Four hundred and ten indigenous villages were burned, razed, completely destroyed (Choy and Borrell 1997; Smith 1990, 1991). Community leaders and Ajq'ijab' as well as Catholic priests and lay workers were frequent targets of state-sponsored terror under the regimes of Romeo Lucas García (1978–82), Efraín Ríos Montt (1982–83), and Humberto Mejía Víctores (1983–86). This period of holocaust also saw army sweeps, scorched earth politics, the institution of civil patrols, and the concentration and militarization of civil populations in "model villages" (resettlement of thousands of people displaced by the violence into new government-controlled hamlets, where they were provided with housing, food, and work) and "development poles" (areas where "model towns" were established, peopled by refugees and controlled by the army).

These horrors of armed conflict deeply shook and traumatized the modern Maya. In many instances the violence eroded economic, social, and political structures, altering the worldview, community life, and traditions of many Maya. For others, the phenomena of displacement of civilian populations and refugees resulted in relations and solidarity with other social groups in exile (Choy and Borrell 1997, 33). In the mid-1980s, as Maya articulated their present and future, the recent past became a political playing field. Jonathan Boyarin's observations about the politics of Jewish memory are relevant: "Walter Benjamin reminds us of the demands of our ancestors who died unjustly; their death is, in a powerful sense, not 'past,' but subject to the meaning it is given through action in the present" (Boyarin 1994, 11). Maya reflection on the suffering, disappearances, and the murders of relatives and communities intensified and redefined strategies for struggle, self-definition, and a viable future.

Vilma Poz amplifies:

During the period of the repression we organized ourselves. We studied and developed ourselves culturally and politically in these organizations. We became more conscious and experienced a new solidarity among ourselves. We recognized a new importance of what we had to do; it was not only cultural or political. It was to do with something deeper. We knew it was spiritual. We began to recognize that Ajq'ijab' had an important role. We also understood that it wasn't time yet.

Small groups of Maya turned to elders and sought in Maya rituals healing, direction, and strength. Thus a people's turn to Maya spirituality occurred at a time of profound personal, communal, and national brokenness. No longer able to bear the alienation, disempowerment, and disillusionment associated with the state and other religious forms, they sought a spirituality corresponding to their own social and religious meaning. They reached deep into their roots to find an expression of faith more concordant with themselves, with their ancestral legacy. In excavating and retrieving this faith system, some would find healing, integration, and hope for their lives.

After the war, a particular combination of forces—processes within indigenous communities and networks of national and international events, influenced by a matrix of relationships, situations, and expectations— yielded the historic space and opportunity to introduce and facilitate Maya demands. Internationally, the global emphasis on human rights was a contributing factor. The newly directed determination of the Maya also coincided with indigenous movements in the Americas; Native peoples organized themselves on local, national, and global levels, some with the support of nongovernmental agencies (NGOs). Indigenous resolve has occupied a higher profile since the 1990s. In 1991 seven Ajq'ijab' organizations reconstructed social relationships in Maya communities. The year 1992, designated as the International Year of the Indigenous Peoples, became symbolic as "five hundred years of indigenous resistance." Rigoberta Menchú received the Nobel Peace Prize; K'iche' Rigoberto Keme Chay was elected mayor of Quetzaltenango. The establishment of the International Year of Indigenous Populations of the World in 1993, and of the International Decade of the Indigenous Populations of the World in 1994–2004, also opened new historical space. Political and significant economic support from European and North American countries, which tied their foreign assistance to Guatemala's human rights records, constructed new international allies for indigenous groups (Cojtí Cuxil 1997a, 135–154). Several conferences held in Guatemala furthered educational and literary concerns, such as the First Congress on Maya education in Quetzaltenango (1994), the seminar on Adrián Inés Chávez (1995), the International Seminar on Indigenous Literature (1997), and the National Congress on Maya Education (1998). The production of indigenous scholarship (as evidenced in publications of Maya research organizations as CEDIM and Cholsamaj) and the publication and distribution of indigenous-owned newspaper weeklies, and calendars made indigenous thinking and perspectives available to the public. The national recognition of twenty-two Maya languages, as well as the Xinca and Garifuna languages in Guatemala, signaled the recognized ethnic diversity of the nation. The cultural promotion work of the complex pan-Maya movement established the first steps toward new equalities in Guatemala (Fischer and Brown 1996; Choy and Borrell 1997; Warren 1998; Zapeta Galamez 1998; Montejo 2002).

These movements also opened a space for the public reclamation of indigenous spirituality. On July 1, 1984, due to local and international pressures, the National Constitutional Assembly was convened to define new laws for the Republic of Guatemala. Important to the Maya movement was the ratification of article 66 (Protection of Ethnic Groups), which refers specifically to indigenous communities: "The state recognizes, respects, and promotes their [indigenous] life ways, customs, traditions, forms of social organization, the use of indigenous clothing of men and women, and languages and dialects" (Cojtí Cuxil 1997a, 25). However, as

Maya theoretician Demetrio Cojtí points out, "The 1985 constitution makes no allusion to political, territorial, or economic rights; this judicial progress has been more a measure of counterinsurgency and a symbolic compensation for the Indian holocaust that began in 1978" (1997a, 26).

The revitalization of Maya spirituality has more directly been stipulated by three documents within Guatemala, two by the Guatemalan state. First, the consensus document Identity and Rights of the Maya People, of the Maya activist group COPMAGUA (Coordinator of Organizations of the Maya People of Guatemala), released on May 11, 1994, affirms that the indigenous peoples have the right to reclaim and preserve their identities and cultural traditions, including the right to maintain, develop, and protect past, present, and future spiritual and religious traditions and ceremonies.

Second, the Agreement on Identity and Rights of Indigenous Peoples, signed by the Guatemalan government and the Guatemalan National Revolutionary Unity on March 31, 1995, was a historic document for the Maya. Negotiated under United Nations auspices, the Agreement established principles which promised to repeal laws and decrees that have discriminatory implications toward indigenous peoples and officially declared Guatemala a "multi-ethnic, multi-cultural and multi-lingual nation." It recognizes "the importance and uniqueness of Maya spirituality as an essential component of their cosmovision and the transmission of their values"; promises "to respect its practices in all of its manifestations, in particular the right to practice, in public and in private, as a means of education, worship and observation"; respects the role of indigenous spiritual leaders; mandates respect for traditional ceremonies and sacred places; promises "to promote the reform of article 66 of the Constitution to stipulate that the State recognize, respect and protects the various forms of spirituality practiced by the Maya, Garifuna and Xinca peoples" (15–16). Third, article 2 of the Guatemalan Constitutional Reform of 1998 set in place national reforms regarding the identity and spirituality of the indigenous peoples and the right to transmit them to their descendants.

In the late 1990s, two independent yet complementary truth commission inquiries were conducted to document testimonies of the former climate of terror. These inquiries were undertaken to facilitate national healing. *Guatemala: Nunca Más!* (Recovery of Historical Memory Project; REHMI, 1999), sponsored by the Human Rights Office of the Catholic Church, reported that the government and its allied paramilitary bands were responsible for 89.7% of the atrocities; guerrillas were responsible for 4.8%. Similarly, in February 1999, "Guatemala: Memory of Silence," a report undertaken by the Historical Clarification Commission (CEH), a project created under UN auspices, blamed 93% of the atrocities on the government forces and 3% on the guerrillas (REHMI, xvi). Exhumations of tens of thousands of bodies in mass graves and respectful reburial of these dead, often accompanied in ritual by Ajq'ijab', uncovered the secret of genocide and opened the way for healing, fueling the urgent demand for human rights for indigenous peoples.

In the resurgent violence of civil crimes in Guatemala since the late 1990s, there have been reports of assassinations of religious leaders of various denominations — Catholic, Protestant, and traditional. Ajq'ijab' have increasingly become targets of robberies, rapes, murders, and in several cases, lynchings. In 1997 Ajq'ijab' praying at mountain altars outside Quetzaltenango were robbed while performing their ceremonies; that same year in July, three women Ajq'ijab' who traveled from the coast to make offerings at these mountain altars were robbed, raped, and left naked. Robert Carlsen reports increasing violence against traditional Maya in Santiago Atitlán, a town of twenty thousand inhabitants. "In late 1996, shamans started to be killed. A pattern to the killings was made apparent on June 23, 1997 when Salvador Quieju, the third local shaman to be murdered, was found hacked to death with a machete on a mountain behind the town." He continues, "Left with the Quieju's body was a note listing some twenty other practitioners of Maya spirituality targeted for extermination" (1997a, 11).

A 2003 U.S. Department of State report documents a number of kidnappings and murders of Ajq'ijab' in Coban, Baja Verapaz, and Chichicastenango. The report states that "while these crimes have not been linked to religious persecution, they represent a disturbing trend of targeting voices of religious leaders who dissent against the corruption and impunity that plague society" (2). Intimidation, discrimination, and racism against Ajq'ijab' continued in 2003. Six Aj'qijab' were murdered; in addition, two Ajq'ijab' in Sayaxché, Petén, were almost lynched, the community having accused them of causing sicknesses and deaths (*Info Maya*). The struggle continues.

In this historical period, the construction of identity is in part a recuperation of knowledge and power. It excavates that which the colonial experience and later liberalism buried and covered, raising to the light that which was hidden in the ensuing oppression. For many, the construction of Maya identity is tied to the emergence and reclamation of Maya cosmovision, and in turn, ancestral spiritual practices. If we consider this historical juncture an open-ended design, the intention and agency of Maya is the exploration and expression of a potentiality for life. The present Maya renewal contributes to the self-determination of indigenous people. Maya spirituality, as Apolinario Chile Pixtún, an Ajq'ij from Chimaltenango, explains, is a resource for living.

> You have to understand that Maya religion is not simply a liturgical act or ritual, but is an understanding of the origin and significance of all of creation. Maya religion, for the grandchildren and children of our ancestors, is the same as life. In studying Maya religion, we have found a methodology to encounter philosophy, science and creation. (quoted in Lima Soto 1995, 21)

Further, Rigoberto Itzep Chanchavac, an Ajq'ij from Momostenango, explains that Maya spirituality leads to ethical activity. "Maya religion is a school for the soul. It teaches the person how to conduct oneself in the world, in life" (quoted in Lima Soto 1995, 20–21). Maya insight and perception of life, then, is but one of many human understandings and constructions of meaning, of aesthetic and ethical activity on earth, but one which many indigenous in Guatemala find consonant with their lives. We now turn to investigate the underpinnings of Maya spirituality.

CHAPTER 2

Maya Cosmovision and Spirituality
Selecting, Examining, and Stretching Out Filaments of Light

One form of knowledge is investigation, as archeology, a science studied
through texts. This analysis uses western techniques, not Maya. Then
there is a life that lives with *caites* (sandals), carrying one's own baggage,
a people with another kind of knowledge. This second kind goes back
thousands of years. It's profound. That's why we have remained here.
We have not disappeared.

RIGOBERTA MENCHÚ TUM, NOVEMBER 2004

Maya spirituality is an inexplicable feeling. It is when one is in contact
with the forces of creation and feels energy, the vibrations of the earth
and of the universe. That is to say at dawn, at the rising of the sun, one
receives energy, feels tranquility, and a profound peace. All the
intentions and words that come from our being are in harmony. It is to
feel what it means to be human.

AURA MARINA COTÍ, OF QUETZALTENANGO

"The theme *cosmovision* is very significant in the life of the Maya today,"
writes Kaqchikel author José Mucía Batz Lem, "because our cosmovision
opens a way to understand those around us. It teaches us how to be with
all created beings that inhabit the cosmos" (1997, 9). In the Maya determination to survive, they are taking up the advice of their elders: "Don't forget the teachings of the ancestors. In their paths we will find hope for the

future" (Montejo 2002, 127). In this revitalization, they turn to ancestral worldviews, expressed in a multiplicity of forms.

Maya cosmovision, marked by various types of knowledge, traditions, and intuitions, provides a template of movement in which human existence and the cosmos are interrelated and harmonic. It is not anthropocentric; rather, the cosmos is the key referent. Maya cosmovision considers, investigates, and respects the order of the universe. Its inclusive logic is fastened to cosmogony, the pattern and movement in the universe where everything is created, interconnected, and in harmony. The construction and ordering of creation, patterns of fourfold markings, cycles of time, duality, mathematical principles, plants, animals, and humans emanate from the same origin. But cosmovision is not only a template; it is a form through which Maya feel, think, analyze, understand, and move reciprocally in the cosmos. For Maya, affection, reflection, and dialogue shape human consciousness, relations, inquiry, discourse, and creativity. This worldview seeks an affective equilibrium within social, cultural, and ecological environments. "Maya cosmovision is a form to understand, relate with, and be human with all the elements of nature," explained Daniel Matul to me one afternoon. "It is the close dependency and complementariness, which is necessary for spiritual and material life and for relation with the eternal."

In this cosmovision "spirituality is found within the interior of each person. It is a particular energy, which moves a person to define and express one's sentiments," write Maya spiritual guides in a chapter entitled "God and Man: An Indestructible Relation." "It establishes the need to feel and to be in intimate contact with the presence of a superior force. This intimate contact provides a deeply felt meaning to one's actions, magnifying them with a particular significance" (Rivera 1994, 35). This statement resonates with German theologian Karl Rahner's *theological anthropology*, in which he shows how humans are open to a positive revelation of the Mystery of God in space and time, that the human person is a cognitive premonition of the ground of being, a dynamic movement *toward* the divine, though always moving *within* the world (1968).

While Maya cosmovision underpins psychological, philosophical, and cultural realities in Maya communities, in the complex interplay of people and place, diverse expressions have developed. Thus cosmovision is not remembered or practiced with unifocal concordance, nor is this cultural knowledge shared with all equally. Further, Western colonial, national, and transnational processes have attempted to erase or erode indigenous knowledge and power. Identities change over time and space, yet clear linkages, continuities of ancient Maya forms, though transformed, continue to inform life. In efforts to recover and assert their ethnic distinctiveness, Maya turn to elements in historical memory and to perceptions in their communities for identity, cultural autonomy, and self-determination.

This chapter follows contemporary Maya inquiries regarding the origin of the universe, human existence, and relatedness. As Maya investigate questions in light of cultural resources available to them, they uncover cognitive perceptions, knowledge, and principles which have guided their people over time.

This inquiry leads us to Mayan understandings of the term *spirituality*. Here I consider models and metaphors of the sacred that emerge in ritual practice and mythic accounts so we can acknowledge the concepts which traditionalists both bring to and use to shape their experience as well as the form in which they report it. These epistemological constructs and ontological commitments, which order experience in differing ways (Katz), will set the foundation for subsequent chapters: how Ajq'ijab' interpret their lives and how they construct and engage with space, with time, and with movement, in other words, their spiritual practices. To represent the persistence of this consciousness, I illustrate how weaving, a vibrant expression of Maya experience, has reflected and transmitted this cosmovision through millennia.

REFLECTIVE MEMORY

Roberto, my brother-in-law, and I were driving to visit another Ajq'ij in a neighboring town. Our conversation that morning meandered in and out of the theme, Maya cosmovision.

"*Jean, there are three phases in our lives: the void, silence, and sound.*" *He elaborated,* "*You can find our understanding in Popol Wuj, not as westerners have interpreted our K'iche' creation account with their emphasis on the word, but in the way we understand our origins. You can find the three phases in the way we reflect on and understand our lives. You can find it in the birth of a word, the formation of an idea, even in the three stages of our rituals.*"

Later that afternoon, I pored over the opening pages of Popol Wuj.

The sky alone is there. There is *nothing whatever* gathered together. It is at rest; not a single thing stirs. There was *silence*, "only murmurs, ripples in the dark, in the night." And then *the sound*, Heart of Sky spoke with Sovereign Plumed Serpent. Out of silence, Heart of Sky and Gucumatz began to speak with one another in the early dawn. They were discussing creation. They talked, then they thought, then they worried. They agreed with each other, they joined their words, their thoughts. Then it was clear, then they reached accord in the light, and then humanity was clear. (D. Tedlock 1985, 72–73)

Roberto's emphasis on the *void* and *silence,* before *speech,* identifies a reflective and dialogic consciousness. He turns to a cultural resource, *Popol Wuj,* to confirm this important perception. Further, he illuminates how this cognitive process informs Maya ways of perceiving and engaging with life. It is in the generative ecology of void and silence, that sound, in this case persons questioning about the origin, relatedness, purpose, destiny, and death of human beings, takes place.

"Today, we are reflecting on the most fundamental questions of philosophy," states Daniel Matul, lecturer and writer on Maya culture. "What is humanity? Where does it come from? How should human beings act toward themselves and others? What are the relationships between human beings and God? What are the relations that harmonize and unite us with the universe?" The question of existence, then, is the starting point.

In their inquiry, to use the metaphor of weaving, Maya are selecting, examining, and stretching out various "filaments of light." They retrieve and investigate ancestral worldviews, recover and construct historical memory to create a future more consonant with their sense of being human. Reflective memory travels to, selects, and contemplates remainders[1] in metaphoric forms. Inquirers turn to communal and mythic narratives, languages, codices and glyphs, agricultural and sacred calendars and practices, architecture, and most importantly the counsel of elders, to understand the ways these multiform and diverse signs are tied and untied in Maya histories and geographies. Rigoberta Menchú Tum explains,

We look at the past with the eyes of the present. We look at the present with the eyes of the past. With the eyes of the past and the present, we look toward the future. If we don't live it in our practical lives, we are lost. (Legion of Honor, San Francisco, November 2004)

Narratives of memory are substantive for communal identity and carry potentials for creativity and transformation. Memory is necessary for personal and communal identity. Bakhtin's rendering elucidates the potential of memory. He writes, "Memory is an unsystematic accumulation of past experience that exists not only for the sake of preservation but also for creative transformation" (Morson and Emerson 1990, 229). He elaborates,

"In one's remembered past and a reassessment of it, one possesses the conditions for creativity and freedom" (230). Narratives of memory are aesthetic and moral resources, which rejuvenate life for a viable future. For example, Komun Tohil, a group of Ajq'ijab' in the Quetzaltenango area, have studied Maya texts, curious to find resonances, even legacies, of their own work. Doña Marta Chávez explains, "For a long time we just burned [offered ceremonies before the fire], nothing more. Just now we are hearing about *Popol Wuj*. We are understanding in new ways."

In this activity contemporary Maya come to these texts as "outsiders," that is, they are located outside the object of their understanding in time, space, and culture. This outsideness creates the possibility of dialogue. In this "creative understanding" of the text or event, they, as interpreters, create a special sort of dialogue which enriches both the text and the interpreters. "The exchange creates new and valuable meanings possessed by neither at the outset" (Morson and Emerson 1990, 289).

The afternoon Roberto opened a copy of the Dresden Codex and identified ceremonial glyphs, Ajq'ijab' poured over the text in animated conversation, pointing to the "drilling fire" glyph (Figures 2.1, 2.2, and 2.3). In that symbol, they recognized a legacy of their own work. Through ceremonial pilgrimages to various sites such as Lake Chikab'al, to altars at Lake Atitlán, Santa Cruz del K'iche', Abaj Takalik, and temple-pyramids at Tikal and Copán, Ajq'ijab' continue to draw strength from their heritage, are reinforced in their ritual work, and reclaim their rights to practice their ceremonies at these sacred sites.

What Is Humanity?

Maya turn to the *Popol Wuj* to investigate this question because in remembered and oral forms as well as in the contemporary written text, the distinctiveness bestowed on humans is illuminated. Humans were to be *givers of praise, givers of respect, providers,* and *nurturers* (D. Tedlock 1985, 79). The Designer and Maker, Heart of Sky and Plumed Serpent, respectively, wanted to create humans to talk, to have hearts, to have minds, to keep the calendar, to remember their maker. After several failed attempts in constructing humanity, Heart of Sky and Plumed Serpent were finally satisfied. In Grandmother Xmucane's grinding of the yellow and white corn, along with the water in which she rinsed her hands, the creation came out human:

> They talked and they made words.
> They looked and they listened.
> They walked. They worked.

FIGURES 2.1–2.3. Members of Komon Tohil examine the "drilling for fire" image in the Dresden Codex.

glyph 3: God Q (shown here) D6b

> They were good people, handsome, with the looks of the
> male kind. Thoughts came into existence and they gazed;
> their vision came all at once. (D. Tedlock 1985, 165)

Once the first humans realized that they saw everything under the sky perfectly, they *felt gratitude* and gave "double thanks, triple thanks" that they had been formed, had been given mouths, faces, that they could speak, listen, wonder, move and know that which is far and near, that which is great and small (166). Unlike the previous attempts at forming humanity, these creatures, these human persons *felt* and *perceived* and *spoke*. The narrators of *Popol Wuj* continue: "They were truly gifted people. They were reverent; they were givers of praise, givers of respect, lifting their faces to the sky when they made requests for their daughters and sons" (169).

Pulling at these narrative threads, we see *consciousness*, that is, the fourfold capacities of remembering, recollecting, feeling, and thinking; the fourfold activities of respecting, praying, nurturing, and providing are characteristic functions of humanness. Humans are *feeling, reflective,* and *dialogic* beings in a stance of gratitude.

Implicit is that humans have a distinctive capacity, *language,* the gift of speech. Guatemalan Lima Soto writes, "The primal function promised/granted by the Creator for the person is the ability to communicate and this constitutes the necessary nexus between the creature and the Creator" (1995, 19). Indeed, language was the definitive factor in which creation was considered concluded, "They talked, they made words" (D. Tedlock 1985, 190).

While language functions as a link between the creature and the Creator, it has a second function. Language facilitates a harmonic participation on a material level. "The Maya resorts to his/her articulated language and other symbols to give thanks, to elevate petitions and offerings, but in reality, the act is syntonic, is a communion with the language of the universe" (Lima Soto 1995, 20). That is, as a communication between creature and Creator, language maintains the speaker in an emotional equilibrium. "When we petition Heart of Sky, we are really starting up a dialogue with the universe, soliciting collaboration." Daniel Matul explains. "We are also grateful when we do this because we sense we are part of the universe" (1989, 150). This dimension of language, according to Lima Soto, contains a primordial function, which is not to be confused with articulated language, appropriate in communication among persons. He explains that to give thanks, to elevate petitions and offerings, Maya draw from articulated language and other symbols, *but in reality, the act is being in tune, is to be in communion with the language of the universe* (1995, 20). Attunement is a special state. As we shall see later, this receptivity has developed specific capacities.

Language has a third purpose: humans participate through language in seeking meaning, purpose, and solutions for practical lives. "Through language," writes Matul, "we sustain and nurture other people" (1991, 15). The blueprint for reflective dialogic activity is found in *Popol Wuj*, where we read that the Creator and Designer "talked, then they thought, then they worried. They agreed with each other, they joined their words, their thoughts, and then it was clear" (73).

Human distinctiveness is also illuminated in the language of the elders. Batz Lem (1997), who consults with Kaqchikel elders on ways of understanding human existence and purpose, delineates four Mayan philosophical principles which order human life:

- Men and women have the responsibility to look after all, as a guardian, as an older brother. But a person is not the owner. The absolute owner of the universe is Ajaw.
- We are in the same category as others, an *awej*, a concept which signifies "a creature with a Superior Being, subservient to its designs, purposes and aptitude."
- Universal laws rule men and women. Each person's period of life varies depending on the mission that has been commissioned within the cosmos.
- All of us fulfill the pre-established cycle for all creation, to come and go, to be born and to die. For this reason, man has the same cycle of life, as that of the ant, the planets, the sun, etc. (12)

This worldview recognizes the givenness of all created life, acknowledges its temporal, ordered, and cyclical nature, yet distinguishes humanity with particular aptitudes, purpose, and responsibility, based, as we shall see, in the 260-day calendar.

How Should Humans Act toward Themselves and toward Others?

In Maya thought, the human is understood not as an individual, but as a *relational* being, that is, one who cannot be conceived of without multiple relations; with one's family and community, the earth, all created elements, other persons, the living and dead, and Ajaw. These relationships evoke and cultivate distinct sensibilities and responsibilities.

Popol Wuj tells how humans were created of a mix of yellow and white corn. "Corn, the center of belief, is a sign of group identity," explains Arias (1990, 1). "Corn is what gives meaning to ethnic identity and to a cultural universe. Corn has a 'mythic' value, not a commercial one. Corn is an emblem for the Mayan community. Individual kernels are of no consequence as such" (Thorn 1996, 1). This sense of community permeates all relations.

In investigating the question "How should human beings act toward themselves and others?" Batz Lem illustrates this interconnectedness from elders.

- If we are eating something, we must share with all that is around us, the persons, animals, the plants, etc. because all form a community.
- The animals hear, the plants perceive, the stars notice our actions. These are some of the expressions that our parents and grandparents have given us of their glimpse, their comprehension, of our relationship, our tie, with the universe.
- For them, there does not exist a classification nor a distinction in those who inhabit the cosmos: the rain talks. A dog, a plant, the wind, a rock, a comet is equal to a person because everything completes its specific function and must be respected with due deference and reverence. (1997, 11)

In everyday spaces my husband Martín, Calixta, and other Maya resonate this attentiveness to interconnection. Martín once explained, "My mother taught me to respect the wind the most. She said it suffers so much. Because it travels everywhere, it suffers. It hits against thorns, rocks, and walls. It bleeds, it cries. But it also listens to everyone. It is always there, always giving humans and all the earth, life." Calixta said something similar to me. "Sometimes, the wind is the only companion I have. It wraps and comforts me in the cold I experience in life. The wind hears our sorrows and carries them to the Creator." In the film *Discovering Dominga* (2003), Ache Jesús Tecu Osorio, survivor and eyewitness to the massacre of 170 Ache men, women, and children at Rio Negro in 1982, says as he recounts how the military threw remains covered with blood, hair, and human flesh into the ravine, "Sometimes it is hard for us humans to bear seeing such things like the day of the massacre. These trees have more memory than we do. The trees saw it all, and so did the mother earth."

What Are the Relations That Harmonize and Unite Us with the Universe?

To answer this question, elders identify principles of familial and communal relations which center on the communal good, on unity, harmony, respect, responsibility, and consensus between parties in decisions. Daily practices reinforce interconnectedness, responsibility, and participation of each member. Further, elders explain that this worldview cultivates a culture of reciprocity. "If one takes care for the earth, the earth cares for us" is often heard. Maya not only care for the earth in the planting of corn, of beans, of fresh vegetation, they nourish her by placing fresh flowers, candles, a bowl of water, and/or fruit on a home altar, or make these offerings in their ceremonies. Traditionally, when one's clothing is worn out and can no longer be used, it is buried in the earth and "returns to the earth to nurture the soil, to give us corn, our life, our sustenance" (V. Poz, personal communication, June 25, 1997). Father Bascilio Chacach Tzoy, a K'iche' and Catholic priest, shares an example of reciprocity from Santa Lucía de la Reforma.

The "huh" prayer is so that all life is abundant. For example, before taking the corn from storage, one has to blow on one's fingers. That's first. Then after you degrain the corn, you have to put the kernels in the pot. Again you blow on the pot. After you take the kernels out of the pot to wash them, again you blow on the area, and again when you have the corn dough made into *tamilitos*. When you put them in the pot, again you breathe over the pot so that the spirit doesn't leave, but that it is abundant, that it multiplies. And when you distribute the tamales for all to eat, you take one out first and put it on the side. This is to maintain the spirit. Then you distribute the tamales. This prayer is an attitude.

A relational and reciprocal sense extends to ancestors, as there is a dialogic connection between the living and the living dead. For example, in summer 2001, we were walking through the cemetery at Santa María Chiquimula with Eduardo León Chic. On this ordinary weekday, the graveyard was alive with families carrying armfuls of flowers or visiting with buried relatives. In the center of the cemetery an Ajq'ij was incensing and praying to the four guardian-mountains to protect the recently buried. Further along, Eduardo stopped to introduce us to two women in their sixties who were sitting near their parents' graves. They were drizzling a little tea, sprinkling pieces of tortillas, and pouring a few black beans over the burial mounds to feed the earth and share the meal with their parents. We learned that every twenty days, these women walk ten miles from their homes to sit with their parents, then return ten miles in the afternoon. "We love our parents so much. They did so much for us. Here we find comfort, solace, strength, and wisdom to go on." In this relation with the dead, ancestors are sustainers and guides among the living. Fr. Bascilio elaborates:

The dead in Maya cosmovision have an intercessory role before God. It is like the communion of saints, we can say. So those who have died, have the power, the facility to ask before God. For example, if I had a rebellious son who didn't respect me, with my wife we would do an examination of conscience of all the mistakes that we have made that have affected our son. Then we would go to the cemetery. We would call all the grandparents. "Grandpa, Grandma, Mama, Papa, older brothers, older sisters, I have a problem with my son. He doesn't want to work. He doesn't want to improve his situation." So yes, I would intercede for my son. I would intercede for my debt, too. In all the problems of life: debts, economic problems, lack of work, lack of ability to help the community, one asks the intercession of one's grandparents, the dead, to help. So the dead are in communion with the community; we are able to ask them for help. First it is God, then the dead.

Communion with the ancestors crosses boundaries, addressing a communal participation from generation to generation. The living dead continue to belong to the living community. In the ancestors, Maya uncover models of wisdom, courage, and patient endurance; the living dead intercede for their children. What ensues is a deep respect and tenderness for ancestors, which in turn supports present and future life.

In sum, distinct principles shape this affective philosophical grounding and undergird Maya spirituality. The principle of *relational complementariness* holds that created life is intimately related in reciprocal ties; *wach'alal* holds that everyone is a relative, "my people, my brothers, my sisters" (the concept "friend" or "companion" is not found in K'iche'); *nawalism* signifies that a guardian spirit who assists the individual maintain ecological equilibrium; the *nawal* helps one discover, through feeling and goodness, the depth and intensity of relations with nature as well as activating the awareness of one's specific identity; and the principles of *equilibrium, balance,* and *harmony* are established and maintained by observance of the 260-day sacred calendar.

"For the Maya, the fundamental part of life is *affective*," explains Fr. Victoriano Castillo González, of Santa María Chiquimula. "It is to feel in the body, to embody in ritual, in all relationships, this affection." To give thanks, that is why there are ceremonies. Rituals are cornerstones of Maya spirituality, the visible activity of the reciprocal relation in which persons maintain connection and harmony.

"TO CONNECT TO THE CENTER IN WHICH WE TRUST"

Maya link cosmovision to spirituality, or say that their worldview is found within Mayan religiosity. We can infer that the term *Maya cosmovision* has an inevitable ontological or religious aspect, however implicit, that expresses the "lived" experience of Mystery from a human perspective situated in historical experience, struggle, and gratitude. Contemporary Maya utilize the term *spirituality* to speak of ways of living their beliefs. Spirituality, in the words of Sandra Schneiders, is the "fundamental dimension of the human being" as well as "the lived experience which actualizes that dimension" (1990, 17). It entails a capacity within the person to come to a fullness of being, that is, to know and experience Mystery or "the incomprehensible ground of being" (Rahner 1968). Spirituality becomes a practical form for living faith.

Yet a distinction needs to be made. The K'iche' concept spirituality does not have the same connotation that it does in the contemporary Western world, where it tends to focus on the individual. Maya think of faith in practical, reciprocal, embodied, and communal terms. "Spirituality is a modern word," explains Roberto Poz. "If we look for some word to express spirituality or faith in K'iche', as in Zunil, Ajq'ijab' say, 'We are going to work. We are going to offer.'" *Faith* in K'iche' is *kojonik*, meaning "putting it on," referring to ritual practice. The term has a second rendering, explains Roberto, "to connect to the center where we trust," meaning an encounter with Mystery.

Having defined spirituality as a practical form for living faith, ritual practice, and an encounter with Mystery, we must investigate who is addressed in ritual, that is, to investigate the models and metaphors of the sacred. From there we come to some assumptions about reality and the Creator-world relation. Some Ajq'ijab' pray to Catholic saints along with Maya epithets; other traditionalists invoke only names derived from a Maya construct. In prayer, Ajq'ijab' address the Mystery in various forms of couplets, each with its own valence.

> Oh, you B'itol, Tz'akol!
> Look at us! Listen to us!
> Do not leave us. Do not abandon us.

Here the first address is "B'itol, Tz'akol," understood as "Father-Mother." B'itol, or Father, is the formative force, which is part of the divine will, which creates; Tz'akol, or Mother, signifies the manifestation, action, or materialization of divine will in nature. The quality of Ajaw, the fundamental principle of time is a duality. Another invocation begins,

> Oh Ajaw.
> Heart of sky, Heart of earth

Here Ajaw, the Owner of all, is rendered and magnified in the couplet: Heart of Sky, Heart of Earth (Uk'u'x Kaj—Uk'u'x Ulew). This presence, as in the earlier prayer, is inherently relational and immanent, male and female. The term *Heart of Heaven* (Uk'u'x Kaj or Alom K'ajolom) points to a immaterial and incomprehensible energy or force and transcendent space. Alom (conceiver) signifies daughter or girl, referring to the feminine part of conception; K'ajolom (engenderer) indicates son, or the masculine force of creation. Perhaps that is why, when I ask Roberto Poz where wisdom comes from, he says, "From Alom K'ajalom comes life, the voice. From here appears space, time, and movement from which information develops."

The other epithet of the couplet, *Heart of Earth*, or "Uk'u'x Ulew" ("which never appears by itself," D. Tedlock 1985, 341), then becomes the materialization of the immaterial energy, *ch'u* (sacredness). Every appearance in nature, then, is an integral part of the sacred whole, that is, a mysterious something precedes everything else. It serves at the same time as the ground of things and as the manifestation of itself. Edgar Cabrera's (1995) interpretation of the creation account *Popol Wuj* illuminates the process.

> There is a spiritual dimension out of which the number one (Heart of Sky) started acting. From this spiritual dimension comes the Creator's strength that develops initially in the sky, the first level. Then, creation continues on earth, the second level. At some point, Heart of Sky abandons the spiritual dimension and enters the material word as Tepew Qukumatz, or the Plumed Serpent, the egg covered in quetzal feathers that explodes giving initial life. Tepew Qukumatz is in itself, interdependent duality: water and fire, two elemental creators. Tepew Qukumatz acts as an entity on two levels, the sky and the earth, which is folded as an expression of the two divine levels in the figures of *Uk'u'x Kaj*, Heart of Heaven, and *Uk'u'x Ulew*, Heart of Earth. The second, the Heart of the Earth, is a feminine nature; the first, Heart of Heaven, is masculine. . . . In this manner, they are the mother and the father of life.

This doubling of Divinity actually allowed the work of creation to continue forward. But the process was detained and could not continue until the sun and the moon appeared, until the sun and moon had risen. The twins, Junajpu and Xb'alanke, the new doubling, go into the underworld and by playing the sacred ballgame, they die; in their rising, they initiate the lights of the universe with themselves as the sun and the moon in full movement. *The material qualities of the Central deity are precisely time, space, and movement concentrated in energy as the primary expression.* Junajpu and Xb'alanke are in charge to define these three qualities. Putting the sun and moon in orbit gains the cosmic movement; the orbit of the sun establishes the march of time. . . . All of this is realized and completed by the twins in the third level, the underworld, *Xib'alb'a.* (86; my emphasis)

This origin story reflects important principles. Physical and spiritual realms are interconnected and interrelated. It illuminates the foundational paradigm in which the material qualities of Ajaw are space, time, and movement concentrated in energy as the primordial force. Ajaw is the giver of movement and measure. This conceptual blueprint assists us in understanding the spiritual quality perceived in the images as temple-pyramids, calendars, and ritual practices built up over time. It establishes a three-tiered universe. Further, it helps us understand that creation is spiritual as well as verbal and numerical, and that it is unfolding or flowering in an orderly yet experimental process. The blueprint for human activity is found in responses of both the twins and the first humans. When Junajpu and Xb'alanke learned their specific capacity and work was as ball players, not as gardeners, they "acted out their self-revelation" (D. Tedlock 1985, 124). They were smarter than their fathers, who died in the underworld. These young twins were not fooled by the Lords of Xib'alb'a; rather than play to win the ball game, they played *trickster,* and defeated all the Xib'alb'ans. Further explanation of the value of this is in Chapter 3.

"THIS SPIRITUALITY IS OUR LEGACY"

"As Maya we realize we have inherited a very profound relationship with the earth from our ancestors," explains María del Carmen Tuy. "We are obliged to live spiritually in relation with the earth. This spirituality is our legacy." What marks this expression as specifically Maya are methods of *communication* and *interaction* with the vital energy in creation. "Our religion is a form of communication," reads the opening address at the First Congress of Maya Education, held in Quetzaltenango in 1995. "For example, in communication with the fire, in our dreams, with the signals in our bodies, we strengthen the relation of humans with nature." Persons shaped by this relational consciousness continue to seek, encounter, and articulate an implicit intimacy and interconnectedness in life. Roberto Poz amplifies,

As humans, we are in a position of encountering all the interactions of the dynamic forces of the universe. We need to see the world with eyes of reason, with the eyes of the body, and with the eyes of intuition. Intuition is more than language and reason. It is precisely the intuitive understanding that gives birth to wisdom and spirituality. With this vision emerges a renovating love for nature and for each person, a comprehension of the spiritual unity of the universe. . . . Spirituality is located within each person and constitutes a sure kind of energy evident in feelings and expressions, establishing the sense of the presence of a superior force with which one is in intimate contact. (R. Poz, unpublished paper, 1994, 12)

We can see from this explanation that Maya spirituality is a *felt* and *reflected upon* experience, that is, one which not only perceives the interconnectedness of life, but which acknowledges and lives, in practical ways, this sense. As will become apparent later, traditionalists have developed distinct ways of knowing related to the calendar, intuitions, dreams, movements in the body over time. Now, to represent the persistence of this life-consciousness, Maya textiles, tactile texts, illustrate how weaving has reflected and transmitted this cosmovision over the millennia.

WOVEN TEXTILES

The traditional woven clothing for women consists of the *huipil* (blouse), *corte* (skirt), *cinta* (hair wrap), *faja* (belt or sash), and *rebozo* (shawl). Men in a few villages still wear the shirt, pants, *capixy* (tunic), *saco* (jacket), and *sherca* (a heavy knee-length apron-like garment worn over pants). The clothing of each village retains its distinctiveness, has its own specific modality, its own forms and conditions of existence, mirroring a particular set of social relations and ways of organizing the world. Otzoy writes,

> The apparel is an element of external identification so that many
> times one can differentiate the Maya from the rest of the Guatemalan
> population. For the reacknowledgement of the Maya as a people with
> all their rights includes the right to wear and weave Maya clothing; it is
> an artistic complement and demand of socio-cultural liberty. This in-
> cludes the respect and understanding of the changes and continuities
> expressed with the weaving and that both involved acts of self-
> determination. (34)

The changes and continuities in the designs and motifs of the textiles not only express the cultural creativity, but also symbolize the ongoing political resistance of the Maya.

"We continue to wear our traditional clothing because it gives witness to the world that we, indigenous women, are still here," explains Lesbia Salanic Poz. "Further, it shows to the world our belief that humans are in the midst of nature. See the flowers and birds embroidered around the collar and shoulders? It is a sign that woman is to be like the sun, giving light and warmth to those around her."

For centuries, woven cloth, designed with symbols significant to the Maya, has transmitted cosmovision, knowledge, and power—legacies which thread from early Mesoamerican practices. The warps that stretch before a weaver are the matrix in which one places the brocade design. The weft passes horizontally over and under warps to build up the pattern. Texts with multiple meanings of identity, history, lineage, and mythology emerge. The process of spinning and weaving textiles creates "a dynamic complex of variables which include the local community, the world beyond, and the deep historical, often sacred roots of the culture" (R. Carlsen 1993).

Pictorial representations as well as a few actual fragments of fabric show lowland Maya in elaborate ceremonial gear from 300 to 700 CE (Morris 1997, 14). In *Living Maya*, Morris writes of clothing in Maya art:

> Since public monuments were intended for viewing by a semiliterate population, the texts are brief. They state the name of the nobles por-trayed, the ritual event depicted, and the date it was performed, much as footnotes to the complex scenes carved in stone. The ritual implement and the costumes worn are the real "text" that the average Maya could read without difficulty. (24–29)

At Yaxchil'an, a Maya site on the Usumacinta River, three lintels found over the portals of one of the temples showed scenes of a bloodletting rit-ual. On lintel 24, Lady Xoc (709 CE) wears a rectangular gown, or *huipil,* that is brocaded with a field of diamond-shaped designs, the embodiment of time and space (Figure 2.4). On this ceremonial garb, the designs rep-resent the four quarters of the world moving through time; the edge of the *huipil* is bound with woven signs for the sky and planets. "Wearing this ceremonial garb, Lady Xoc symbolically stands at the crossroads, at the center of the world, where she can communicate with her divine ances-tors" (Morris 1997, 14).

On the next lintel, 25, a double-headed serpent coils before Lady Xoc, and from its maw emerges a warrior wearing a jaguar-skin helmet. The design on her garment is a four-petal flower, symbolizing the mouth of Cauac, the reptilian earth monster (Figure 2.5). In the center is a braided knot, the glyph for royalty. "Lady Xoc," Morris writes, "wears what she sees—a royal personage emerging from the jaws of the underworld" (Morris 1997, 30). In the final lintel, 26, Lady Xoc wears a *huipil,* as in the

FIGURES 2.4–2.6. Lady Xoc of Yaxchilán. Lintels 24, 25, 26, drawings by Graham (1977: 53, 55, 56), selected and cropped from Tate (1992, 98 and 99).

first scene, but instead of the earth symbol, there is an image of a toad in the center of the diamonds (Figure 2.6). Of the toad, Morris writes:

> The toad is commonly associated with the beginning of the rainy season, when the newly planted cornfields are filled with toads singing and mating in the first spring showers. The toad symbolizes the rains that bring life and fertility to the earth. Its curled legs resemble the pictograph for accession, the crossed legs of the king seated on the stone platform that serves as his throne. The toad motif is worn by the queen as an emblem of prosperity under Shield Jaguar's reign. (30)

Weaving persists as a dynamic expression of Maya experience, though innovations such as wool and the treadle loom[2] (Rowe 1981), as well as acrylic and metallic thread, have been introduced. Designs today have become public statements about an emerging consciousness of identity. Visual semiology—meaning and messages encoded in the form of sign-vehicles—continues as new motifs develop, and becomes a form of communication, a discourse. For example, icons for one's day of birth or for the entire twenty-day signs woven on Maya textiles in the last decade reflect the reclamation of the Maya calendar. Since 1987, many women and young girls in Zunil have asked their weavers to compose and interweave the Maya day glyphs, specific to each woman's day of birth, conception, and future, into the vertical lines of their green *cortes* (woven skirts) (Figures 2.7–2.9). Fifty miles to the east, in Patzun, women embroiderers brocade the Chol Q'ij's twenty-day signs circling the neckline of the *huipil* (woven and embroidered blouse). In Santa Catarina, around Lake Atitlán, textile artists interweave Maya day signs on their celestial blue-and-white striped *huipiles*. Estuardo Zapata explains that jackets with embroidered Chol Q'ij designs

FIGURES 2.7, 2.8, AND 2.9.
Designs on these contemporary
cortes in Zunil have the young
girl's or woman's particular day-
signs of the Chol Q'ij woven
into the fabric, while patterns
on the *huipil* from Yaxchilán
(709 CE) mirror the quatrefoil
world moving through time.
Lintel 15. Drawing by Graham
(1977, 39), from Tate (1992, 198).

have been popular for commercial consumption since the mid-'90s. Women embroiderers often produce the designs knowing they can demand a fair price, but do not understand the significance of the days (personal communication, 1998). The new and the old have the same ties. Like their ancestors before them, weavers design with purpose the universe into Maya cloth, creating continuity between the old and the new.

Irma Otzoy, a Kaqchikel scholar, writes, "The attitude toward conserving textiles permits the Maya to dress in a kind of clothing that satisfies their artistic, moral, and spiritual feelings, and also distinguishes them culturally" (1996, 14). In *Maya' b'anikl Maya' atzyaqb'al (Maya Identity and Maya Clothing)*, Otzoy analyzes the use of Maya apparel as a cultural element which represents the processes of historical struggle, cultural creativity, and political resistance. She explains, "To dress in Maya clothing, the Maya woman demonstrates her identity and at the same time imports a reading [lesson] of active cultural resistance. The Maya *traje* (clothing) provides the world a text to be read, a living library" (27).

The *huipil,* a mirror of the universe, encloses a woman in sacred space, announces her positionality and dignity. Clothing is linked to spirituality and ceremony in multiple dimensions: the motifs, the colors, relations of colors, symbols, and designs. Aura Marina, an embroiderer, social worker, and teacher in Quetzaltenango, explains that a Maya woman weaves out of her spirituality.

> When I am working with women embroiderers, I ask them, "How do you feel in your heart?" "If you feel happy, you will reflect that beauty in the brightness of the colors you choose on the *huipil*. If you are sad, you will choose darker colors; if you are not in equilibrium with the cosmos, you will not balance the colors and designs well. When you commission a weaver, you want to know that she is spiritually well.

Aura Marina continues, "The *corte* and *huipil* reflect the elements of the ceremony. They reflect the woman's feelings in her heart, her sense of beauty in the world around her in the flowers and animals she chooses." Pointing out how the four designs around the collar of her elaborately woven and embroidered Quetzalteca *huipil* reflect four days of the Chol Q'ij, she explains, "These are to keep us in balance."

The signators of the Agreement on Identity and Rights of Indigenous Peoples pledged to respect and guarantee as a constitutional right the use of indigenous clothing in all aspects of national life and to struggle against all discrimination regarding the use of indigenous clothing. They also agreed to "the conscientization of the population regarding the Maya,

Garifuna, and Xinca cultures in their distinct manifestations, and to inform the public of the spiritual and cultural values of the indigenous cloth and their due respect" (17–18).

Modernization and global processes are shifting the use, and in some cases the accessibility, of the *huipil*. One effect of the civil war was that widows who had to assume the planting and harvesting responsibilities as well as caring for their children and household no longer had time to weave. Recently, as more young Maya attend secondary schools, these private schools require young girls to wear uniforms, Western in design. In cosmopolitan areas, younger women find sweatsuits, tee shirts, and jeans more economical, comfortable, and warmer for certain activities. For example, one young woman, fifteen, who works in the San Lucas Tolimàn reforestation project, explains to me, "I do not own a *huipil*. There is so much dignity, pride, and identity in our *huipiles*, but I do not have money to buy one. So I buy tee shirts. I want to save money for a *huipil*; it reflects our world." Most young women, however, in formal and social events, are proud to present themselves in the *huipil*, *corte*, and *faja* of their village.

To conclude the chapter on cosmovision, I want to return to another Sunday afternoon with the group of Ajq'ijab' in Zunil, to an incident which, I think, reflects the openness, inclusiveness, and concern for future generations in Maya thinking. When I am in Guatemala, I usually visit with members of Komun Tohil, sometimes sharing videos of Native American ceremonies, sacred places, or cultural ways. When I show the same films to students in U.S. universities, they typically express perceptions of "otherness." Ajq'ijab', by contrast, immediately draw parallels to their lives and discuss what they can learn from the videos, how they can improve and hone their ceremonial practice to make it more beautiful and effective.

In June 1997, I approached Komun Tohil about doing a film with them in collaboration with Patricia Amlin on the reemergence of Maya practices. The purpose, I explained, would be to illuminate this new cycle of light, the renaissance of visible Maya spirituality through ethnographic interviews, ceremonies, and an animation of calendric cycles. The intended audience would be the people of Guatemala, so they can understand beliefs, ceremonial work, and responsibilities to the community of the Ajq'ijab'.

"Our ancestors had glyphs," Doña Marta began. "We should leave something for our children. We should use contemporary technology."

"Someday we are going to die," added a woman of twenty-eight. "But our children can see it. We should do it so they will know our ceremonies."

Berta, eighteen years old, spoke to us in K'iche' through Roberto. "Utz, compadre. This is good, compadre. We never know from one day to another if we will be here or not. But we can leave this for those who come after us."

"The call we have," Roberto said, turning to me, "we don't understand until years later, until after years of prayer, ritual, and service to others. Education for other people is important so they will know who we are and that they will understand that what we do is not bad."

"This understanding that we have," began Faustina in a quiet, gentle voice, "that our ancestors have left with us, helps us in our difficulties." She continues, "Their teachings help us wake up in our difficulties. So we know we owe something to Mother Earth. One way to give thanks is the use of incense, or pom, as a way of giving thanks very profoundly. The ancestors' words are a memory for future generations. If we make this movie, when we leave the earth, we will leave these ideas, and our children will see this material. They will see the decision is in me, but they will recognize that they have the seed in themselves. We have an oral tradition. It is sacred and secret. But we thank Mother Earth and give those aromas to her."

What I found very moving in this conversation was that all but one of the women who spoke was either single or married without children due to miscarriages. Yet each woman, childless, spoke lovingly of the children to come. Further, each utterance was placed humbly before the reality of death.

The men and women conversed excitedly with one another in K'iche' and I saw as they nodded in agreement, they had come to a consensus about something. Doña Marta turned to me and spoke for the group: "Doña Juana, we need a ceremony to purify the machines. Before filming, we need to ask the nawales, the guardian spirits, to protect the work. We need to ask them that the message be strong, so the viewer can feel this 'call' to be within the spirituality of life."

Maya approach to life is practical. Several weeks later, on the selected morning of Aq'ab'al, we (the original film crew), carrying aromatic offerings in our backpacks, followed five Ajq'ijab' up through the cornfields toward the pine-surrounded cave, Xe' kega ab'aj. This altar, east of Zunil, is the site of a fresh spring, a place of initiations. During the ceremony, Doña Marta and Roberto held the camera over the fire, saturating it with its white smoke. Indeed, all, in this case even the camera, is included in Maya cosmovision!

This discussion on foundations of Maya cosmovision provides the bridge into the next chapter, where we shall hear contemporary Ajq'ijab' illuminate their obligation, their way of living and working before B'itol, Tz'akol, Heart of Sky, Heart of Earth.

Part 2

A CULTURAL INHERITANCE

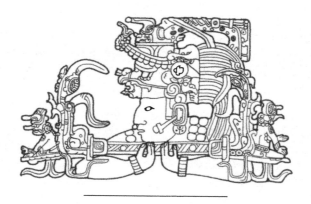

CHAPTER 3

Ajq'ijab'
"To Enter the Mystery Is Our Reality"

Calixta Gabriel Xiquín was twenty-seven years old when I asked if she would share her life story with me. That was October 1980. At twenty-six years of age, she fled alone from the highlands of Guatemala north to San Jose, California. Her three brothers had been assassinated within eighteen months of each other in 1978–79, and her parent's adobe home and cornfield had been burned; the family relocated to a government-designed "model village." This young woman fled to the United States for refuge, assuming the names "Eugenia," "Domitilia," and "María" in exile.

In Guatemala, she had been a social worker, catechist, and teacher of literacy and Maya culture in her village of thirteen thousand, and a coordinator of a Catholic radio program in Kaqchikel, her native language. In California, Calixta worked in a rubber assembly plant and later in an auto parts assembly plant; she etched her pain and loss in poetry, claimed hope and life in song, and actively lectured and spoke for the dignity, culture, and suffering of her people.

We sat together in her bedroom in San Jose. On the wall behind Calixta hung a turquoise banner she had put together in memory of her family. Photos of her sister weaving on a backstrap loom and of her three assassinated brothers were carefully placed with pinecones, wheat sheaves, flowers, and an ear of corn. She had glued the words "Weaving the Life" to the cloth. On a small table beneath the banner, a single flame burned from a white candle.

Calixta sorted through a pile of loose papers scattered on her bed and selected the handwritten page before her. She knelt down on the hardwood floor, tucking her corte *neatly under her. I sat cross-legged facing her. As she read, the intensity of her face lightened, her words resonating as if warmed with a ray of sun. Through her generous smile and deliberate reading, she spilled her poetry.*

> When I see your faces in the portraits
> of those shadows
> my soul soars,
> my heart pounds.
> I sigh for pain,
> for happiness,
> for the immense space and void that separates us.
> We hold back the tears in each other's eyes.
>
> I feel lonely.
>
> I walk alone carrying the pain of evil,
> which is like the heat of fire
> that whips our souls,
> empty of mourning for death,
> for the martyrdom of enduring hunger and
> the cold wind of poverty.
> I sob for the wreckage
> of the very rites of the breath of life.
> I want to see you.

She finished reading and wiped her face, catching some of the tears which streamed down, missing others which dropped on the embroidered flowers on her huipil. *That* huipil, *hand-embroidered with birds, flowers, stars, sun, and lightning, echoed Maya knowledge that their lives are in the midst of the cosmos. What endured in that cloth was the collective permanence created in the centuries of the Maya weaving, reflecting their astronomy, mathematics, and mythology.*

Then Calixta raised her head, smiling through her tears. "It's very difficult to understand, but these hardships help me to grow in my spiritual life. I think it's really very hard to be the kind of martyr that dies. But it's even harder to be a martyr and live. I feel I'm in exile in the United States. There have been tremendous shocks for me—the murders of my brothers and my people—as well as trying to understand the people in the United States.

"For the Maya, the most fundamental thing is life. We can tolerate being robbed or being poor, but when they start taking away life . . ." Her voice

quivered, her eyes filled with tears. "I would like to make many people aware of my people, but in the United States people are so inclined toward materialism and individualism . . ."

Calixta was among the hundreds of thousands of Mayas who fled the Guatemalan highlands to Mexico, to the United States, to Canada during the massive repression and massacres from 1978 to 1982. Exiled, grieving the loss of her three brothers and of her displaced parents, hearing news of increasing numbers of murders of her people, and trying to construct her life in the United States, she was often overwhelmed; surges of sadness, heartbreak, and anguish swelled her being. She entered the labyrinth of her memory for some warmth, some flicker of light. She sought out friendships across ethnic, race, gender, and class boundaries: she became an avid spokeswoman for Maya displaced and exiled, and in her numerous invitations to speak, she denounced the Guatemalan army's massacres of Maya peasants. Her brothers dead, her parents far away, she often found herself desperate, alone; "everyday life confronts me with the reality of mourning in my soul," she once wrote.

Calixta entrusted her soul before a fire; here she encountered sustenance, warmth, and courage. She entered a ritual ceremony, either alone or with her friends, in her backyard or in the San Jose foothills. The fire, fed with sage, cedar, copal, and sugar, became her steady point of reference, the ancestral conduit of her people.

She explained to us. "We go to the mountains to pray. God is in nature, so we leave our villages and go the mountains to give thanks, to beg pardon, to ask for a blessing. We light candles, burn incense, make offerings. Some burn an ear of corn so the smell will rise and carry their gratefulness to the Creator.

"We don't even have a word like religion in our language. For us it is life itself: respect, dignity, love for one's neighbor. All these things are the presence of God. One way the Maya prays is by blowing 'huh' into one's hand. [She breathed into the palm of her cupped hand.] It's like saying 'Excuse me' or 'Pardon me.' The Maya does this 'huh' and continues on his or her way. For example, when we slap the tortilla dough we do it. Or before a man cuts down a tree, he asks permission from the earth by saying 'huh' because the earth is his mother. My parents taught me this prayer, and even now I do this prayer for many things. But it doesn't translate well because it doesn't have words. It comes from the heart."

In exile, Calixta found herself in a liminal space. She sought ways of accommodating: learning English, earning a living assembling rubber or auto *parts, adjusting to formalities and time prescriptions; but she remained conscious of her displacement, the "bifocality" that characterizes locally lived lives in a globally interconnected world. "I am alone," she wrote.*

> I find myself alone,
> everyday life confronts me
> with the reality of mourning in my soul.
> The fibers of my being broken and torn
> from the injustice,
> the struggle that springs from the blood of innocent people,
> the collective martyrdom of Latin America,
> the shadows that amass on our journey,
> the ringing of the bells of our being . . .
> It's not my calling,
> neither have I chosen it.

The "aloneness" she writes, "is not my calling." Displacement can be devastating. Displacement is not merely about attachment to place as a sociopolitical context, but an inner, much deeper uprooting from a geography, a sense of time, a language, a people which sustained one's soul. Calixta reached out to new people, and they to her. She found herself emerging at an intersection of multiple communities: Chilean and Argentinian "widowed women of the world," religious groups of women, migrant workers from Mexico who also resettled in San Jose as well as Hopi, Navajo, and Arapaho elders who also shared a profound sense of a loss of territorial roots, but also connected with their spiritual sources. She accompanied the elders in ritual sweats and peyote ceremonies; she sought solace and healing from Doña Andrea, a visiting Huichol curandera *from northern Mexico. She found herself in a "multiplicity of attachments that people form to places through living in, remembering, and imagining them" (Malkki 1992, 38), rethinking difference through connections. While Calixta's network of friends broadened and deepened in the Bay Area, she was becoming clearer that she could not sustain her soul in the deep uprooting from her geography and sense of time, from her people and language.*

In her dreams and in indigenous ceremonies, visions emerged directing her to her homeland, warning of great risks and of accompanying protection in the many trials. In 1985 Vinicio Cerezo had been elected; killings of dissidents by death squads declined, and she decided to return to Guatemala.

"I feel so contaminated in the United States. People don't respect life. They don't give thanks. I cannot survive here."

Friends questioned her, "But aren't you afraid you might be killed?" Friends warned her, "You might be arrested."

But her response was firm. "*I would rather die among my people than die little by little each day here.*"

She sought a context for the problem of her soul.

For Calixta, her experience was a daily death; the angst of her soul, her loneliness, her search for depth, increasing visions, the image of her work, and the advice of Native American religious women and men all played into the forces of cultural gravity. Though she drew strength from multiple communities and hybrid rituals, what made sense for Calixta were her people's models, metaphors, stories, and images, which shaped her principles and values. Calixta sought the "metaphysical and moral valuation of roots in the homeland." Simone Weil wrote, "To be rooted is perhaps the most important and least recognized need of the human soul" (1952, 7–8). For Calixta, that rootedness meant a return to the Guatemalan highlands, to be immersed in and to embrace Maya life ways.

In 1987, seven years after her arrival in the United States, Martín and I bid her farewell as she departed for Guatemala. Weeks earlier, she had written this poem:

> California is beautiful.
> It's a paradise.
> It covers me when there's sun
> and caresses me when I'm happy.
> But California leaves me uncovered when it gets cold,
> and in the dark when the night comes,
> and all alone when I become sad.
> That's why my mind never lies down here.
> It never rests day or night
> because I am thinking only of my motherland.
> I miss her warmth and her mantle.
> I want her to blanket me with her beauty even in death.

Though she left California soil, Calixta linked many of us with the Maya, their cultural ways, depth, and their struggles. In conversations, questions and affections were planted which would have lives of their own. As Breckenridge and Appadurai write, "Diasporas always leave a trail of collective memory about another place and time and create new maps of desire and of attachment" (1989, 1).

In Calixta's case, she returned to the Guatemalan highlands; she sought healing from her accumulated darkness and pain under the guidance of a K'iche' woman Ajq'ij. After months of preparation, Calixta was initiated as an Ajq'ij, beginning to learn ancestral wisdom, culturally constructed

perceptions of the sacred in the cosmos, the accompanying rituals and re-
sponsibilities. In 1996 Calixta published her first book of poems, Hueso de la
Tierra. In 1999 she received the degree of Licentiate in Social Work from the
University of Rafael Landívar, with a thesis on the social function of
Kaqchikel Maya spiritual guides. She continues to serve her people spiritually.

In my case, this work on Maya spiritual practices was initiated by Calixta's
words:

> When the Europeans came to Guatemala, they met a strong culture and
> colonized it with the Catholic faith. It appears we accepted the faith,
> but this is not really so. We already had the faith. It was a way of life for
> my people. It's like we just changed clothes and put on a mask. Our faith
> is profound within us.

"TO ENTER THE MYSTERY IS OUR REALITY"

The Ajq'ij understands his or her spiritual work, undergoes training, offers petitions and thanksgiving in rituals, and illuminates according to the
Maya sacred calendar and worldview. "To be an Ajq'ij, in our Tz'utujil language, is to be 'of the days,' 'in charge of the days,'" explains María del
Carmen Tuy, from Sololá. "It is much better to say 'Ajq'ij,' not Maya
'priest' or 'priestess,' as these are Spanish terms. They don't express what
we are. It is a person with the destiny to serve the community." Other
K'iche'-speaking villages, such as Santa María Chiquimula, use the term
chuchqajaw,[1] meaning Mother-Father, which is understood as the media-
tor between person, nature, and Ajaw, or the earlier term, *zahorin*, in San
Antonio Ilotenango (Falla).

Ajq'ijab' (plural of Ajq'ij) use the Chol'Qij ("the day count"), the symbolic 260-day calendar system, which serves as an orientation instrument.
They guard the values and knowledge of this calendar and transmit them
in counsel and in ceremonies. To be a spiritual guide is one's destiny, a
power that is determined from one's birthdate. "One is born an Ajq'ij, it is
not something one chooses," explains Roberto Poz (Figure 3.1). Ajq'ijab'
observe and understand the days and dedicate themselves to a relationship
with B'itol, Tz'akol, Constructor and Former. Scholars have identified
Ajq'ijab' as daykeepers, priest-shamans and shaman-priests, priests,
Working People, or ritual specialists.[2]

The Ajq'ij is not the only kind of spiritual designation. Maya thought is
formed by positive and negative, a complementary duality, and the Ajitz
(*itz* means "of the obscurity") is a person whose "day" obligates her or him

FIGURE 3.1. Ajq'ij Roberto Poz Pérez prays before the fire.

to balance between sicknesses, confusion, even death. This person may enter pacts with sinister forces. In taking on the obligation of "darkness," an individual does not become bad, but powerful and dangerous. "It is part of their destiny, the work they must do," explains Roberto. There are also the *ajnawal mesa*, or *ajmesa (mesa* means "table"), individuals who concentrate at a special sacred place or in front of a table, and communicate directly with ancestors and spirits. "The work he or she does is good," explains Roberto. "When we began Komun Tohil, we saw many spiritual mediums [instruments for the voice and will of the spirits that possessed them] in Zunil and Samayac. In the mountains, the energies or spirits call. We think it is because of all who have gone before, who have suffered and died in this area. Their spirits live here."

The commitment of women and men Ajq'ijab' is the focus of this chapter. Ajq'ijab' speak about understandings of their obligation, their work. The framework for the present discussion is M. M. Bakhtin's *Toward a Philosophy of the Act* and *Art and Answerability*. Both texts offer a comprehensive and unifying theory positing that an individual establishes a relationship to the world with a specific "field of vision," in a unique time, space, and culture. This theory of authoring, answerability, and unfinalizability from the standpoint of aesthetics, and of ethical responsibility, provides the paradigm I will use for the *answerability* of the self, the *transformation* of the self, and finally the *responsibility* of the self to the community.[3]

In Bakhtin's theoretical constructions, everything is approached from a particular point of view, "time and space as embodied in a particular human at a particular time and in a particular place" (1990, 145). Thus, one sees the world from a *horizon*: "the world gives itself as immediately around me, as circumscribed by the angle of my vision, as a surrounding full of specific meanings determined by my own ends" (xxxix). Bakhtin says of self-activity: "The problem of the soul, from a methodological standpoint, is a problem in aesthetics" (xl). Aesthetics, he writes, is "a form of embodying lived experience" (xl), "for everything that is aesthetically valid encompasses not a void," but is the struggle to achieve a whole, positional, and relative construct; it is "the persistent . . . directedness to meaning on the part of an act-performing life" (xl). Thus for Bakhtin, to be human is to *mean*, to live a determined life. "I become the instrument for assigning specific value to time and space" (xxix).

But a full self-accounting is impossible; consummated wholes can never be absolute, but are toward a larger value. Bakhtin writes that outside of God, outside of trust in absolute otherness, self-consciousness and self-utterance are impossible. Trust in God is an immanent constitutive moment of pure self-consciousness and self-expression. "As trust and tones of faith and hope gain immediate actuality, aesthetic moments begin to penetrate into self-accounting... and one begins to change from an *I-for-myself* into the other for God" (xxxvii).

As Bakhtin develops his theory on aesthetic self-activity, he delineates the determined, emotional-volitional activity and unity of *answerability*. Parts are developed into wholes.

> The individual must become answerable through and through: all of his constituent moments must not only fit next to each other in the temporal sequence of his life, but must also interpenetrate each other in the unity of guilt and answerability. (2)

With this brief theory of authoring, answerability, and aesthetic activity in place, we can now consider the aesthetics and ethical responsibility of Ajq'ijab' from their horizon, their angle of vision, of space, time, and human activity.

ANSWERABILITY

Since 1985 an increasing number of women and men of all ages, as young as fourteen and as old as seventy, have been publicly initiated as Ajq'ijab'. Their lives span a diversity of professions: weavers, educators, merchants, agricultural workers, community workers, university professors and students, carpenters, midwives, bone setters, orthodontists, journalists, lawyers, and those who dedicate their lives entirely as spiritual guides. I have also observed that homosexual men find in this tradition a space to express their faith, and to be respected for and function publicly in their spiritual roles. A growing number of Ladinos, Europeans, and North Americans have also been initiated.[4] Ajq'ijab' are a living legacy to the first K'iche', who were great knowers, guides, penitents, and sacrificers.

In investigating the roles of the Momostenango daykeepers (Ajq'ijab'), Barbara Tedlock reviews the anthropological and ethnographic materials of active religious practitioners of Mesoamerican communities.[5] Tedlock concludes that "shamanism—defined in the strictest possible manner by William Madsen as necessarily involving direct communication between spirits and the diviner through dreams, visions, or spirit possessions—exists in Maya communities" (1982, 50).

The shaman is the person, male or female, who experiences, absorbs, and communicates a special mode of sustaining, consulting, and healing power.[6] The shaman's call has several distinguishing characteristics in his or her numinous encounter. Contact with the numinous is initiated by spirits. Within many indigenous traditions, contact with numinous power often produces an illness, whose cure instigates the shamanic vocation.[7] Transformative dreams are often able to give form and order to this chaotic situation. After this experience, and often after undergoing an initiation process, he or she brings the sustaining energy to the community. Aware of both hidden and manifest spirit presences, shamans maintain their communications with the spirit world, through silence, prayer, abstinence, and ritual practice. Tedlock notes that Momostecan daykeepers and mother-fathers are not only shamans, but also priests, that is, those who serve as an intermediary between man and the gods (1982, 24).

Ajq'ijab' iterate this twofold aspect. Roberto explains:

> I received a call, a connection with all the ancestors, with the mountains, with altars, so sacred, with ancestors of tremendous power and intelligence. In ceremonies, we connect ourselves with the ancestors and in this connection, we feel very happy. As humans when we are alone, we are worried. In prayer, we can be very tranquil. Within our call, with all the ancestors, such as the mountains and the temples, we connect with the Father Sky and the Mother Earth to feel this love that we so much need.

María del Carmen Tuy, a community educator, says:

> An Ajq'ij is a person who comes with a mission to help humanity. One is in charge of the days. One is an important person, as one guides others, depending upon one's ability. One could have the ability to cure others, to solve family problems, to give advice. There are different abilities. Both men and women are called to serve as Ajq'ijab', not only men, not only women. Some problems must be attended by men; others must be attended by women. But we all have to complete the mission we received from the moment of our birth, our mission to help humanity.

Edgar Rolando Ixcot, a journalist, explains that Ajq'ijab' held great authority in earlier times.

> Ajq'ijab' are spiritual guides. We have a hierarchy, and the Ajq'ij' is the authority. In previous times, the Ajq'ij' advised in political and social matters. And this was the construction of the ancient understanding. For example, in a town, the Ajq'ij looked at the sign of the birth to decide different roles. If one was born on Noj [a day of wisdom and understanding], that person could be the mayor; if born on Tzi'kin

[day of fortune], that person could be appointed treasurer to create a good economic base for the community; or if one was born on Tzi [justice], that person could be the lawyer, treating everyone equally, without favoritism.

Tomás García, a K'iche' and Catholic priest in Cantel, explains:

> Ajq'ijab' have received an authentic vocation; it is the power to convey. One is a servant, as an *alcalde* (mayor) in the Maya structure. It is an inheritance. The Western priest inherits scripture, Catholic, Jewish, Greek, Latin, and Spanish traditions. But the Maya inheritance is more authentic. It's a call within the living cosmos. — *chosen*

I recognize Ajq'ijab' as individuals informed by "a sense of faith," which Bakhtin writes "is an integral attitude . . . toward a higher and ultimate value" (Morson and Emerson 1990, 61). This attitude establishes a relationship to the world within a "horizon," that is, in a unique time, space, and culture, and it initiates and sustains one in a specific and meaningful life. Persons who understand, maintain, and embrace Maya cosmovision interpret their destiny within the 260-day sacred calendar, which is the "field of vision" or horizon from which they understand the full capacity of their lives. "They become the instrument for assigning specific value to time and space" (Bakhtin 1990, xl) within an inherited construct. A person receives this capacity[8] and obligation from the day of one's birth. Thus their birth date on the 260-day sacred calendar, to which they assign specific value, is the dynamic icon from which they chart their lives. María del Carmen Tuy interprets it as follows:

> A child receives this destiny from the moment one comes into the world. His or her parents often know it and raise the child accordingly. Many things happen in one's life as child, as a young person, which prepare one for this destiny. Things will happen in life, which will manifest this destiny in different forms; then the person will need a lot of attention from the parents and the spiritual guides so this person can develop. This person will encounter many problems, so we have to help the person to walk so he or she can help humanity. But there comes a moment when it is a person's "time" to receive it.

Maya say that the *time to receive* their obligation is manifested through dreams, visions, spirit possessions, sicknesses, and personal problems that cannot be solved.[9] They explain that problems manifest because a person hasn't attended to his or her day, his or her *nawal*, that is, energy or mission (Figures 3.2–3.5).

FIGURE 3.3. María del Carmen Tuy, from Sololá.

FIGURE 3.2. Calixta Gabriel, from San José Poaquil.

FIGURE 3.4. María Antonieta Cofulum, from Quetzaltenango.

FIGURE 3.5. Male Ajq'ijab' from the highland region.

According to Roberto Poz, "The day you were born on the calendar carries the 'it's my time in it.' There comes the time to manifest itself." Most frequently, those suffering physical illness will first seek the help of a medical doctor. But when nothing cures the illness, they will seek an Ajq'ij. While individuals experience this obligation at all ages of life, I have found that girls and women tend to arrive at this point younger than men.[10]

While ethnographers have recounted that physical illnesses, dreams, visions, and spirit possessions are catalysts for this vocation, in my ethnographic work, I have also met individuals who have undertaken this path from a restlessness, a sincere search for depth, or as a way to better serve their community. They desire to live out the fullness of their capacities and potentialities; they *seek* to become Ajq'ijab'. Individuals speak of an intense restlessness or constant nightmares and problems and will seek advice from an elder Ajq'ij, who studies the date of birth, the dreams, illnesses, and struggles, and consults the fire and *tz'ite'* ritual to help determine whether or not that person might become an Ajq'ij. Further, the elder advises whether the time is right for the individual to begin training. Although Ajq'ijab' offer diverse accounts of their realizations of this obligation, they share in common the lengthy and often extreme burdens of illnesses, family misfortunes, nightmares, visions, or restlessness and desire for a deeper commitment. Each explains this in relation to his/her date of birth. Physical torment, infirmity, and even death plague the initiate until he/she responds to this call. The urgent nature of such sicknesses is revealed by Pablo, of Panajachel:

> I began working because of so much sickness. They told me I had to work in ceremonies. But I didn't want to. I was afraid. What will all the people think?

A husband and wife Ajq'ijab' in San José Poaquil explain,

> We had so much pain. We went to Ajq'ijab'. "You have to work," they told us. We didn't want to do it. That's why all died: the cats, the dogs, the turkey, the children. Then we made an offering. Now we have three daughters. We have to continue this work.[11]

Berta, who became an Ajq'ij at the age of fourteen, recounts,

> It's because of a sickness. When I was young, I got really sick. I had lots of diseases for two months. They tried to heal me. Even different Ajq'ijab', but they couldn't find it. We went to different *curanderas* and doctors. They gave me herbs and things, but nothing helped. At age twelve or thirteen, I became so sick. I couldn't get well. "It's the spirit," my parents said. "It's a bad power in you and they can make you sick." But I became so sick. "Why don't you go to another person or a center of spiritists?" they said. At night I got so sick. Three days later, I became gravely ill. I went to see an Ajq'ij. They asked me to accept it, but I didn't want it. Finally, I paid for the training to become an Ajq'ij. My father borrowed the money. It was so hard for me because my Dad had to borrow money. Little by little, I became better. My mother asked, but this Ajq'ij said, "It's her day."

Francisco, a carpenter, former catechist, and now an Ajq'ij in Zunil, explains his prolonged illness, doubts, and the dream in which he decided to become an Ajq'ij. In his narrative, we hear his wife's doubts and mother's support.

> In my past during the time when I was going to the Catholic Church, I never had any problems. No. I got married. Three years later, I had big pains. I became so ill. When I had two children, I got very sick. I had just a simple cold, and then I became well, then worse. But in another time, I was so sick for twenty days. I was so ill for a month. It was the festival of Santa Catarina. I became so sick for two to three months. I became so sick. I also had a family, and I didn't have money for firewood. It was

important. My father said, "Don't worry about it. We'll give you some corn, some firewood." My wife asked, "Why did this happen? You know Ajq'ijab'. Ask them."

They said, "I think it's his day. "No," my wife said, "it's an illness."

"I'll become an Ajq'ij. It's too bad that we have gone so much to Catholicism," I said.

"No, it's a lie," my wife said.

"If I die, I'll die," I thought.

My mother said, "The old way is true."

In my case I accepted it myself. Because of the pain and the thought of dying. "Oh, What am I going to do? Just become an Ajq'ij, a *brujo*."[12] But I kept asking myself, "Is it ourselves or not?

"I had my first ceremonies, three times, and then I was calm. I had a dream that it was right by my day. So I decided to become an Ajq'ij. I know some people say, "Oh they just want to make money." I didn't want to become an Ajq'ij to make money, because I already knew how to make money. But it was my gift. I see it is important in my life. I heard, but it's like I was sleeping and I woke up. I am an Ajq'ij. Ten years I have been an Ajq'ij. Thanks to God. I have not been sick at all with any illness.

Others speak about a persistent desire to commit themselves to their community at a deeper level, accompanied by personal problems and dreams. Victor Lem, a musician and member of the former National Commission of Spirituality, explains,

I suffered a restlessness, the need and desire to work at another level. I encountered tests, physical tests and spiritual tests in dreams. I felt afraid of the great responsibility. An Ajq'ij has a role, but the way is very open and deep. It is all of the energies, and an orientation to give to others, to your family, to the people. It is to be a guide. At that stage I felt this necessity, this desire, but also a terror because there are questions one has to look at. One is not independent of energy. You have to understand duality, complementariness, and balance within the cosmos. It is a tremendous responsibility.

Roberto Poz recounts multiple manifestations of his "call."

There was a stage in my own life when I could not find a road to follow. There was no alternative. In the midst of this, I felt that I had a great sickness. *This is the call.* I went to another Ajq'ij to guide me because other Ajq'ijab' had said something. But this other Ajq'ij also said, "You are confused. You have a vocation, another destiny." Through all my trials, I came to know that I needed to have a deeper relationship with life. I missed something in my life, an energy, some clear direction. I had the same dream three times, that I was getting married again. But I loved my wife. I tried to heal myself from this dream, but it didn't work. When I went to an elder Ajq'ij, he explained I was being called to work in the community. For nine months, I prayed with this Ajq'ij to see if I had the gift. I waited to see if it was for my life. When the elder priest told me, "You have the gift. You'll respect the gift. You have enough energy to become a priest," I put myself to the task. I knew the gift has a strong power to cure, to give advice and direction in life. I continued praying, studied the Maya calendar, and talked about this with our relatives, who accepted the predictions. Finally, after I made many ceremonies and sacrifices, I was ready to accept the gift.

Other individuals, such as Calixta Gabriel, experienced this *growing obligation* when they were outside Guatemala. She recounts, "I was in the exterior for seven years in the United States. The most important part of this time was that I found myself and I encountered the depth of Maya ways."

The multiple manifestations of illnesses, visions, dreams, and problems reflect the enervating quality of this formative phase. These sicknesses, interpreted as more than ordinary illness, are a forced preparation which limit the individual's social interaction and s/he turns toward inner psychic activity. The dream-calls initiate her/him into the powerful world of cosmic forces. Ajq'ijab' reflect on why a person experiences such suffering, illnesses, and problems when the time to receive it comes. Q'anjobal Ajq'ij Matías explains it as a purification, a cleansing of negative energy, so "light can be understood within the person." He says,

> The person, the Ajq'ij, is born as any person who is born and grows up like others. There comes a moment when his/her day arrives, the day of enlightenment. It is the moment that the light wants to be understood within the person. This is when the light begins to ignite. In this moment, when the light is kindled, it requires purification because to be an Ajq'ij implies you will have positive energy, energy of happiness, of joy, an energy of medicine. So one can't continue as one was. One must eliminate as much negative energy as possible. This process of elimination of the spiritual dirtiness is an immense pain that one experiences. It is something that is fighting, attacking your body. It is an experience of pain that is so immense, so immense that it is incomparable. One says, "Never, never have I experienced such pain." One is passing through the field of the fire. Also when you pass through this field of the fire, there is a

happiness that is incomparable. One also says, "Never, never, have I experienced such joy and happiness." But how beautiful, how lovely, how immense is the life. One smiles, one lives a new quality.

Vilma Poz cites this initial phase as preparation for understanding and assisting others in their problems.

As an Ajq'ij, one wonders why it is that in the beginning things are apparently bad. Why is it that we have to pass through so much suffering? Why? The "why" is that we pass through so many sufferings to understand others. If an Ajq'ij was perfect, he or she couldn't help another. If someone comes here seeking help, I wouldn't understand. I would look at another level. If I didn't have economic problems, I wouldn't understand. It is so one can pass a crisis, so one can help others. It is something so beautiful, so wonderful.

For many Maya Ajq'ijab', before they can accept this ancestral capacity, they must *reassess the discourse* imposed by colonialism and other global processes, which internally colonize, imposing Catholic or evangelical belief structures, controls, disciplines, metaphors, and icons. They must also *reconsider the spiritual aspects* of their own experiences, the advice of the ancestors, the role of ceremonies and rituals, and the sacred calendar system. Some are afraid of what the community around them may say; others hesitate, recognizing the great responsibility of service to one's community. This reassessment can best be explained by means of Bakhtin's hermeneutical process, which Thorn develops in *The Lived Horizon of My Being*. She writes that this process of self-fulfillment and reconciliation includes the following:

1. The absorption/internalization of outside, generally prejudicial, opinion concerning the individual;
2. Assessment of the *self*, relative to that outside influence, which is essential to reconciliation and situating one's *self* ideologically;
3. A metamorphosis that begins with a conscious volition to change;
4. The growth of a modulated and self-sustaining person, which represents a shift outward from moral and ethical contemplation and consideration to speech and individuation;
5. Finally, the projection of that *self* into the world at large, through praxis. (Thorn 1996, 14)

Each of these individuals have at some moment assessed their experiences from within a Maya worldview, accepted their "obligation," "their "destiny"[13]—an activity that we might call in English "faith"—and through a willed decision, begun a metamorphosis.

"Faith" in *K'iche'*, as mentioned earlier, is *kojonik*, meaning "a center where we connect to trust" or "putting it on." This faith, informed by an inner determinateness, facilitates gratitude and a connection with Mystery, with the ground of being. Roberto Poz explains that for the Ajq'ijab', "To enter the mystery is our reality." On trust in God, Bakhtin writes, "Where I overcome in myself the axiological self-contentment of present-on-hand being, I overcome precisely that which concealed God, . . . a place for God is opened up" (1990, 144). Faith now informs life.

In this worldview, a person connects intuitively with the rhythms and thoughts of the universe, with ancestors, and takes on a responsibility to others.[14] One navigates from cultural and psychological constructions in which one inhabits his or her body and experiences it, and perceptions of life, in ways very different from those shaped primarily by Western reason and rationality. Now in frequent ceremonies, before the fire, a woman or man expresses his or her obligation to the Creator, asking pardon and permission, giving thanks and petitioning for help. In this process, he or she begins more clearly to identify and accept potentials, capacities, and emerging knowledge.

The other mien of *kojonik* relates to performing regular rituals of thanksgiving, petition, pardon, and permission, which followers of this way believe is essential work. As one responds in faith to the "center where we connect to trust," a woman or man takes on this road, undertakes ritual work, and assumes the purifying process and charge of light, which is also the responsibility to serve others.

This acceptance ushers in a transformation which hinges on the ability of the individual to come to terms with his/her life—past, present, and future—and take responsibility for it (Thorn 1996, 31). Bakhtin writes that the act of answerability establishes a unity within the person. "The heart of all human action is the problem of achieving wholeness of one kind or another out of parts of different kinds"(1990, xxviii).

> But what guarantees the inner connection of the constitutive elements of a person? Only the unity of answerability. . . . I have to answer with my own life for what I have experienced and understood . . . so that everything I have experienced and understood would not remain ineffectual in my life. (1990, 1)

When individuals finally say "Yes" to this commitment, they begin a formal preparation lasting from six to nine months, to sometimes years, under the direction of an Ajq'ij to develop the special qualities and skills needed to be spiritually effective. That is, they learn to contact and relate with forces through cultural techniques. This preparation varies from region to region and depends on the advice of the teacher and the candidate's age, character, experience, and financial ability. In some villages, a grandparent Ajq'ij trains a grandchild. The training consists in learning by memory the 260-day sequence of the Mayab' Rajalb'al Q'ij, the significance of each day, that is, the *nawal*, the spirit, of each day. "It is our obligation to know the sacred calendar," recounts María del Carmen, "because from this we work, from the calendar we advise others. It is our spiritual base."

The preparation is often done with much precision, as one might prepare for a traditional wedding. The individual accompanies the teacher regularly to ceremonies, learning the powers of the variable days and of specific sacred sites such as caves, forests, springs of water, lakes, or convergences of rivers. The initiate is presented in these sacred places so the hills and valleys get to know him or her, and so the initiate will know where to do the ceremony to "clear the road" for spiritual life. The teacher instructs the initiate on food practices, fasts, and the periods of sexual abstinence required for particular ceremonies. Depending on the region and on the teacher, the initiate must also complete nine, thirteen, twenty, or sixty ceremonies at different locations, all in accordance with the specific powers of each day and its accompanying number.

In a ceremony the person develops the enstatic reciprocity needed for communication with the spirit in the natural world; it is the basis for "walking this way." In the words of a young Ajq'ij, "To be an Ajq'ij is to have a tremendous energy. One has to control energy. But this role has to be supported by the community, by the natural world." Roberto Poz concurs: "An Ajq'ij carries a great energy. To maintain this energy, you need your ceremonies." One comes before the fire, then, to ask for authorization for this service to the community and to develop energies. Through this ritual practice, the initiate learns to overcome personal fragmentation, to gain a particular spiritual strength and psychic understanding so that he/she will become capable of healing others in ritual. As Roberto Poz discloses, "This practice and discipline allows the other dimension to penetrate us more." During this period of formation, the initiate may also begin to receive and learn to interpret different manifestations of energy. The manifestations include interpreting dreams, recognizing the signals that are awakened in his/her body, called "lightning in the blood";[15] reading the *tz'ite'* beans; and perceiving the significance of the flames of the ceremonial fire. It is important to note that each individual Ajq'ij receives different capacities to interpret the manifestations and movements of energy, and at different stages in the process.[16]

In the western highlands, on a day chosen by their teacher—often Wajxaqib' B'atz'[17]—a person is initiated as an Ajq'ij'. Here before the fire, the Ajq'ijab' make their offerings—their petitions and thanksgivings—and receive their *vara* (a Spanish term), a small folded cloth or small bundle which contains 260 *tz'ite'* seeds *(Erithrina corallodendron)* (Alvarado 1997, 167). This bundle, one's inseparable companion, considered the spiritual partner of the Ajq'ij, can also contain crystals, rocks, or plants. The bundle and the Ajq'ij are in a union for all of his/her life, like a spouse, engaging in a mutual promise to care for one another and together to serve other people who ask for spiritual help (167). "This *vara* is a companion. It is a protection in all your life. The *vara* is an instrument with which we do the consultations, and it is very mysterious," discloses Roberto Poz. "Just as we count [engage with] the rocks and beans, so they give us energy." The word *vara* has two other meanings, both of which designate authority, civil and religious. First, the *vara* is the scepter in the Maya community, which the mayor carries, designating his authority and word. It also refers to a tool for measurement.

At this initiation ceremony, one also receives a *sutib'al su't*. This is a ritual headscarf that designates authority. In earlier periods, the headscarf represented the elite; "to tie a headband" is the phrase of accession, suggesting movement toward Ajaw. The initiate also receives a table or altar, and a cross. Many have explained that at this initiation that they grow in health, understanding, and equilibrium, with a new connection to the universe and themselves. Each initiate has indicated an experience of love, an acceptance of mystery and a commitment with B'itol Tz'akol. Again, I connect this with Bakhtin's idea of "answerability"—reconciliation with "one's lived horizon of being."

María del Carmen shares her memory of her initiation.

> When I received it, I was very happy. I felt that I had a crown. I felt it, but it didn't weigh anything. And I was that way from the morning. That's how I was. I kept feeling like I had something, but I didn't see anything. I said to my friends, "I feel happy and I have something on my head, that I can't see." They told me, "Today is your wedding," they said, "and your partner is very happy." When they say "your partner," that is the spiritual.

Gerardo, an Ajq'ij from San Juan Ostuncalco, speaks at length of his initiation process. The final ceremony, which he calls his "graduation," was eight days of ritual processions to four regional mountains. This ritual procession relates to Maya ritual circuits around spaces as much as it does to the Postclassic Maya "ritual circuits" which were performed in their quadripartite world.[18] Gerardo speaks first of his realization in becoming an Ajq'ij, then narrates his eight-day ritual procession.

The first hill we went to was Santa Rita. It's the one over there. There, I burned *copal*, made a fire, and set off fireworks. The women carried the food for us. People played the violin, the guitar, the *chirimía* and *tambor*, and the *chinchin*. They played melodies of very long ago. They play that music to say to God that we'll be coming. The priest carries the *copal* in his incensory. I follow, the rest are behind us. Half a block before the altar they play two or three melodies to say to God we are coming. The initiate dances a very special *son*,[19] nine times forward, nine times back, for the purification of the person. God receives the person with all love. The dance is a demonstration to ask pardon from God. After the dancing, they open the cloth with the ceremonial materials, and make a fire with *copal* and the candles. They sacrifice a rooster if the initiate is a man; they sacrifice a hen if it is a woman.

He points out the ritual directions originating in the East and describes the elaborate ritual of the fourth night.

Every day they select a different mountain for the ceremony. First, in the East, then the West, then the South, then the North. The initiate never sleeps much; the elder chooses where to go. On the fourth day at night, things are prepared at the house of the priest. The priest and others dress as they did sixty or seventy years ago, in a borrowed black tunic, an embroidered belt, and carrying a small *manta* [cloak] on the left arm. The next day they take those clothes off. Then we go to the place where my crosses and *vara* are, about four blocks away. The *chirimía, tambor*, and *chinchin*[20] go ahead of me. The women, dressed in yellow *huipiles* and black *cortes*,[21] with their hair down, processed with us. One woman carried a bowl of *copal*, the other a bowl of cigars. There I reflected on the table and all the materials that I would use. They made a platform and had me sit on it before the altar. I took off my shoes and meditated before the arch made of pine branches, bananas, pineapples, peaches, cacao. Oh, the aroma is very, very sweet! They decorated a crown with white roses and ribbons; Don Pedrito, eighty years old, put the crown on my head. He cleansed me, all my face in the middle of the night. They told me, "Go." And they carried me down one block with music and incense into a patio and left me alone. There it was like a "Mass" between God and myself in the darkness and obscurity. I called on the presence of God and closed my eyes. Later I called everyone to come; the women covered themselves with their shawls. I invoked the presence, the existence of God in the obscurity because one calls God not only in the light, but also in the darkness.

Then they put the table in the middle of the room. "You are going to have a revelation and see the sky yellow, yellow," they said to me. I saw, but it was so beautiful, a yellow, but a beautiful yellow, perhaps a color one could not even imagine. Where they left me, they came for me. They set off fireworks three or four meters away. "Don't be afraid," they said.

Then they took me to the altar. There in front of the altar, each came to kiss my feet, from the youngest to the oldest. Each expressed gratitude and respect toward God. They said, "Give a little to everybody," handing rum and wine. "Toss some to God, then to all and give coffee." Then we made a sacrifice. We sacrificed a turkey, a big turkey. "All the blood, throw it on the altar." Then I burned *copal*. With the smoke of the *copal*, they incensed the altar, the chairs, my *vara* nine times. In the morning, we set out for the other hills.

The fifth day, we went to a spring of water. We left three crosses, burned *copal*, and planted pacaya leaves so all would be green, in harmony with life.

The eighth day, at dawn, is the last ritual. One asks for tranquility and gives thanks. My life has changed. It is complete. The community begins to take apart the arch, giving away the fruit to all the families. Then they cleanse the altar. They peel the bananas and distribute the fruit to all. At the end, I set off fireworks to see if the smoke would make a crown. Everyone waited. It made a beautiful crown, then disappeared at three meters. They said, "It was worth it. He won't do anything bad. Congratulations!" Because of this sign, I had to drink eight inches of rum! Imagine after not sleeping so many days, I wasn't tired. They said, "Yes, you have strength. You didn't fail." They put me through many tests to see if I really love God. Many cried, they were so happy. "Yours was beautiful!" they said to me, "even if your family wasn't there." Three days after I "graduated," the first person came to ask for my help. I've been a priest now for eight years. I don't pay much attention to the social or family life. I dedicate myself to know God.

Something rich, complex, and beneficial seems to be going on here and deserves our attention. What is important in this initiation period and ceremony is what comes out of it. The public initiation is an affirmation of an inner determinedness of the initiate's unique place, a unity of wholeness, as well as of his/her commitment to "walk the road." To be human is to mean, is to live a determined life. Bakhtin writes, "In the deepest part of myself, I live by eternal faith and hope in the constant inner miracle of new birth" (1990, 127). He identifies this "answerability" as "my non-alibi in Being that transforms empty possibility into an actual answerable act." Yet, it is "unfinalizable," "something-yet-to-be achieved" (1993, 142).

TRANSFORMATION

The newly initiated Ajq'ij engages in ritual practice, attentive to signs in dreams, in the ceremonial fire, in reading the *tz'ite'* beans, in attuning to the signs moving within his/her body as interpreted through the matrix of the 260-day calendar. This is what identifies the religious experience as specifically Maya. Further, this answerability is coupled with a trust in absolute otherness, of spiritual forces, of the Creator and of the ancestors' teachings. Through this engagement, the former self is gradually and painstakingly transformed into an emerging neophyte.

Two processes are at work here. Traditionalists both bring to ritual practice a dialogical interaction and use it to shape a personal transformation. In the introduction to Judith Thorn's *The Lived Horizon of My Being*, Arturo Arias explains Bakhtin's disclosure of an ethical interaction for modern human beings:

> Through dialogical interaction, a subject transforms him/herself, becomes a self-created subject, thus defeating selfish individuality. To be a valid subject, our lives have to have meaning. To have meaning, we as individuals have to express intentionality and purpose. . . . In this process we reach temporary truths as we continue a never-ending process of personal transformation that is the result of continuous interaction with others around us. The subject, thus, is always a temporary stage in which elements of his/her own voice interact with elements of the voices of many other subjects, kaleidoscope-like, in a process of seeking personal responsibility and accountability. (1996, 6)

This now "answerable" individual engages in an intentional reflexive and reflective process of reconciliation and self-transformation in relation to his/her cultural and spiritual horizon.

I remember entering the spacious unfurnished white adobe room of María and Pablo in Panajachel (mentioned in Chapter 1). María led me to a large three-tiered altar constructed in steps, painted a bright red (Figure 1.4). "In my dreams, the table showed itself to me in steps," she explains. "The dream showed me how I was to build my altar. So you can learn step by step. That's the way of Maya spirituality. They have to tell us how to progress."

Gerardo also speaks of the stairs that one climbs after receiving one's *vara* and *mesa*, what he calls one's "graduation." He identifies the first step as the "graduation"; the second occurs when other people come seeking one's help; the third as one occupies oneself with only spiritual things; the fourth as one does one's individual work and helps others through ritual and advice; and the fifth step, as one receives one's gift, specialty, and has very "elevated" dreams. "We compare the steps of Maya spirituality with the steps of the temples," Gerardo says. "Every person constructs their own steps, according to one's personal spiritual energy."

Speaking of a spiritual progression, Roberto Poz reached for a conch shell and held it before himself. "Our way is like this conch. It is deeper and wider into mystery," he said, running his fingers along the spiral. "It's beautiful to reach a high level as an Ajq'ij because in the levels of energy one learns and is given a great capacity to teach and assist others." On another occasion, he picked up the black-painted eight-inch wooden cross from his altar. The equal horizontal and vertical branches of the cross were set on a square platform with three ascending stairs on each side. He pointed out how the symbol of the cross set on the three-stair base is a representation of the Ajq'ij's life: as the Ajq'ij progresses in life, his/her knowledge and wisdom becomes more focused and complex. Elaborating, Roberto says,

> An Ajq'ij has a symbol: the Maya cross. The Maya cross signifies the process of the Ajq'ij. The four extensions of the cross are equal. The base with three stairs represents the spiritual progress of the Ajq'ij. On the first step the wisdom is wide. But as one continues in life, the wisdom is distilled and clearer. One's wisdom becomes more complex, more pure, clearer, more profound in life. The Mayan cross is a symbol of the Ajq'ij's life. The cross is not a Christian cross, but a Maya cross for the four directions. It is from one of the temples in Palenque so it is very clear that the Maya cross has its origins in Mesoamerica. It's the foliated tree of life.

When an individual progresses, "takes the road," or "walks" a long time alone, *in that process,* his/her emotional-volitional consciousness is transformed. I connect this forward motion with Bakhtin's idea that a true self is "yet-to-be." "What constitutes my inner self-confidence, strengthens my back, lifts up my head, directs my gaze forward" is the knowledge that "the center of gravity in this world is located in the future, in what is desired, in what ought to be" (1990, 98). He also writes, "My relationship to each object within my horizon is never a consummated relationship; rather, it is a relationship which is imposed on me as a task-to-be-accomplished, for the event of being, taken as a whole is an open event" (98). The creation of an integral self is the work of a lifetime, and although that work can never be completed, it is nonetheless an ethical responsibility.

On this progressive "road" within the Maya cosmovision, the Ajq'ij enters a deeper, more complex connection with the universe, deepens in receiving and interpreting dreams, visions, and various manifestations of spiritual energy as well as assuming a responsibility to the community. Here the manifestation of the sacred, perceived through a cultural lens, becomes concrete for the Ajq'ij. Bakhtin explains that the outside world becomes determinate and concrete for us only through our willed relationship to it (1990, 4–12). He further explicates the transformative process in faith.

> The more the moment of *trust* and the tones of faith and hope gain immediate actuality, the more certain aesthetic moments begin to penetrate into self-accounting. When the organizing roles pass from repentance to trust, an aesthetic form, a *concord,* becomes possible. I change little by little from an *I-for-myself* into the other-for-God. I become naive in God. (145)

At this stage, Bakhtin explains, "prayers have their place; rhythm becomes possible, a rhythm that cherishes and elevates the image, etc., in anticipation of beauty in God, tranquility, concord, and measure become possible" (145). To walk in this "beauty" and with the burden of transforming energy requires a continual purifying to allow a place for light, to surmount content with "loving form," which in turn has the capacity to enlarge perception and affect others.

Men generally spoke of the purification and transformation as an incremental perception and attunement to physical manifestations, the enlargement of the spirit, and an increase of energy; women tended to narrate their purification and metamorphosis as a preparatory process leading to understanding and sharing with others their sicknesses, problems, sadness, and happiness. The following selected narratives exemplify this pattern. Miguel Matías reflects,

> After the initial purification, one continues, continues to climb the ladder, to clear the mind, to ask for wisdom so you can go to another stage. You have to get rid of another spiritually unclean part. Another torment, another torment, but you must pass through it to go to another level.

They want to give you a tremendous amount of positive energy and happiness, so you need to eliminate the negative part. You say, "Now I see! Now I understand! But still I feel like something is missing." So one continues going to the altars to ask for wisdom and science. And then comes another attack, stronger and stronger. It always shows itself. But as one becomes more conscious, one learns that is how it is.

But one arrives at another level of spirituality. "Oh, now I understand! Incredible, but the fire is clearer. Before the fire didn't speak, before it didn't speak." No, it is not that the fire didn't speak, just that before the person had some uncleanliness in his or her heart.

Every person experiences suffering. The measure of suffering is the same measure as the measure of happiness. If it is a small suffering, it will be a small happiness. If one wants to be wise, to understand life, well, excellent. But to arrive at this understanding, it is your calamity. If you don't have this brokenness, then you won't understand life. To understand life, you will have many trials you will have to pass through in this road of brokenness. But this brokenness will also give you light. So in this brokenness, you will construct life and continue on.

Calixta Gabriel interprets her understanding of suffering.

When I understood happiness and suffering were one, that death was life and life was death, I accepted the struggle with myself. I had to purify myself. To purify myself, I had to have a universal love. I had to lose all that was personal that was my family. My brothers were lost [murdered or disappeared]. And in this I learned to love humanity. Also it is a struggle because sometimes one is proud or selfish. And this is the daily struggle, to become humble, to share the good, the happiness, but also to share the tears of the people, of the people when they are sick, of the people when they are sad. One has to understand this. This is what I have learned in the road of spirituality: to feel the pain, to feel the suffering of the people. I give thanks to God for what I have learned.

Audelino Sac Coy, an Ajq'ij in Quetzaltenango, identifies the warmth and wisdom that manifest from walking this road.

That's why I always say institutions and universities give us diplomas, understandings, sciences, the ability to reason, technologies. But wisdom doesn't come from any place except walking in life. Wisdom doesn't come from any university. One walks alone for a long time, and then gains one grain of wisdom. Those who have not walked a long time just have information and knowledge, and it is cold.

Wisdom, perception from the heart, warmth, intuitive knowledge, and intelligence are human qualities valued among the Maya. Two of the models for obtaining these characteristics are Junajpu and Xb'alanke, of *Popol Wuj*.

The afternoon in 1988 after our daughter Joanna's ceremony, I asked an elder Ajq'ij', Don Tino, of Totonicapán, why the hero twins, Junajpu and Xb'alanke, survived the trials in Xib'alb'a, the underworld. He breathed deeply and began.

"The tests of the brothers. They had no house, so they are in obscurity. They didn't have any tools or any weapons, according to what my mind thinks and my hearts feels." Then pausing, thinking deeper, he continued. "They protected themselves with their minds and their eyes. Yes, their minds and their eyes helped them to get through. The warmth of their bodies helped them in the darkness."

"How did they survive the House of Cold?" I asked.

"In the House of Cold, as they prayed, they created warmth. Then the warmth of the place where they prayed sustained them. And their eyes and mind helped them out of this house, too."

Like Junajpu and Xb'alanke, who after many tests in Xib'alb'a become transformed into the sun and moon in the mythic narrative, Ajq'ijab' also undergo trials and sufferings. One Ajq'ij' explains, "We live the trials of Junajpu and Xb'alanke every day of our lives." As they draw on the inner resources of intelligence, reflection, imagination, endurance, and prayer, acts of survivance, they assume the charge of light in their communities. In this process of transformation, the Ajq'ijab' affirm and look within the collective memory that has informed generations. The collective memory, then, becomes a creative source.

RESPONSIBILITY

And Maya spirituality is so beautiful. It is the theory of the mirror. I am you; you are me. There is a great humanity. In the European culture, first it is me; then in the second place it is you. But if I affect you; he is me and you are him.

PROFESSOR VICTOR RUBEN OVANDO

The inner transformation and its concurrent experience of capacity and potentiality urges and compels Ajq'ijab' to serve their communities. Perhaps they come close to the first humans envisioned in *Popol Wuj*, "givers of praise, givers of respect, providers, nurturers." The first humans, who carried out great sacrifices to Tohil and oriented their people in the migrations and led them in the conquests of new territories. They assumed their roles as penitents and praisers, guides and leaders. Contemporary Ajq'ijab', as inheritors of light and energy, continue this legacy.

"The Ajq'ijab' have an authentic vocation," explains Father Tomás García, a K'iche' Catholic priest.

> They are servants, as mayors in the Maya structure. It is an inheritance. They have a vocation, "from your mother's womb you are called." These Ajq'ijab' have a call of God and have a generous response. They are servants; they feel it in themselves. They are not bitter, not complicated. They have tranquility and harmony, but also know sufferings are part of the call.

María Carmen Tuy concurs.

> The Ajq'ij has a responsibility before the community and family. The community has confidence in an Ajq'ij to cure, to give advice, to orient. So many people depend on you. So many people consult with you before they take on a decision. We ask the Creator and Former for help so we don't confuse people in the consultations, so they can walk on this great path.

This life of service to the community echoes Bakhtin's understanding that "it is only from my own place that self-sacrifice is possible, that is, the answerable centrality of myself can be a self-sacrificing centrality" (1993, 48). In the Ajq'ij's answerability to this obligation, s/he also discovers the distinct way his/her destiny is to be played out in the community. Roberto Poz explains it this way:

> The change in a person is not physical, but it's spiritual. After the ordering of life, there is the birth of responsibility. Now ordered, one must go deeper and arrive at one's gifts and specialities, a security with one's self. The capacities, to meditate, to consult, to cure, are very particular and are related to one's destiny.

It is a responsibility, the "ability to respond," that is within one's day of birth. The person may be meant to be a farmer in a cooperative, a healer or midwife, a public spiritual guide, a political leader, a musician, an interpreter of dreams, a community worker, or an educator. Or the responsibility may be for oneself or for one's family. But every Ajq'ij I have spoken with indicates an awareness of his/her capacities and commitment to the needs of his/her family and community or, on a wider level, to national or global needs.

María Antonieta Cofulum, an Ajq'ij in Quetzaltenango, mother of three, and merchant in the central market, explains:

> It's a great responsibility. You have to be an example, sometimes a hero. You are not free of mistakes. No. No. But the responsibility is very great. All around are looking. You are a spiritual guide, so what kind of example are you giving. I think it is a great responsibility. Fifty percent of my responsibility is in the community.

Roberto Poz, who works full time as an Ajq'ij', recounts:

> It's not a commercial thing. People ask for prayers, for their families, for their studies and businesses. We even are asked to pray for the national bus companies, for the safety of the drivers and passengers on the highways. It's a need in the community and I have to give my time to others. Sometimes I do two or three ceremonies a day.

Though not an Ajq'ij, Aura Marina Cotí forms her life by Maya beliefs and rituals. Here she also distinguishes the diversity of gifts.

> One person cannot be good in everything; but is good for something specific. Some are good at healing, at investigating, or others at understanding the signs of the elements, like the fire, the beans. Not all have the same energies.

Victor Lem links responsibilities of the Ajq'ijab' of today to both the past and future generations.

> As a representative of the Maya, for a time I felt afraid, very attentive to a great responsibility. The wisdom is of the ancestors. We have to present them, to identify their posture, their ideology. It is a political work. It will impact the future generations. We are in part responsible for the future.

As the Ajq'ij's "answerability" to an all-encompassing real and mysterious presence ushers him/her into a transformation and service to others, death, too, can be a form of the aesthetic consummation of a person (Bakhtin 1990, 131). "We are like other elements of the universe," says Roberto Poz. "As they die, we, too, must die." If this act is embraced aesthetically, it is transformed into a consuming act. As Bakhtin writes, aesthetics is "a form of embodying lived experience for consuming action so that it may have the meaningfulness of an event" (1990, xl). Father Tomás García narrates a beautiful story of the final days of Don Santo Pom, in 1996, who was both an Ajq'ij' and a devout Catholic.

Don Santo Pom called me two days before he died. I finally arrived at the house and knew the other Ajq'ijab' gathered saw Catholicism as a competition. But Don Santo was an Ajq'ij and also a Catholic.

When I arrived, he said, "Yes, I am gravely ill."

This man went to Mass with respect. But when he knew he was to die, he gave a public confession, a value that we have forgotten of the old ways. In front of the women and men, his wife, his family, he told all he had done before these people, humbly, simply, and profoundly. This keeps us in equilibrium. We know we have to give an account. It is not like death before a judge, but before God as a Papa, who always loves his children.

In this last public accounting of Don Santo, we see how Don Pom's utterance resonates with Bakhtin's notion that one's last word is a surrender "to the mercy of *the other.*"

And within myself, as well, this insanity of faith and hope remains the last word of my life: from within myself in relation to my own given-ness—only prayer and penitence are possible, that is, my givenness ends in a state of indigence . . . In my last word, I turn to the outside of myself and surrender myself to the mercy of *the other.* (1990, 128)

This understanding of consuming love for one's people is embedded in Maya mythic traditions. *El Kanil: Man of Lightning,* a story from Jacaltenango, reflects this process: the *answerability,* the *transformation,* and *responsibility* of a young Jacaltecan. I am familiar with this story because Victor Montejo, a Jacaltecan, in his youth a refugee in Mexico, then later in exile in the United States, and professor at the University of California, Davis, has paid special attention to the story. He transformed it from oral teachings into a written form. In the story, the protagonist, Xuan, gives his life for his people. "The allegory here is related to the actual use of light and subsequent enlightenment and the responsibility for the good of others, which is inherent in the use of light" (Thorn 1996, 94).

At one point in the story, "the strongest men from every valley and hill gathered in the main plaza before Jich Mam, First Father, as with a heavy heart he announced the invasion of a strange people and called the people to battle." As Montejo tells it, young Xuan, "too small to be a warrior, but unlike those first chosen strong enough to carry both his own pride and the sleeping mats and pots of sorcerers, shouted 'I'll go!'"(31). Thinking how he loved the Blue River, the mountains, the fields, the families and children of Xajla', he ran from mountain to mountain "leaping like a deer through the hills," seeking power to save his people. He finally arrived south to the magnificent K'anil.

The great K'u leaned over him like a cloud.
Xuan shouted, "Give me your powers, great K'anil."
K'anil answered, "Xuan, tell me why you ask."
"I want to save them!"
After the great K'u heard his story, he asked, "Are you ready to abandon all you have and never return to your people or change your mind?"
"I have made that choice forever," Xuan answered.
"Then lie down on this earth and receive my powers." (35–37)

Xuan lay down, and as the sky grew dark and roared, lightning everywhere danced through the darkness. "Get up now and put on this yellow shirt that holds all the powers you asked for." Xuan went into battle humbly as a waterboy, but with a heavy burden on his back, he covered his secrets, hid his powers (38). As Xuan and his friend Juan Mendez, disguised as the two porters, marched toward the shining sea, a young man appeared, smiling, greeted them as friends. He said, "I am your brother from Chiapas. I dreamed of your mission and like a dream I've come" (53).

The narrative of this brother from Chiapas, who received and recognized a charge in life from a dream, discloses the importance of visionary phenomena among the Maya. The dream revealed a work he was to accomplish. Upon understanding the dream, the Chiapan travels days and nights across the mountains to join Xuan and Juan Mendez, and pronounces, "Accept my help and now give me the first blow" (53). Xuan and Juan Mendez recognize the sacred manifestation of his dream; they accept him as their ally.

Their acceptance is rewarded as the Chiapan brother gives the first blow. "The sky burned with lightning, thunder exploded and a crackling ray threw back the seas. Xuan saw the enemy uncovered and leaped. Then Juan Mendez. Lightning fell everywhere" (56). The enemy was defeated.

Though the other Xajla' warriors wanted to "to feast them for three days and give them royal quarters and our highest honors" (57), the three, preferring the peace of humility, answered, "Do not think of us. We are thankful to have fought as promised. We ourselves think only of returning home" (56).

Upon their return toward Xajla', Xuan and his companions, knowing they had promised that after using the power they could no longer live again among their people, hid themselves in the great southern volcano,

El K'anil, "We shall live with our father who gave us our power and look down on all Xajla'."

> They now live in the peak of El K'anil, no longer like us. They are K'ues, men of lightning from whose sight Xajla' and Chiapas shall never vanish. They are no longer ours but we are theirs. From the height of El K'anil their blazing rays will always protect us. So they have promised and so it will be. (59–60)

Like Xuan and his companions, Ajq'ijab' emerge as powerful and creative forces among the Maya communities. The Maya legacy of a tie to one's people, of self-sacrifice, and of an everlasting relationship and responsibility toward the community precedes them. In *Popol Wuj,* too, Junajpu and Xb'alanke, after many trials in the Xib'alb'a, ascend "straight on into the sky, and the sun belongs to one and the moon to the other. When it became light within the sky, on the face of the earth, they were there in the sky" (D. Tedlock 1985, 159–160). Xuan and his companions, Junajpu and Xb'alanke, and contemporary Ajq'ijab' exemplify the inherent use of light: the responsibility for the good of others.

CONCERNS OF INAUTHENTICITY

There are concerns internal to practitioners of Maya spirituality. First, there is a concern that people view this resurgence as "popular" or as a fad. Outsiders may dismiss it as a folkway, an advertised tourist attraction, or an invention of the pan-Maya movement, rather than understanding the vital and legitimate importance of this work. Second, conversants warned of their unease that an increasing number of persons are becoming Ajq'ijab'. They described the liabilities: insufficient preparation, self-magnification, political or economic motivations—all of which jeopardize and imperil the authenticity and capacity of Maya spiritual work. The danger is that some Ajq'ijab' appropriate and misuse their position for personal gain: power, money, or fame, thus abusing this role in the community. This is in part, because some individuals become Ajq'ijab' too young or are not properly prepared.

Carlos Escalante, of Quetzaltenango, feels that people becoming Ajq'ijab' is now a popular fad. "They are not well prepared ritualistically, nor do they understand the spiritual energies. If they are not well prepared, the work will not be well done." He suggests that it takes ten years to be well prepared:

> First, one should know the origin, the cultural and historical processes of the Maya. Second, one should study the Maya cosmos, that is, the

relation of an individual's life to astronomy. This has been lost. There is a great loss in our understanding of this relationship. Third, individuals need to learn the rituals and understand one's role in the community.

For years, the circle of those who practiced these spiritual traditions was very closed. When the circle opened, say in the mid-'80s, it lost control. I think, about 35% are not well prepared. They are too young, don't know the counting of time, lack understanding, and are not associated with any organization. Spirituality is profound; it guards mysteries. The problem now is it is becoming a popular thing. This phase is static; it's not going forward, it's not going backward.

Edgar Rolando Ixcot says that some individuals utilize this tradition because they want to be "the new protagonists of the history of the Maya." This thread of deceit and personal magnification has a long history. *Popol Wuj* warns of the pitfalls and defeat of each one who engages in self-magnification and deceit. Seven Macaw, a vainglorious scarlet bird, decked out in jade, metal, jewels, gems, the source of his brilliance, proclaims himself the sun and the moon. The Hero Twins, Junajpu and Xb'alanke, see "evil in this" and see that his "fiery splendor is merely a matter of metal." They invoke the help of the ancestors, "a truly white-haired grandfather and "a truly humble grandmother," who are healers. They yank out his jeweled teeth, replacing them with white corn so that his face sags, and pluck out his metal eyes. Seven Macaw is defeated and dies (D. Tedlock 1985, 77–81).

As in most religious systems, there are traces of fundamentalist "purist" interpretations of appropriate ritual practice by zealous new "traditionalists" and of dogmatic, essentialist teachings from individuals who assume prominent and authoritarian roles as "priests." I have witnessed a few individuals assume positions of authority, inventing and dogmatizing teachings and concepts regarding the significance of colors, of directions, fatalistic interpretations of day signs, and ritual purity. These authoritarian discourses and processes undermine the nature of Maya religious expression, which is relative, flexible, and individualized (Earle 1995, 7).

Interpreting inauthenticity through another lens, Bakhtin calls "the pretender" one who lives "representatively" and "ritualistically." Such a life is one "washed from all sides by the waves of an endless, empty potentiality" (Morson and Emerson 1990, 31). This action runs counter to the answerability inherent in the lived horizon of one's being, an integrity that demands an ethical responsibility. This inauthenticity and self-magnification breed lovelessness and indifference, is nonproductive and destructive.

Lovelessness, indifference, will never be able to generate sufficient power to slow down and *linger intently* over an object, to hold and sculpt every detail and particular in it, however minute. Only love is capable of being aesthetically productive; only in correlation with the loved is fullness of the manifold possible. (Bakhtin 1993, 64)

The work of the Ajq'ijab', though transformed, has endured through generations; it is the inheritance for the future. "One fundamental part of Maya existence is the spiritual dimension, to give thanks, in attitude, answering, waiting, in patience, in courage," explains Fr. Victoriano Castillo González, S.J., in Santa María Chiquimula. "It is through this spiritual life that they have resisted crises, economic and political violence. If with faith in God or in yourself, no problem can destroy or break you, even more so with a people who have faith. This is the key to Maya existence."

Part 3

THE AESTHETICS OF SPACE, TIME, AND MOVEMENT

CHAPTER 4

Sacred Geography
Reciprocity, Ritual Sites, and Quatrefoil Mapping

On April 31, 1997, my husband Martín and I were driving across the plain of Urbina, the mesa where the first great battle between Tecum Uman and Pedro de Alvarado occurred, trying to find our way to the home of the marimba maker who lived in the aldea of San Ramón. We often encountered crossroads, and at each wondered, "Which way?"

At one junction, we met a woman and a man, the man carrying large bundles of palms. "Oh, it's maguay!" exclaimed Martín. "They're getting ready for the Day of the Cross." May 3, I learned, is the Day of the Cross, popularly called the Day of the Construction Workers.[1]

The following night, May 1, our relatives appeared at our house with tayuyos, tamales made of ground maize. The corn dough is rolled out very thinly; a paste of black beans is spread over it, and then the dough is rolled up tightly and wrapped in cornhusks. Lesbia, my sister-in-law, handed them to me, "So you won't be old!" she laughed.

As I unrolled the tamale and examined it, she explained, "Tayuyos are shaped like the snake, and today is the day we believe that snakes change their skins. We hang a tayuyo in the tree so the birds and animals will come. It's so all elements will share in the abundance of life."

That morning I had passed La Democracia, a market in Quetzaltenango, and noticed indigenous women and children assembling crosses ranging in size from six inches to three feet. They stapled double-maguey palms along the vertical and horizontal beams and inserted purple stasis, burnt orange and red strawflowers, red carnations, or yellow mums between the palms. Then they peddled the foliated crosses in the market for 3–10 quetzales. These crosses would appear the morning of May 3 on the front doors of homes, over rooftops, in front of construction sites, or fastened onto the front fenders of trucks.

Three days later, on May 3, we arrived before dawn, by truck, for the Day of the Cross ceremony at the village of San Martín Sacatepéquez, the trail-head for our pilgrimage. We prepared to hike up an ancient volcano cone, in whose hollow lay our destination, Lake Chikab'al ("good or sweet place" in Maya-Mam) or Chicabal (Spanish version), situated in the tropical shelf of the South Coast. Approximately fifty women and men Ajq'ijab' quickly sorted, arranged, and wrapped ceremonial materials and food in woven cloths, then balanced the bundles on their heads or tied them on their backs, and we set out in small groups.

I began the ascent with Lesbia. "Juana, let's get started," she began. "I'm not really used to walking these mountains; the other women are really used to walking and will probably gain on us. You see, we believe that if you are one of the last ones, you have to carry all the energy of those before you, and it's a hard walk. So let's get going!"

We set off along the rocky path that cut up through foot-high corn plants, greeting young children ducking and laughing in the cornfields, then wound up through fields of young green potato plants. A mantel of white mist rose over the rolling valleys and hills as the morning sun warmed the face of the earth.

Three women from Zunil soon caught up with us. "We don't want to carry the energy of all those before us," one laughed, as the trio joined our gait, and soon passed us. Lesbia and I continued on. At a small clearing the pilgrims at the head of the line had stopped and gathered under the trees, resting and waiting for the others. I recalled the words of Martín that he had learned from his people: "That no one stays behind. Not one, nor two, nor three. That all of us go forward."

As the ascent steepened, the earthen path narrowed through the thickened flora and fauna. We entered a different world, eerily disturbed only by the soft buzz of insects or the screech of parakeets. Our gait slowed. We zigzagged through the dense fern forest, avoiding tree roots coiled underfoot and bending below vines hanging like snakes from trees. We stepped through the moist underbrush, grasping branches, anchoring our feet on thick roots or protruding rocks. Conversations dwindled as each pilgrim preserved his or her breath, hearing only his or her heart beating and pounding on this pilgrimage. The wind murmured gently in the branches of the pines. Mothers with infants and *a few elders trailed behind, although others assisted them by carrying their food and ceremonial materials.*

Lesbia leaned against a tree and stopped to catch her breath. "Roberto wouldn't carry my material or food," she sighed, adjusting the bundle on her back. Then in a more resolved tone she continued, "He said we each had to do penance for our sins."

I remembered what I had learned on a nine-week pilgrimage to Israel and Assisi years before: "You are cleansed, purified, by the length of the road."

Lesbia took off the baseball cap she was wearing, wiped her brow with the sleeve of her huipil, then explained, "As you sweat and strain, you are cleansing yourself of the negative, preparing yourself for the ceremony. The longer the walk, the farther away, the cleaner you will be, and often the stronger and purer the ceremony will be."

We continued on, the fifty of us now strung along the trail. At one point, concerned murmurs, breaking into an anxious warning and directive, traveled from those last in line toward those up front, "Don't forget to stop and ask for permission." "Don't forget," each passed on to the one in front of her, "Stop and ask permission. Don't forget."

I wondered. Were we on private property? Was it a regional park? I dismissed those thoughts. Perhaps I had to learn a new sort of association with the land. Could they mean we needed to ask the Owner of the mountain, the Guardian of the lake, for permission to enter? I remained quiet. I would find out.

Thirty minutes later, someone in the lead group whistled out from above, the sound echoing slowly down through the thick, humid forest. Silence, then a whistle from the end of the group traveled up through the vines and thick ferns in response.

We slowly, but deliberately, climbed through denser vegetation, insects buzzing in the thick, humid air until we arrived at a small clearing at the summit. I looked around. We were standing on the rim of an ancient volcano! Each Ajq'ij set his/her bundle of materials on the earth, then knelt and kissed the earth, the face of the earth, as if at a threshold.

I understood! With arms extended in prayer, each working person thanked and asked permission from the Guardian, the Owner of the Mountain, to enter the sacred place of Lake Chikab'al. In closing, each Ajq'ij one by one kissed the earth again, sealing prayer and heartfelt gratitude into the face of the earth, then quietly picked up his or her bundle. We stepped along the path, which dropped precipitously through the thick, moist forest and then soon *broke open to the lake's clearing. What a sight! Dozens of small crosses, foliated with white, yellow, red, and purple mums, lined the lake's rim. At the shore in the silence, I listened to the ebbing and flowing water lap and splash against the adorned crosses planted on the water's edge.*

Contemporary Ajq'ijab' conceptualize their interrelation with the earth and with Ajaw (Owner of the Earth, or Earth Lord) and render mappings of their sacred geography. Ancient referents and modern Maya configure places and landscape features differently. Some continuities remain, but they are transformed. Glyphs, murals, and architecture in conjunction with the Popol Wuj narrations show how reciprocity was central to Maya ancestors long before the Spanish invasion.

Geological formations are sacred places. These designated sites, places of encounters and revelations, and accompanying mythic narratives, with their ritual practices, were long hidden because of Western religious constructions and impositions, but are now accessible to understanding as centers of Maya personal and communal spiritual life. Geological formations such as caves, mountains, and water springs are holy sites. Sacred places are not only "storied places," as Lane suggests (2001, 15), but are designated as sacred through an embodied, interactive engagement with place. They create an alternative world of consciousness.

A distinct component of Maya physical space is the cross or quatrefoil map, which marks all Mesoamerican cartographies. To understand its root importance I must trace its presence and significance in architectural structures, codices, territorial boundaries, and mythic narratives. This quadrant cartography, a transformed continuity, informs the landscape of contemporary ritual practice, cultural activities, and, most recently, Maya curricular and pedagogical design (Mendoza and Mendoza 2002). It emerges as a text for entering Maya space and time.

"THE FACE OF THE EARTH IS NOT OURS, WE ARE JUST RENTING IT FOR AWHILE"

We cannot live without the earth. An aesthetic is needed then, which connects our selves with the power of the earth. In the sacred book, *Pop Wuj*, the Creators say, "Let us make humans, first, so they can feel. And after, so they can think." In Maya culture, first is the capacity to feel. So when humans found themselves in the middle of this lush paradise, that is Mesoamerica or Central America or Guatemala, their feelings prayerfully overflowed, "Let us give thanks two times, three times for creating us," they prayed. The feeling of deep gratitude comes from one's feeling toward the earth.

DANIEL MATUL

To understand the gratitude that Matul feels for the earth, a translation of the word *nature* is necessary, which can open for a Western reader something of the K'iche' world vision. The concept *nature*, Chomb'al juyub' tay'j (*Chomb'al*, it's alive; *juyub'*, mountain; *tay'j*, lowland), imaged in the duality of high and low, is interpreted as "a place of much happiness and energy," "the happy house where I live," or "the green of the earth." Language here reveals the sense of being in an alive universe. What is internal becomes external; respect and gratitude are made visible in the practice of everyday life.

As a farmer plants kernels of corn, he first exhales on the palm of his hand a "huh" prayer, asking permission to open the earth. Ajq'ijab' carry bundles of aromatic materials to present at the altars, to recognize and give thanks to the earth. Before the exhumation of a mass grave to identify village members disappeared and murdered during the late '70s and early '80s, an Ajq'ij asks permission to open the earth. Before a family constructs a house, the family speaks with the earth, asking permission, explaining to the earth their need to dig holes, to plant poles in her surface for the house's foundation. They address the earth: "We are just passing through this life, but we need shelter. We need a place to sleep, to be protected from the rains and from the dangers of night. Please understand us, that we are asking permission to change your face, the face of the earth. We are only passing through."

"My people say, 'the face of this earth is not ours,'" explains Martín. "We are just renting it for a while. We just pass through it, then we are gone." In a traditional K'iche' perspective, the earth is a territory maintained by the Owner, Ajaw (*rajaw juyub*, "mountain owner"), who owns the land and everything on its surface. The universe, then, sustains us while we are here. This perspective is shared among other Maya. According to the traditional Tz'utujiles around Lake Atitlán, Mam, the Lord of the Earth, is a proliferative sacred being who is "felt" by his people because he is an animistic presence (Stanzione 1999).

Other Maya refer to the earth as *our mother*. María Antonieta Cofulum, of Quetzaltenango, says, "The earth is our mother. She gives us corn, fruits, flowers. Her waters wash us clean. At the end of our life, she opens her entrails and receives our bodies. So she must be respected and loved."

Whether the earth is understood as a *territory*, maintained by Ajaw, the Owner, the Earth Lord, or seen as a *mother*, the land is alive and needs to be cared for and fed. Matul explains that in *Popol Wuj*, "the Creators said, 'Let's make humans to be the providers and nurturers.' As humans, we establish a guardianship of the earth." As humans "just passing through it," men and women not only cultivate the earth, but also offer aromatic gifts, thanksgivings, and petitions to maintain a reciprocal relation with the sacred earth, this sacred place. This concept of reciprocity—to receive something of value, you must give something of value—permeates the Maya worldview.

Further, embedded in this cosmovision are beliefs about how particular offerings accomplish certain tasks. For example, in Cantel people bury the hooves of a sacrificed goat in each of the four corners of the house and the head of the goat in the center as a present to the Owner of the Earth, so the foundation of the house will be stable and strong (Lesbia Salanic Poz). Traditionalists of Santiago at Lake Atitlán believe that as long as the Flowering Mountain Earth is "fed," it will continue to provide sustenance. Rituals such as burning *copal*, dancing sacred bundles before the fire, and praying can feed the ancestral form (Carlsen 1997b, 51–52). Stanzione writes that during Holy Week of the Christian calendar, fruit is carried up from the coast and given as a gift to both Mam (the Earth Lord) and Ma-Nawal (Jesus Christ) during the elaborate rituals of sacrifice; the New Year is regenerated through the sacrifice of Mam and climaxes in the flowery rejuvenation of the world through the sacrificial blood and body of Ma-Nawal Jesu Krista' (2000, 20). In contemporary ritual practice, making offerings, "feeding the fire," continues to be foundational to religious aesthetic activity of Ajq'ijab' (Figures 4.1–4.5).

This fundamental value of reciprocity is exemplified by the following story, narrated in 1997 by Fr. Bascilio Chacah Tzoy, a K'iche' Catholic priest.

He said, "Two years ago, the people of Santa Lucía de la Reforma asked me to celebrate the Holy Mass at a spring of water in the community between the trees and rock. They asked me to celebrate a Mass there because the spring wasn't giving enough water. The elders, because of their wisdom and because they are the ones who first benefited from the spring, explained that the people first had to desire her. Within Maya cosmovision, we encounter the need of a reciprocal desiring. 'Forgive us, forgive us because we have treated you badly,' they prayed before the dry spring. 'Forgive me because I put something dirty [in it] and it made this place dirty.' The whole community had to reconcile; we asked forgiveness first.

FIGURES 4.1 AND 4.2. Reciprocity, feeding the fire with aromatic elements, underlies Maya rituals. Here sugar and incense are offered to the fire.

FIGURE 4.3. Each of the four directions, marked by flowers in white, purple, red, or yellow, is fed a cup of *atole* and sweet bread.

"Second, after asking forgiveness of the water and of God, we talked to the spirit of the water. 'Oh, we hope you come to us.' But God is first, right? So they said a prayer. Third, they asked me for a Holy Mass. The priest has to understand the cultural consciousness of the people. Maya cosmovision is the underpinning of all of this, before Catholic or evangelical rites. It is an encounter with the water. So what does the water say? We need enough water. What the ancients used before was salt.

I asked, "I don't understand. What do you mean, you need salt? Is it for a blessing?"

"No," he explained. "You need to throw the salt into the spring. If there was no water, one had to bring water from the sea or from a large river. What was important was to bring live water, live water. It must be from the sea or from a river that is sufficiently large. So they would bring a large jug of water from the river and then one could see what would happen. They offered prayers, and one would put incense, candles, song, and throw salt. After we did this, the spring was fine. The spring is now full of water.

I inquired, "So in this story you are talking about the spirit of a place?"

"Yes," he said.

"So, if you give something, the spirit of the place will give life?"

"To give life, yes, this is it. But it is also the belief and conviction of the people. The person asks the God of Creation sincerely from the depth of his or her conscience, not with hate or resentment. The clean heart and prayer multiplies the capacity of the spring to provide sufficient water. So that there is enough water, you have to throw salt, as salt

FIGURE 4.4: Ajq'ijab' dance, purifying and strengthening their sacred bundles before the fire.

FIGURE 4.5. Glyph of self-sacrifice. Drawing by René Humberto López Cotí.

comes from the sea. It is to say that the salt is the spirit of the sea. Because the salt is of the sea, the salt is something of the sea; it carries the spirit of the place. So when you throw this salt it provokes sufficient water, even abundance, in the spring. It is the same if you bring a jug of water from a river, because the river is living water. It is for abundance. For this reason, the elders said that you have to plant water. You have to plant water. Do you see?"

Reciprocity has been central to the inhabitants of this place for thousands of years, representing a natural trajectory from the prehistory of this region. For the people of the highlands, a certain kind of attunement between themselves and the earth built up over generations. Ancestors interacting with the land configured the earth not only as a spatial territory or cultural landscape, but also as sacred and living.

Paleo-Indian life in the Guatemalan highlands dates back to as early as 15000 BCE, lasting roughly until 5000 BCE (Lovell 1992, 38–39), when a gradual but persistent shift occurred from hunting and gathering to a more settled agricultural life. By 1500 BCE, sedentary village life was a cultural reality. In trading and migrating, settling, and working the land to cultivate corn, beans, and squash, inhabitants developed a sense of the vitality of the earth. Brady and Ashmore write that the material legacy of Mesoamerica, in architecture, settlement patterns, agricultural ways, and ritual practice bears witness "to repeated or re-crafted strategies for acknowledging the earth, for honoring and working with its vital forces" (2000, 126). Ancestors configured terrestrial landscapes, spatial cartography, and mythic narratives to mirror the celestial events of the night sky. From 250 to 850 CE, architects mapped astronomical space and laid it over geography, aligning architecture, settlement patterns, and ritual practice with solar, planetary, and lunar events. The construction and layout of temple-mountains at Chich'en Itza, Copán, La Venta, Palenque, Tikal, Utatlán, Uaxactún, Zaculeu, and other cities present strikingly literal maps of the sky on dates associated with the Maya creation or with important events in each polity's history. Dawn, dusk, the equinoxes, and the solstices at specific geographical locations were viewed as sacred; these time-spaces provided entrance to the sacred. At these sites, at designated times, people performed rituals interlocking themselves with cosmic cycles.

Archaeological work has revealed offertory caches containing human and animal sacrifice and offerings of vegetal material. Eric Thompson writes that the large quantities of incense burners found in caves indicate that the elite and peasants made pilgrimages to caves, considered portals to the underworld. Here they made offerings for rain and the fertility of

bloodletting
(CPN St I, D5)

sacrifice + Copan Emblem Glyph
(CPN St I, D6)

fish-in-hand + manikin cap
(CPN St I, D1)

FIGURE 4.6. Ceremonial offerings (from Proskouriakoff 1993).

the earth (1970, 182–183). Serpents found in Maya art connect the personification of a cave tunnel or passageway, indicating that caves, with their long winding tunnels of enormous size, were places of offerings and encounters with the deities and ancestors (Bassie-Sweet 1991, 127–156). Priests smeared blood of the victims on the face of the (stone) idols with the idea that the deities needed to be strengthened (Thompson 1970, 181). Offerings to bodies of water have been recovered from lakes and from cenotes in western Yucatan, where lakes are not known. Children were sacrificed for rain. La Farge and Byers describe a 1920s Year Bearer ceremony in which a turkey was sacrificed and its blood was burned (1993, 178). Ritual sacrifices made at the convergence of sacred time in sacred spaces opened up arenas for both religious and political activities.

The ceremonial nature of many of the activities depicted in architecture, stelae, lintels, and codices indicate that royalty and priests offered sacrifices at specific times and places for the renewal of the earth and time: New Year's ceremonies, dedication rituals, and royal accession events all required sacrifices.

Among the earliest glyphs recognized were those for offerings; these were frequently pictorial: fish and iguana, the head of an oscillated turkey, the bound haunch of a deer (Kelley 1976, 143). Murals of Bonampak and Chich'en Itza, lintels of Yaxchil'an, stela of Piedra Negras, and burial remains of Tikal all depict various forms of ceremonial offerings. Precious substances such as *copal*, maize dough, rubber, and jade contained soul and were burned in huge braziers for their smoke; they became a form of sustenance the deity could understand (Freidel et al. 1993, 204). In *Popol Wuj*, the K'iche' lineages offered blends of *copal* honoring the first dawn, "crying sweetly as they shook . . . the precious *copal*" (Tedlock, 161).

However, human blood was ranked the primary conduit of *ch'ulel*, the life force or soul. Priests raised obsidian blades, plunged them into flesh, and extracted hearts. Men of elite families drew cords through holes pierced in the penis (Madrid Codex); women and men of royalty drew cords through holes in the tongue (mural of Bonampak), ears, fleshy parts of the arm, and penis, and allowed the blood to fall on sheets of bark paper or gathered it in dishes and offered it to the gods (Thompson 1970, 176). The pictograph of the hand-scattering gesture, liquid in the form of a scroll trimmed with drops that fall from one's hands, is found on a number of stelae, lintels, and codices (Figure 4.6). Whether deciphered as blood, *copal*, or corn, the hand is scattering "drops" of offering (Bassie-Sweet 1991, 65–70). Another hieroglyph figure, showing the lower portion of a kneeling human figure with a "smoking" *cauac* sign in the area of the groin, representing self-sacrifice or ritual bloodletting though genital mutilation (Figure 4.5), appears on the back of Tikal stela 31. It refers to a bloodletting event on a date of unusual importance (Fahsen 1987). Federico Fahsen, a Guatemalan archaeologist, writes:

> Self-sacrifice is now recognized as an important element in rituals dealing with accession to power by Maya rulers, with war or period-ending date celebrations. In both contexts the ruler is representing his people in front of gods, either in a role of propitiation or in some sort of fertility rite where blood is equated with semen or with menstrual flow. (1987: 1–3)

Sacrifice is understood as a strategy for acknowledging the earth, for honoring its vital forces; sacrifice creates an aura pleasing for supplication. It is necessary to establish equilibrium with the earth, although transformed in practice and nature.

What follows demonstrates an early twentieth-century interpretation of reciprocity in which human offerings were presented to a place to stabilize the construction of bridges, dams, roads, and tunnels. Some Maya have perceived acts of construction, such as changing the course of a river or building a highway, as violent disturbances to the earth, and believe that the Owner needs sacrifices to be compensated for the injury. Further, they believe that to accomplish good works, for construction projects to be stable, "the sacred earth, the sacred place, needs a present."

Residents of local communities narrate stories of architectural structures which were sites of human sacrifice in the 1910s–1940s. Rafael, of San Pedro de Laguna, shares how his grandfather told him that in the construction of the Bridge of Belize, now called the Medici Bridge, they planted a human head in each of the columns to stabilize the project. Martín Poz explains, "In Nahuala, several people were sacrificed in the construction of the two bridges for the Pan American highway that passes through the town. Twenty people were sacrificed during the construction of the tunnel outside Zunil; people were sacrificed at the dam at Santa María de Jesús to stabilize the structure."

Martín Poz relates the story:

There is a story from my town. There's a road near Zunil, past the tunnel, which goes to the Pacific Coast. Every week, a group of vendors would come from the mountains and go down to the coast with jars, pots, and pans and sell them on the coast, and then come back from the coast with bananas, pineapples, mangos, and things like that and take them to their towns in the highlands to sell them. And they would do this every single week. These people would go through little towns that other people couldn't get to. They even used to sleep on the front porch at my father's every Friday night. They made a fire and heated their tortillas at night, and then traveled again. But the people before that, they were also travelers who went along the same road. The road wasn't paved at that time. In that area the travelers wouldn't travel alone. There were always four or five of them traveling together. They were afraid of the person, the "head-cutter," who would grab them and make them disappear. They were saying that there were people who were killed because someone was looking for people to sacrifice. The person who was doing it would get paid to get people's heads and bury their heads in the construction of the dam. They would say, "The place needs a present."

They were constructing a dam near Santa María de Jesús sometime between 1910 and 1920, but they had construction problems. They would construct it; then it would fail. They would construct it; then it would fail. The company that was working there was losing a lot of money because the project kept failing. In my people's way, the big head [the foreman] might gather the workers together and ask, "What is happening? What can we do?" They would answer, "Well, we might need a present. We might need to get some people buried here as a present."

So the company paid a man who was a "head-cutter." He would take people and cut off their heads and throw the heads into the dam. So their story is that some people disappeared there. The only things they found along the road were the things the merchants were selling. The people had disappeared. They also said the foreman would drop tools into deep pits and then ask these people to jump in and get the tools. But when they jumped in, he would have his workers pour cement over them and bury them alive. My people would say it is because the Mother Earth needs a sacrifice, a present.

The tunnel outside Zunil was constructed by German engineers in the 1920s. I heard the workers had to sacrifice a lot of people there because it wouldn't stabilize. The contractors were German, but the Germans didn't know what was going on. The workers sacrificed people because they understood that Mother Earth wanted them to be sacrificed there.

The evening we were discussing this story, Roberto explained to his son, "Tepew, they did this during the period that Maya ceremonies were prohibited. Now we have our ceremonies to put our lives and projects in harmony with creation." He then explained that in the construction of a highway in Totonicapán in 1998–1999, work crews had an incredible number of obstacles: machines broke down, then stopped; the asphalt wouldn't adhere.

> The people understood. They knew the project was bothering the many sacred sites in Totonicapán. They asked a number of Ajq'ijab' to perform ceremonies, to ask permission and to give gifts to the places, so the sacred sites would be in agreement and the construction crew could continue. We performed ceremonies all along the way of the proposed highway, interceding with the sites, giving them gifts, so the road, which the people need, could be completed. After many ceremonies, the project was completed. It is about ecology, about the earth demanding her rights too, so that all creation is in harmony. We have to respect her.

Presenting offerings to the Owner continues to be the underpinning of many religious activities in the highlands. It's simple: reciprocity is sharing, giving back. Eduardo León Chic, of Santa María Chiquimula, in the Totonicapán region, writes,

> For our grandfathers and grandmothers, the sacred offering was a present to Ajaw. For us, indigenous, to give to another person is to give from the most sacred interior of your heart, to give part of your heart, because this is how a present is given. It's born from the heart. The gift we present is a symbol of the love in our heart for Ajaw, Mother-Father, for Mother Nature, for the spirit of life, the spirit of cold and the wind, and the spirit of life of the animals. The sacred offering we present to Ajaw is nourishment for the wind and the cold; it is nourishment for our Mother Earth, is nourishment for our grandfathers and grandmothers because they have suffered hunger and thirst to care for us. We give our sacred offering to Ajaw, to our grandfathers and grandmothers, and to the Mother Nature as a sign of our deep gratitude for the life of our daughters and sons. (1999, 47)

Today ritual speech, prayer, and sacramental substances such as liquor, candles, small branches of aromatic plants like laurel or rosemary, *copal, ensarte, cuílco,* chocolate, honey, sugar, sesame seeds, eggs, sweet bread, lemons, and flowers are offered in traditional ceremonies and adorn altars, similar to the Tolzoltil ceremonial practice of southern Mexico (Gossen 1999, 84). Through heat, smell, sound, smoke, and warm feelings, Ajq'ijab' "feed" Ajaw, the Earth Lord, and the ancestors. On certain occasions a hen, rooster, or mourning doves are offered in the fire. In highland Catholic churches, such as in Chichicastenango, Santiago de Atitlán, and Santa María Chiquimula, honoring Jesus, Mary, and the saints, adorning them with prayers, incense, fragrant flowers, local costume, and candles, are Christian in form, but Mayan in meaning. While the Catholic Church intuited something similar, Christian forms often came to be the storage receptacles of ancient Maya cultural information, in this case, reciprocity (Figure 4.7).

Maya ecological reciprocity is not the same as the Western understanding of deep ecology and environmental ethics, which necessitates a reconciliation of humans with the earth for a sustainable and harmonic relationship. Rather, it has a distinct rendering, shared with other indigenous peoples of the Americas. Native American scholar Vine Deloria Jr. helps articulate the perception. "The sacredness of land is first and foremost an emotional experience. . . . It is a feeling of unity with a place that is complete, whatever specific feelings it may engender in an individual" (1999, 251). Daniel Matul explains, "We don't talk in terms of Western ecology. You might say for the Maya it is *ecosophía,* because it is a felt love of the cosmos." For the Maya, the basis of this relationship lies in the transitory nature of all creatures, and the conviction that we are not owners, but *renters* of this earth, and part of a larger cosmos.

"WE RELATE TO THE EARTH, THE EARTH RELATES TO US"

Geological Formations: Sacred Places as Centers of Communication

All Ajq'ijab' go to the mountains. Some mountains are so pure. That is where the spirits manifest themselves more. This has not been destroyed, erased, or forgotten in our history. For this reason, many people have faith in particular altars because of the answers given, because of the signals given in the fire there.

AURA MARINA, QUETZALTENANGO

FIGURE 4.7. Christian forms often came to be the storage receptacles of ancient Maya traditions. Here an Ajq'ij prays with a censer of smoking *copal*, creating a cloud of thin, sweet aromatic smoke at the entrance of Santo Tomás Catholic church in Chichicastenango. This church was first built in 1540 on the site of a Mayan altar, then rebuilt in the eighteenth century.

We present ceremonies in the altars, at the volcanoes. We give thanks to God. As we do it, we feel the forces, the wisdom of God. One presents oneself at the ceremony, and one feels happiness.

MARÍA, PANAJACHEL

Before the day stirs, Ajq'ijab' give thanks and intercede at their home altars. Others, carrying their ceremonial bundles, ride buses, drive pick-ups, or tread earthen paths away from their villages to tens of thousands of sacred sites in Guatemala. They quietly pass along the edges of cornfields, the long leaves tossing as they pass, and continue on. It could be toward the low places: bubbling springs, lapping river, or lagoon edges, or a convergence of waters. More likely it is toward the high places: the summit of high mountains, close to cave entrances, or a mountain ridge.

Ancient peoples of the highlands marked territorial boundaries in distinct emotional-volitional tones, transforming spatial horizon into a homeland. Mountains, caves, and water—local *mystical geography*—were and are important foci for settlement, social organization, and ceremonies (Brady and Ashmore 2000); they influenced the placement and construction of temples, dwellings, and tombs. Temple-pyramids were modeled as mountains extending toward the sky with inner sanctums reaching to the Underworld. Then ancestral bones were placed within to accumulate the vital forces from the Underworld, where humans were reconstituted, as at the Temple of Inscriptions at Palenque (J. Carlson 1976; Freidel et al. 1993). Generations in this Mesoamerican region have shaped a singular universe of meaning in relation to the land that has informed conceptual lives, cultural identities, and life ways.

Geological formations are linked to this aesthetic envisioning of a people's relationship to the earth. Specific topographical features have accumulated value and meaning through human narratives, memory, and history as sites for ritual practice, as portals to the sacred. For thousands of years in Mesoamerica, water, mountains, and caves—locations that corresponded to critical junctions between the planes of sky, earth, and the underworld—have been ideational landscapes (Ashmore and Knapp 1999; Miller and Taube 1993). Limestone caves which open to the earth's interior, recognized as mouths of the Earth Lord and portals to the underworld, are a complex of powerful animate forces (Bassie-Sweet 1996; Brady and Ashmore 2000; Freidel et al. 1993; Vogt 1981). Zetina writes that trees comprise one fourth of the sacred sites. In the mountains around Lake Atitlán, seventy-one sanctuaries have recently been documented, of which three altars—Tzip, Xe Abaj, and Manamel—in Sololá were dedicated to deer hunting (2001, 2). Bones have been found at three of the sites; they, metaphorically as flowers, are planted and can germinate. In Chiapas, wooden crosses at the edges of waterholes and at the entrance to caves provide means of communication with the Earth Lord. These crosses serve symbolically as "doorways" or "entryways"; that is, they are means of communication with deities as well as boundary markers between units of social space, between the world of the living and the dark underworld (Vogt 1981, 137). In Zunil, Berta, an Ajq'ij, says, "We know caves are places to contact the ancestors. There before the fire, we communicate with Heart of Sky, Heart of Earth." These physical geographies understood as sacred sites are integral to the maintenance of people's identities and spiritual traditions.[2]

Some ritual sites have origins and history reaching back as far as five thousand years; others were constructed between 250 and 850 CE, an era which scholars name the Classic Period. The importance of these sites is documented in *Popol Wuj* and *Chilam Balam,* as well as in contemporary oral and written narratives. Present understandings of sacred places have roots in the cosmology of the ancient Maya world, which Mayanists envision in three vertical layers: the starry arch of heaven, the stony middle world of earth, made to flower and bear fruit by the blood of kings, and the dark waters of the underworld below. All three domains were thought to be alive, interrelated, and imbued with sacred power (Schele and Freidel 1990, 66). Both topographic and architectural sites have provided access to the upper and below worlds.

This three-dimensional model of the world was simplified in order to conceptualize horizontal space; the sky was associated with the North, the earth with the South, and the journey of the sun with the East and West. This model of the world was concentric as well as quadrangular. "Running through the center," continue Schele and Freidel, "the Maya envisioned an axis called *Wacah Chan* ('six sky' or 'raised up sky')" (66). The tree, which symbolizes this axis, coexisted in all three vertical domains. It was rooted in the nadir of the watery underworld region, its trunk traveled through the middle world, and its branches soared to the zenith in the highest layer of the heavenly region (67). This center axis, envisioned as a tree or as a cross, connected the three worlds, and "could be materialized through ritual at any point in the natural and human-made landscape" (67). Thus sacred sites, as a center axis, are considered portals to these worlds. Contemporary K'iche' explanations of the three vertical layers will be amplified in Chapter 6, on ritual practice.

The Spanish understood the importance of sacred places to the Maya. In fact, they built Catholic Churches over Maya altars, for example, in Chichicastenango, Esquipules, Santa María Chiquimula, and Momostenango, in order to convert the Maya. "It's not a syncretism," clarified Federico Fahsen. "It's a place where the ancestors live."[3]

Legacies of this worldview, then, continue to shape understandings of geographical sites as sacred places. We turn to stories which are the narrative fabric in which Ajq'ijab' disclose how selected geographical sites are sacred places. Michel de Certeau amplifies the role of stories, making a valuable distinction here between place and space. "Space is a practiced place," he writes (1988, 117). *Place*, a location, implies stability; on the other hand, *space*, composed of intersections of mobile elements, is constructed by activities within it, activities that orient, situate, and temporalize it. Space is determined through actions, the daily practices, of historical subjects in a specific place and through the narrations, the stories, which articulate the experience. "Stories thus carry out a labor that constantly transforms places into spaces or spaces into places" (118).

Contemporary Ajq'ijab' convey through their stories how a geological place is experienced as a space of spiritual communication and power. Here, their narrative fabric enlarges conversations on the meaning, characteristics, function, and selection of sacred sites. Ajq'ijab' perceptions resonate with emergent phenomenological approaches, which insist that all human perception of landscape is relentlessly interactive, inviting mutual response (Lane 2001, 41–45, 52–58).[4]

Ajq'ijab' distinguish sacred places as *encantos*, places where one is more likely to encounter a spirit or where a specific, personalized, maybe anthropomorphic manifestation appears, or as *altars* (*kojb'al*, "a place where you go to give something") where one says his/her prayers, but doesn't necessarily do a ceremony. However, both *encantos* and altars are places of contact and communication with Ajaw, portals where people are engaged with the sacred.

Each geological formation and place has a distinct Uk'ux, heart, owner, *nawal* or guardian spirit, and possesses some determined energy, making communication with the sacred possible. Thus distinct places are portals to the sacred. "Places have a *nawal*, better to say a spirit or a heart," explains one Ajq'ij. "It's like the essence of the place." Stories and folktales, too, reveal cultural beliefs of the *dueño*, the Owner of hills, mountains, and forests (Sexton 1992; Montejo 1984).

Further, a site, part of a larger geological and spiritual system, has a force that operates as a transmission channel between humans and spiritual sources of power. Ajq'ijab' utilize contemporary technology references—a satellite, a telephone, a communications network, or a bank branch—to explain ancient phenomenon. At most altars, they have set a wooden cross, which is understood as the doorway for spiritual communication.[5] Roberto Poz explains sacred place this way:

> It is always a sacred place because of an attraction; something is more profound there. With the spirit present in this place, our words go more rapidly. To say it another way, a sacred place is like a satellite; it takes our petitions, the message, and distributes them. The place transmits it in this way.

In the cemetery of Santa María Chiquimula, an Ajq'ij faces and offers *copal* and intercessory prayer at each altar in the four forest-topped mountains: to the East, *Wajxaqijb' B'atz' Pa qachoch*; to the West, *Kab'lajuj tijax Pa iquel*; to the North, *Kab'lajuj k'an, Iklaja*; and to the South, *Kab'lajuj kyej Pa chaj*. The four mountains are solicited to work together as a team to provide strength and sustenance for a particular ceremony.

The insightful perceptions of Tom Hart, a native of Ireland who has lived in Guatemala since 1994, are relevant here. He has chosen to stay in Guatemala, the best place to deepen in Maya spirituality. Tom and I would occasionally talk over cups of instant coffee, around his small wooden table, sorting out our experiences and interpretations of Maya spirituality as outsiders. Informed by his extensive spiritual training and practice as an Ajq'ij and his ethnographic work, Tom elaborates,

> Ajq'ijab' of the highlands explain that altars are telephones. You ring in from the nearest telephone and you are instantly connected to the network. And that's right. There are altars that are set to directly communicate to one another. They are hills rather than altars, but they are sacred. At night one sees lights going from one hill to another as if they were criss-crossing messages from one hill to another. People say that the hills are husband and wife. There are all sorts of ways sacred places can communicate.
>
> There is an Ajq'ij who uses the image of altars as bank branches. He said, "It's like I pay into my account; I bring offerings, my candles, my prayers, my incense, and I take out. I take out messages, balances, and happiness. I've got my account here in this sacred place but I can go from one place to another, from one account to another." The places are like a network.[6]

Some Ajq'ijab' speak of a place as inherently powerful because of forces associated with its location, others because of its anomalies in the earth's electrical system, or because of its alignment within a larger geological system. The activity of a sacred place as a site of transmission has also been translated to more domestic settings, such as a home altar, a glass of water, a crystal, or to the image of Mam, the Earth Lord (Carlsen 1997b; Stanzione 2000). Ajq'ijab' recount that some people who consult with them, particularly evangelicals, feel more comfortable to pray in these domestic places rather than in a public space.

These places of encounter and revelation are approached with respect, as one would approach another person. Roberto Poz explains the protocol. "It's as if you have to adorn the heart, the spirit, the head, the body of the site so the place can feel good. Then the place will become present for the ceremony. We don't see with the eye, but with the other eye, the eye of contemplation." He continues, "In a sacred place, you feel more perceptive, because of the attraction, but also because of all the persons who have transmitted power in this place." We see how K'iche' traditionalists attach meaning to place through their own embodied, interactive participation with it. They not only perceive the physical features, tonality, or mood of the landscape, but also feel, recognize, and respect a dimension intuited: the heart or spirit of the place. This intuitive perception is recognized through culturally conditioned sensibilities.

> Every mountain has a spirit, and the spirit translates what one needs to Ajaw. In the mountains, there is silence. No sounds. You can invoke the spirits in silence. You invoke. You don't have to shout. No strong words, you can ask pardon. You say "[Name of the altar], I've brought this gift to you. Please receive it in memory." And you pray until they tell you how many times to return or where to go for the next ceremony.
>
> MARÍA, PANAJACHEL

A place has a distinct energy because of its physical shape, its position as on a hilltop or a cave, the organic material that is there, what has happened before at this site, and what will go on in the future. Thus, the spiritual function often resonates with its geological formation. Some altars are designated for curing, others to ask for personal equilibrium or economic well-being, or to resolve a problem. If it is near a river or spring, it may be selected for the presentation of a child or the initiation of a project. If it is in the mountains, it is often for penance, to ask pardon, or to give thanks.

One afternoon, a young Ajq'ij and spiritualist accompanied by her mother, who receives her daughter's channeling, and I, had finished a ceremony at one of the favored altars in a cave called Kojb'al (altar) Xe kab', outside Zunil. We were threading our way through the well-worn muddy footpath, which wove through young cornfields and plots of green onions standing eight inches tall, back to the highway. I turned to Berta, and asked, "Berta, what do you know about altars?"

"Altars have spirits," she began, "they have souls. They have positive and negative energies."

"What about this altar?" I asked.

"Kojb'al Xe kab' is a very strong altar. What you ask, for a child, for health, for a project, the fire is always very strong. It is very happy. Some other altars are just regular. Nothing really powerful comes. Chuwi pek is also very strong."

Dual Energies of Sacred Sites

The principle of duality in Maya cosmological vision also transfers to physical places, which have both positive and negative energies. In this geographic energy system, some places are designated as "good" or as "bad." Ajq'ij Juan explains, "We have a perception in which we understand that a particular place is for healing or balancing, and another place can be used to 'tie someone up.'"

Aura Marina enlarges this perception:

There are altars that don't reveal anything, because bad things have happened there. There are people who do bad things at the altar. If you go, you arrive, and with your positive energy, you can pick up the negative energy and it will affect you. So I feel sometimes that the purer it is, the more real. I had an experience in El Baal. A friend wanted to go. She needed to go do a ceremony. But when I returned I had a headache. I felt so sick. I felt the negative energy that was in this place. So I said to her. "It was something bad; I felt sick." And she said what happened there was that someone had come earlier to do something bad in that place. "Because of this you feel bad." She told me I needed to cleanse myself with lemon. What I came to understand is that there are some altars, which are very beautiful, but they can also carry another energy. Pascual Abaj is a very beautiful altar. One feels the place, the peace. I wanted to go to feel this peace. There is another altar, here in Quetzaltenango, close to Los Vahos, where hardly anyone goes. Another altar, El Kiej, in the hills, behind the hill, Candelaria, has very good signals.

Tom Hart amplifies this sensibility:

I think there are two reasons why I feel uncomfortable with a place. I think first it is what people use this *encanto* for. I think all sacred places have a residue, what people have asked for there, what people have done there. If it is precisely the same place as where the Ajitz [one who deals with negative energy] worked, I think you have to be pretty expert so that the energy doesn't seep through. There are neutral places. I think there are places I've been where I have seen people doing evil work, places where one has known people have done bad things. The other reason why I think there are places I feel uncomfortable is because places are very specific. Each place has its own spirit, its own essence. There are places which are for curing, places which are for defense, for asking for the rain, and places which are to be visited on specific days on the calendar, like Imox or B'atz'. And I think if one isn't very aware of these distinctions, it contributes to a sense of uneasiness.

Some sites have two altars: one embodying good energy, where the Ajq'ij performs the good ceremonies; and the other, set off to the back, embodying negative forces, where the Ajitz throws curses or tries "to tie someone up." Aura Marina continues.

In the case of Hun Noj [an altar in Quetzaltenango], people don't like to go there. There are two altars, one a good place to ask for money, for economic success, but I hear people don't like to go because of recent robberies. From what I know, they say, "The other altar at Hun Noj, which you need to climb down a rope to get to, is where you have to get the work done by an Ajitz, and of course that is the place to offer babies, to offer cats, to make a pact with the devil." So that is a place, which possibly only because of repetition of blood sacrifices is a pretty serious, pretty heavy kind of place. During the presidency of Ubico, which ended in 1944, Hun Noj was ordered to be excavated by local authorities. They found quite a number of remains there.

Selection of Sacred Sites

Ajq'ijab' select ritual sites as appropriate for particular ceremonies following distinct methods. These methods include *embodied memory* of a "storied" place; *ritual association* with particular sites; *intuitive perception* of a place as a site of power due to its physicality or its geographical remoteness, often passed on to generations through teachings; and *discernment* of revelations in dreams or ritual practice.

Some places are sought out because they possess topographical features—mountains, caves, springs of water—distinct in their powers. Other sites are selected because they have a history of efficacy for a particular need. Juan, of Zunil, explains, "All that we know, we learned through teaching, through oral transmission. The elders always said, 'This is the place to cure. This is the place to ask pardon. This is the place to ask for money.'" Other sites are selected because of their remoteness, and thus sacredness and purity. The pilgrimage to the site, the length of the road, is a cleansing experience.

> To go to the altars, you have to walk a long way. It is part of the sacrifice that helps you to concentrate when you are making offerings. If a person walks a long way carrying his/her ceremonial offerings, it cleanses the person from distractions so s/he can communicate more humbly, clearly, and sincerely." *(Ajtzijonel Especial el Regional 1996, 9)*

At these remote, often peripheral, places, Ajq'ijab' are able to access the Uk'ux, the Heart of the place, through acute concentration, cultivated through meditation, prayer, and careful observation. Here the Ajq'ijab' perceive and interpret signs in accordance with the calendar and ritual system.

Other sites are selected because people have prayed there for generations. Some Ajq'ijab' have experienced paranormal energies breaking into the ordinary, and their ritual or local stories recount that ancestors witnessed the appearance of the virgin, as in Santa Lucía de la Reforma, Jacaltenango, or Santa María Chiquimula; the narrated experience of the place is passed on through the generations. Yet other remembered or reclaimed "storied" places, such as Abaj Takalik, El Baul, or Lake Chikab'al, on the Pacific Coast; Utatlán or Pascual Ajab in El Quiche; or the caves of San Jorge near Lake Atitlán are sites of origin, migration, or encounters with powerful forces, passed on in oral accounts. More recently, groups of Ajq'ijab' have traveled to Tikal, Copán, and Palenque for ceremonies. On other occasions, Maya traditionalists select sites, some well known, others new or forgotten, because they are revealed in dreams or visions,[7] or through ritual practice, specifically in interpreting the fire, "reading the beans," or discerning the movement of the "lightning in the blood." In the following narratives, Roberto Poz shares the acumen of "the lightning in the blood," a distinct form of embodied discernment.

> When we have to do a ceremony, we have to put down the beans and ask: "Where do I have to do the ceremony?" The body will also tell me where I have to go with another person for a ceremony. How does the body say this? For us, we have many indications in our bodies. It's a training to learn to read the body.

Roberto continues, explaining how he intuitively dialogues with a place regarding its use for a ceremony:

Let's say I have arrived at a place, but my body tells me this is not the right place for this particular ceremony. I say to the altar, "Excuse me, but this is not the place." I move to another place, and the Heart of the Place understands. Let me give you another example. A particular place doesn't want you to do the ceremony there. So I have to ask permission. I clean the place. I use a flowered water to harmonize the place, so then the site receives the ceremony. You see, the same earth is informing you. The earth, the specific place, indicates if it is right to have a ceremony there.

One morning, I asked Tom Hart how he had come to understand sacred places in Guatemala:

I think places become imbued with prayers. I think, as I was saying before, the Mystery has more to do with an emotional than an intellectual state. We think for a moment what prayers are. Prayers are much more emotional than intellectual. Here in Guatemala, when I first started going to ceremonies, I was almost embarrassed, especially if the ceremony was in K'iche' or Mam, to see the petitioner break down and cry. Now I have seen that so often, it looks absolutely normal.

But that's the depth of emotion, when people are talking to God. They are bearing their souls, and they are telling God their problems. Their deepest fears, worries, insecurities are being verbalized and those words have to hang in the air. If the prayers go down to Mother Earth or if they go up to Father God in the Sky, then they go and they leave a resonance in the air, they leave a resonance in the stones and in the altar itself. And I don't think that dissipates, ever. I think that's probably why some places like the dolhman in Ireland or the temple of Carmac in Egypt are other places that I have heard had very much the same sense. Generation after generation, emotions are accumulated, tears are accumulated in a place, and the place takes on a pattern of emotion, which makes it sacred.

Of the relation of spirituality and land, Vine Deloria Jr. writes:

Religion cannot be kept within the bounds of sermons and scriptures. It is a force in and of itself and it calls for the integration of lands and peoples in harmonious unity. The lands wait for those who can discern their rhythms. The peculiar genius of each continent, each river valley, the

FIGURE 4.8. Ajq'ijab' line their foliated crosses along the shore of Lake Chikab'al
on the Day of the Cross, May 3.

rugged mountains, placid lakes—all call for relief from the constant
burden of exploitation. (1999, 30–31)

What emerges in these narratives is *an attunement,* an intimacy with the
earth, perhaps a latent intuitive potential in human perception, a strategy
for survival developed over time in encountering and engaging with one's
environment.

In summary, we have seen how Ajq'ijab' relate to sacred sites, and that
their ritual engagement at specific geological places is linked to their envisioning of the world, to the maintenance of their cultural traditions, and
to their survival. Walker writes that sacred sites are "natural maps that
provide direction to life and shape to the world. They give order to both
geographic and social space, and by ordering space they order all that exists within it" (1993, 111). While transformed in meaning over time, geographical sites are accessed by Ajq'ijab' as sacred sites, as communication
sites with Ajaw, with the Sacred Earth, and with ancestors through ritual
practice. By means of interpretation, Ajq'ijab' enter into and appropriate
the world of meaning that the site projects, and they are thereby changed.
What ensues is an engendered respect for, attachment to, and dynamic engagement with geographic place (Figure 4.8).

THE QUATREFOIL: BOUNDARIES AND TERRITORIES

Let us return to the Day of the Cross at Lake Chikab'al, its shore lined with foliated crosses. Some Ajq'ijab' carefully unpacked their six- to twelve-inch wooden crosses set on three-step square platforms from their bundles, adorned them with mums and stasis, and planted them firmly at the lake's edge. Soon, new yellow, white, purple, and crimson foliated crosses hemmed the shore, water lapping at their bases. In the distance, diamonds of light bounced off the rippling water. Other Ajq'ijab' prepared the ritual space on the sandy shore, opening small plastic bags and drizzling sweet sugar granules over the face of the earth from East to West, along a vertical axis from North to South, then encircling the quadrant. They arranged incense and other aromatic materials within the ritual circle. Finally, they planted candles and flowers of designated colors at the cardinal points: red in the East, black in the West, white in the North, yellow in the South, green and blue in the center, splitting the middle into two directions, up and down, like a tree grounding roots to the underworld and lifting branches to the heavens.

Doña Marta called us together before the circular space, now built up of and adorned with pom, candles, incense, laurel, flowers, and chocolate upon the sugar base. "Today is the day of the cross," she began, extending her arms wide open. "It is the day we remember the cross in the sky; but also the day to remember the cross we carry in our bodies. We carry the sacred cross of thirteen numbers in our bodies," she continued, pointing to each of the thirteen major joints of her body. "And with this cross, this cross in our body, we have a connection with the Heart of Sky and with the Heart of the Earth. Today is the day we bless our crosses."

To begin the ceremony, participants knelt, facing East to greet and show respect for the guardian of the East, then shifted in turn to each of the other directions: the West, the North, the South, naming and honoring them, then calling upon the guardians of the mountains, rivers, and lakes. We called on the Creator and Former, also named B'itol, Tz'akol, and on the spirits of the grandmothers and grandfathers for good health and welfare for their children and grandchildren. Doña Marta raised her arms, face, and voice to the sky, then turned to the earth, addressing the Source of all Being,

Oh Ajaw
Heart of Heaven, Heart of Earth
Hidden treasure, which fills heaven and the earth
and the four corners of the universe
Only before you is there peace and tranquility.

She bent over and lit the center blue and green candles, then each candle for the four directions. The materials caught fire; soon the flames sizzled and raced across the sugar paths to join the cardinal points. The ceremony began.

The quadrant schema appears in multiple highland icons. Wooden crosses mark altars at springs, in caves, along lakes, in cornfields, or in family homes. Fields of diamond-shaped designs, the embodiment of time and space, are often woven into women's *huipiles*. Ritual space is usually organized as quadrants within a circle, with flowers, candles, and corn of designated colors in the cardinal points. María, an Ajq'ij from Panajachel, placed a large ceramic angel on each of the corners of her altar. "St. Michael, St. Gabriel, St. Rafael, St. Seraphim, you know, the Archangels, the four directions," she explained. Gerardo walked for eight days, from East to West, then South to North, from mountain to mountain around his town of San Juan Ostuncalco, offering ceremonies for his initiation as an Ajq'ij. Ajq'ijab' refer to their bodies as crosses. Roberto Poz uses a quadrant chart aligning the twenty day names with the four directions in counseling and advising people. "It's our psychology," he explains. Contemporary Maya say they remember their grandparents never positioned their beds or *petates* (mats) facing East. "They said never put your beds so that when you wake up you face toward the East. It's a matter of respect toward the sun. All our lives we are looking toward the East; only in death can we be placed toward the East. In cemeteries you will find the buried facing East." Today, educators and community activists often design a brochure, announcement, or banner with the Maya cross configuration. The quadripartite organization and vertical layering is the contemporary ritual "model for life," as discussed in Chapter 6. What is the underpinning of this thought-image, this four-directional authoritative symbol?

The cross metaphor is a mapping devise that has organized Mesoamerican geographic, social, political, and religious image-space. This *text*, enduring in architecture, codices, narratives, and ritual design, opens up a "window" on the regional ideational logic of the ancient world. For example, the word *Pop* signifies *petate* (a square woven mat). In *Popol Wuj*, the Aj Pop (authorities, those with great consciousness) sat upon the woven mat to do consultations, gathering the advise of the four cardinal points: the rising the sun, the setting of the sun, the side of the earth, the side of the sky. The four cardinal points also consulted with one another; this model or basic principle has shaped Maya community organizations throughout history.

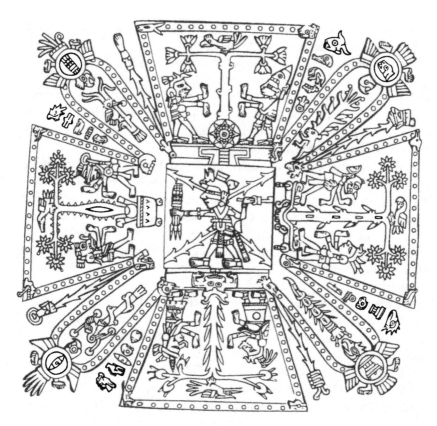

FIGURE 4.9. Quadripartite division of calendar and associated trees, birds, gods of four world quarters on page 1 of *Codex Fejérváry-Mayer*, from Mixteca-Pueblo area (from Milbrath 1999, 132, after Krupp 1983, 291).

They mirrored the structure of the cosmos to permit contact with its power. The power of cosmic order energized and organized human affairs. Four sides, cardinal orientations, or directional placement, they could mobilize any setting into service as a sacred world center or as a world-quarter shrine. (Krupp 1997, 20)

This structure of the cosmos was theological and ideological, which people constructed and lived within (Figure 4.9).

The source of the cross metaphor is variously interpreted as *the cardinal directions, the solstital positions,* or *the sun's path.* Yet Maya attention to astronomy laid the foundation. The sun's movement is the primordial root. As we trace the genealogy and aesthetics of the cruciform space, we find that florescent embodiments of the cross metaphor come into view:

quadrant architectural structures; the fourfold siding, fourfold cornering of the world in narrative accounts; the quatrefoil image in the codices; directional colors, stones, corn, bees, flowers, trees, symbols, and incantations in glyphs; world-quarters marking territorial boundaries, political and social image-space.[8] Further, the crossroad in mythic and literary accounts discloses a people's perception of plot in narrative.[9] The cross form today marks personal, communal, and ceremonial itineraries; it emerges as a text for entering Maya space and time.

This Mesoamerican cartography, produced as astronomical-religious positioning, was also utilized as a paradigm to define political territory. The Utatlán settlement, the K'iche' political and religious center of the highlands from 1250 CE to 1424 CE, was composed of four major subsites; however, the K'iche' conceptual world was in fact geographically much larger than the central area, incorporating such distant places as Tula in Mexico, the caves of Alta Verapaz, and the volcanoes of the southern axis. Carmack writes that "the central area per se was conceptualized more in social than in ecological terms. Nevertheless, small territorial divisions within the area were viewed as squares extending in the cardinal directions, the symbolic corners *(retal)* being formed by prominent mountains" (Carmack 1981, 78; Recinos 1957, 62).

In "Sacred Journeys and Segmentary Politics in Mayan Culture," Garrett W. Cook and John W. Fox (1994) present a map orientated to the four cardinal directions, with Utatlán as the axis mundi of this cosmogram. This map, a schematic version of sacred geography which defined the borders of the pre-Hispanic K'iche' segmentary state at its most expansive phase, suggests the frontiers of a united sphere of interacting highland Maya peoples. It extends from Utatlán in the center, northeast to Cobán, southeast to Esquipulas, south to San Jorge and Santiago Atitlán, southwest to Zunil and the volcano of Santa María, northwest to Chiantal and north to Cerro Negro. Cook and Fox suggest that visitation to these general locations has pre-Hispanic roots, both because these locations define the old borders as noted above and because Postclassic sites are located near most of them. However, I found curious continuities of this quatrefoil in the contemporary landscape. The afternoon Roberto Poz and I conversed about altars around Zunil, he said, "Jean, let's go to the cemetery and talk there." I would find that a quatrefoil model marked the town, but it was no longer transparent.

The cemetery of Zunil is located at the top of the central hill overlooking the village behind the Catholic church. So, from his house, Roberto and I crossed the bridge over the river, through the valley, traversed the plaza, walked up the winding cobblestone path, passing block and adobe homes, and entered the western gate to the cemetery. The cemetery resembled a city. Tiered vaults flanked the central avenue, which led west to east atop the hill. Hundreds of low earthen mounds, most oriented toward the East, were bordered with either turquoise, a "jade-green color which affirms they are treasured" (Becom and Aberg 1997, 129), or with whitewashed roof tiles planted upright around the graves. Bunches of calla lilies or marigolds cascaded from glass jars set before the wooden crosses marked with K'iche' names. We walked along the dirt pathways between earthen mounds and tiered vaults. In the center of the graveyard, Roberto motioned to a small cleared area, blackened from ashes and soot. A warm, fine white smoke was rising from the hot ashes of a recent ceremony (Figure 4.10). "This is the center of our village," he said, "where our ancestors are."

From this spot, then, Roberto mapped out major altars at the four corners of the town, indicating their special capabilities. When we later diagrammed the altars, the Zunil cosmogram looked like the cosmogram shown in Figure 4.11. At that point, I realized that Joanna's "giving thanks to the mountain" ceremony in 1988 had been in the East, at Xe' kega ab'aj, a place of beginnings.

Roberto and I left the cemetery and walked along the outskirts of town, visiting designated ceremonial sites: springs of water, rock outcroppings, and caves, as he explained their significance and histories. We stood for a long time in front of the lower altar of Chuwi pek, in the West, where we had an expansive view of Zunil. "This is the good altar of Chuwi pek," he explained. "The other altar of Chuwi pek is higher up, but we won't go there. It is designated for the work of the Ajitz."

As we headed down the rocky path toward the village, I thought that most of the seventeen thousand inhabitants of Zunil probably knew about some of the caves. But I wondered how most of them, outside of the Ajq'i-jab', interpreted their meanings, given that other kinds of discourses and practices have been inscribed in their world through layers of time.

Questions of land or site ownership, right of entry to sacred places, management of archaeological sacred sites, and of safety for Ajq'ijab' at these sites emerge as global, national, and local interests privatize and develop for profit, land, and natural resources. The Agreement on Identity and Rights of Indigenous Peoples pledged "to recognize the historic value and protection of the temples and ceremonial centers as part of the cultural, historic and spiritual inheritance of the Mayas and of all indigenous people" (16). The Agreement applies not only to the frequently visited

FIGURE 4.10. White smoke rising from the "center of our village" in the ceremony in Zunil. A father and son from a neighboring village carry firewood along the central avenue of the cemetery.

```
                              East
                         Xe' kega ab'aj
                      "under the red rock" (1)
                              red


      North                   Centro                  South
Pa roq'ib'al xik (4)         Cemetery              (3a) Pa minas
 "the place of the                                   b  Pa musmul
song of the eagle"                                   c  Pa kalpul
      white                                            yellow


                          Chuwi pek (2)
                        "in front of a cave"
                              black
                              West
```

1. *water source spring:* "under the red rock": ask for good health.
2. *cave:* "in front of a cave": to heal illnesses, place very big, large spiritually, near Poza Negra
3. a "place of the mines": to beg for money, social situation
   b "place of the drizzle": to get rid of infirmities, of craziness
   c "place to offer": to offer for the family, people, special days
4. "the place of the song of the eagle" to ask so there is not so much wind

FIGURE 4.11. Cosmogram of four major altars in Zunil.

tourist ceremonial sites, but also to the tens of thousands of sites linked to a people's personal and communal survival.

As a result of the Agreement, the National Commission of Spirituality was established. Four Maya Ajq'ijab' and four representatives of the government formed this commission. The work was charted in three phases. From January 15 to April 15, 1997, they were to define *sacred place,* and then begin to solicit lists of sacred places from each village throughout Guatemala. From April 15 to December 31, 1997, they were to establish an agreement with other commissions on the form of their work. In the third phrase, from January 2, 1998, through April 2000, they were to design a legal plan for the designation of official sacred sites, for the purpose of conservation and administration of the temples and ceremonial centers of archaeological value. However, after several years the commission was dismantled due to irreconcilable differences, how to manage ancient Maya cities being one of them. A new commission was established in 2000, with similar results. The government is beginning to regulate the access of Maya Ajq'ijab' to archaeological sites. Further, it is providing certificates to Ajq'ijab' for access to sacred sites. Both actions have been boldly criticized.

At the same time, reports of local management of municipal parks such as a Chikab'al volcano and lagoon are exemplary (Secaira). Chikab'al is an important ceremonial site, with at least twenty-six Maya altars around the lake. It is an important region of biodiversity, with forty-three species of threatened plants, a shelter for rare and threatened birds, and migratory birds along the Pacific volcanic chain. In 1999, when active management and protection of the area was initiated, a process of dialogue was begun with Maya Ajq'ijab'. They interceded through ceremonies for the conservation of nature in this region and suggested that swimming, bathing, and fishing in the lagoon be forbidden out of respect for its sacredness. While Ajq'ijab' have made some strides in guiding the management of this protected area, conflicts remain. Nevertheless, their participation represents an important step.

In sum, Maya traditionalists believe that the universe sustains us and that as humans we have a transitory passage on earth. This perception informs their reciprocal relationship with the land. Geological formations, storied and ritualized sacred places, long hidden under Western religious constructions and impositions, are accessed today as centers for personal and communal spiritual life. Further, the ideational cross image-space, a transformed continuity of the quatrefoil map which marks Mesoamerican cartographies, is claimed in the cultural landscape of ritual practice and as a marker of cultural identity. Some highland groups have been inspired by the model of the Aj Pop consulting on the woven mat in *Popol Wuj* and structure their basic principle of communal organization on the quatrefoil (Macleod 1998, 141–143). This quadrant image-space continues as a text for entering Maya space and time.

CHAPTER 5

The Calendar

Unbundling, Interpreting, and Appropriating the Chol Q'ij

"It's all about time," begins Roberto Poz late one evening as we sit in his small, benighted office, saturated with deep, warm scents of copal and a single burning flame. "To comprehend and deepen in understanding the calendar takes time. The basis of our spirituality is the Chol Q'ij, our calendar of twenty day names paired with thirteen number names, equaling a count of 260 days. The Chol Q'ij is mathematical and metaphoric; it coincides with the time a fetus is in the mother's uterus and it also possesses all the elements of life. Here, let me show you," he says as he pulls out a small paper from his pocket, unfolds and straightens it, revealing a handwritten chart of the twenty day names.

"Would you explain the meanings of the days?" I ask.

"Of course. However, you will just begin to understand. Today, for example is 4 K'anil, or seed. The characteristic of the day is the germ of life, the origin of all life, of plants and animals. K'anil is the nawal, *the guardian, of all kinds of seeds. It is an auspicious day to ask for an abundant harvest for any project we begin. It's a good day to start a new job, open a business, or plant a field. We also see that a person born on this day is like a seed: energetic, astute, and intelligent. This person has a young spirit, is fluent in speech, and likes to struggle. However, he or she can be self-occupied. His or her challenge in life is to discipline him- or herself to finish projects he or she has begun."*

Roberto clears his throat, nods reflectively, then proceeds slowly to delineate each of the days and to amplify its metaphoric meaning—its nawal—*and its practical application. "As you begin to understand the days," he* explains, "their meanings clarify, deepen, and broaden—like a giant spiral, like a dynamic weaving. They unfold like the petals of a flower.

"All spirituality takes time," he says. "To know the calendar, and then to deepen one's understanding of the calendar, takes time. That is, time to get the threads of one's life straightened and in order. Time to understand the relationships in life. Time to know one's capacities and to deepen one's life. Time to feel the forces of spirituality. After a while, you begin to feel the calendar in your body."

If there exists a contemporary, living embodiment of ancient Maya understanding and discernment, it is the 260-day calendar, known in K'iche' as the Chol' Q'ij. At one time this 260-day calendar was in use in much of Mesoamerica,[1] but it is now utilized only throughout the Guatemalan highlands, and in some communities in Veracruz, Oaxaca, and Chiapas (B. Tedlock 1982). The calendar has been recorded in the memories of ancestors, who conserved the calendar over the centuries, transmitting it from generation to generation, helping persons who have sought and looked for peace for themselves or for their people. This lunar calendar is a dynamic sacred matrix that traditional Maya utilize to maintain equilibrium in their lives as well as in relation to other persons, to nature, and to God. This inherited calendric method of spirituality remains foundational to traditional Maya everyday life, discernment, and ritual practices.[2] It is "the heart of the wisdom of the Maya people" (León Chic 1999).

In this chapter contemporary Ajq'ijab' interpret and appropriate the calendar as well as elucidate their work as "keepers of the days." They make transparent the Chol Q'ij and its function as the foundation of traditional highland personal and communal life. After establishing the primacy and sacredness of time among the Maya, and Ajaw as the fundamental principle of time, we will look at the centrality of the calendar and the role of Ajq'ijab' as interpreters of it. Next, we examine the question of the origin of the calendar, how and why the period of 260 days was used, with the subcycles of the thirteen numbers and twenty day names.

With this understanding in place, the calendar is presented as a textual world possessing qualities as well as a referential field so that it functions as an orientation instrument. Ethnographic narratives unbundle the significance of the calendar text, the meaning of each of the twenty days and of the numbers 1 to 13, to elucidate the complex potential of this paradigm. Finally, an Ajq'ij demonstrates a calendric consultation. In advising the individual, the Ajq'ij illustrates the complex mapping of a personal life and further makes transparent the underlying matrix used for advising a person in a marriage partner, friendships, and vocational choices. What emerges is a spiritual paradigm with ancient roots, reappropriated and reinterpreted as a discernment schema, a paradigm of meaning, for identity, for political memory, for personal and communal lives.

TIME AS THE CENTRAL MATRIX OF CULTURE

The primacy of time among the Maya is well established. Written evidence for the use of the calendar goes back to the sixth century BCE. Ancient Maya observed and measured the lunar cycle and solar year, lunar and solar eclipses, and the risings of Venus and Mars with great accuracy. They interpreted time not just as a quantitative calculation, but as saturated with meaning for human affairs. From 250 to 850 CE, the Maya devised ways of recording the passage of time, naming days and establishing significations and linkages between days, events, and ruling lineages. Stellae, monuments, and lineage houses in the lowlands in the Peten are inscribed with the history of the Maya elite, introduced and situated within the Long Count dating system. Four remaining pre-Columbian Maya ritual books—the Dresden, Madrid, Paris, and Grolier codices—record calendar computations used for divination and prophecy. These texts provided prescriptions for rites, ceremonies, and history (E. Thompson 1970, 5–12; Love 1994).

In *Popol Wuj*, the Former and the Architect plan, worry, think, and speak until they create humans, who will be givers of praise and respect, "keepers of the days." Bishop Diego de Landa, one of the first outsiders to see written Maya texts, showed that the knowledge of highly sophisticated methods for conceptualizing and recording the passage of time was the peculiar possession of specialists in the Maya society (Tozzer 1966, 63–64). The British scholar J. Eric S. Thompson identified one of the important elements of Maya civilization as "the overwhelming preoccupation with time" (1954, 37). Scholar Miguel León-Portilla writes, "It would be more appropriate to call the Maya worldview a chronovision, . . . to ignore the primordial importance of time would be to ignore the soul of this culture" (1988, 62–63 and 109–110).

Like the other peoples of Mesoamerica, the Maya developed various forms to measure time; it is ordered socially, agriculturally, and religiously. They developed three ways to count time. The Choltun, or Long Count, an era-based calendar, "counted whole days accumulated since the day zero, which they apparently conceived of as the beginning of the current manifestation of the cosmos, the fourth version of creation to exist" (Schele and Freidel 1990, 81). The beginning date can be correlated to

August 11, 3114 BCE, in European notation (82).[3] The count of days is marching toward the end of an immense 5,125-year cycle of history, when the 13th Baktun of the Maya calendar will draw to a close in December 2012, on the 20th, if using the Guatemalan 584283 correlation, or on the 22nd, if using the Classic period inscriptions of 584285 (Macri, phone conversation, August 2005). After that, a new cycle of time will begin. John Major Jenkins notes that "December 21st, 2012 CE (13.0.0.0.0 in the Long Count) will be a close conjunction of the Winter Solstice Sun with the crossing point of the Equator of the Milky Way and the path of the sun, what the ancient Maya recognized as the Sacred tree" (John Major Jenkins website).

Another record of time, called the Haab by Yucatec Maya and *macewal Q'ij* by the K'iche', is the agricultural measure, organized in eighteen months of twenty days (360 days), with a five-day terminal period called Uayeb at the end of the year. The third calendar, the Chol Q'ij, or sacred calendar, is a lunar count. This cycle of 260 days, composed of thirteen numbers consecutively combining with twenty day-names, is the subject of this chapter. The two cycles, the Choltun, lasting 365 days, and the Chol Q'ij, lasting 260 days, mesh to provide a fifty-two-year cycle, called the Calendar Round.

AJAW: THE FUNDAMENTAL PRINCIPLE OF TIME

Kaqchikel José Mucía Batz Lem's (1996) work "*NIK*" illustrates a recent investigation which sifts through particular signs in codices, monuments, stela, and other archaeological remainders to uncover and interpret the ancestral understanding of time. Batz notes that the figures of the flower, the seed, the conch shell, the zero, and the profile of a face, which he identifies as the glyph for Ajaw, have the same functions in Maya mathematics. The numerical flower is identified as the Maya zero, and has the function of being central. The other figures—the face, the flower, the shell, and the seed—have particularities and by definition are very different, but they possess qualities that are similar (Figure 5.1). For this reason, they are designated to complete the same functions of the beginning and the end, which is Ajaw (47). Numbers, he concludes, are like shadows of things. Time, then, is an attribute of the sacred. He writes:

> Ajaw is the fundamental principle of time and space, as other well as of other unknown dimensions. At the same time Ajaw is the trustee of all wisdom and scientific disciplines, Ajaw is the beginning that initiated mathematics. This signifies that the counting of time began with Ajaw. (11)

FIGURE 5.1. Figures of Ajaw, of the beginning and end. From José Mucía Batz Lem, "NIK": *Filosofía de los Números Mayas* (Guatemala City: SAQB'E, 1996), 22.

Scholars of Maya history and philosophical thought concur that time is an attribute of the sacred. León-Portilla writes that Maya attribute divine nature to *k'in,* sun-day-time. *K'in,* as sun, as time, as day, has important variants: the old god with the solar eye, the four-petal flower, the jaguar mask, the monkey face. "So we know that the *kinh*—sun-day-time—was not an abstract entity but a reality enmeshed in a world of myths, a divine being, the origin of the cycles which govern all existing things" (1988, 33).

> In a word, *kinh* appears, as the heart of all change, filled with lucky and unlucky destinies within the cyclic reality of the universe and most probably inherent to the essence of divinity itself. (33)

In these interpretations, we find that time is an attribute of the sacred. Numbers are metaphors, shadows of things; the calendar, in "the counting of time," then, is an engagement with the sacred. With these foundational understandings in place, we turn to the Chol Q'ij.

MAYAB' CHOL Q'IJ

The Chol Q'ij was remembered by Maya ancestors, who conserved it over the centuries, helping people who desire and seek peace for themselves, for others, and for their community. "The calendar is a spiritual guide for discernment," writes Victoriano Castillo González, S.J. "If we incline ourselves to drink of this font of spirituality of our ancestors, we will be capable to understand better our faith and to put it into practice" (1998, 4).

The 260-day calendar refers to two continuous repeating cycles, the set of twenty day names, and the count of thirteen days. This calendar is the basis of traditional highland personal and communal lives. Perhaps the following examples will make the Chol Q'ij more transparent as we begin to see the significance of the days worked out in daily, practical life and in ritual practice.

Each day is sacred, to be respected and kept. Before the ceremonial fire, each of the day names is directly addressed thirteen times and fed aromatic gifts. Shopkeepers may open their business or a farmer plant corn on 4 K'anil, the day of beginnings, the seed. On 8 No'j, a couple may intentionally try to conceive a child. On 5 Ajmaq, people visit altars to ask pardon and remember their ancestors. On 13 Imox, one Ajq'ij might decide not to travel on a major highway after noon; another would just be more cautious in traveling. A couple understands their marriage problems may be due to the mismatch of their day signs; they would need more effort through regular ceremonies and understandings of one another to have a happy marriage. Ajq'ijab' are usually initiated on 8 B'atz. In Santa María Chiquimula, the *cofradía* of Cristo of Esquipules washes the clothing of the saints at midnight four times a year: on 12 Kiej, 12 No'j, 12 Iq', and 12 E. National bus companies hire Ajq'ijab' to offer ceremonies every nineteen days for safe bus travel both on the Pan American highway and in rural areas, ensuring the benefit of the specific energy of each of the twenty days of the calendar. An Ajq'ij interprets and renders a dream distinctly, depending upon which calendar day it occurs, and whether it was visualized before or after midnight. The calendar becomes a matrix around which people organize their lives. Ajq'ij Miguel Matías says, "It is learning to live, to pray, to work within the rhythm and advice of the calendar that a person progresses deeper and wider in Maya wisdom."

An Ajq'ij is "of the days" or "in charge of the days." These calendar keepers are the trained and often wise persons who utilize the Chol Q'ij, the symbolic 260-day system of values, as an orientation cosmogram and instrument. They assist other persons and their communities to arrange the days as threads, to manage an individual's life from birth until death, in accord with the day and sign which corresponds to his/her moment of birth. They teach that if we understand the calendar, we can reason from that to our own inner structure.

The work of Ajq'ijab' as "keepers of the days" and the function and metaphoric understanding of this calendar text can be elucidated by archaeological, ethnohistorical, and ethnographic studies. This calendar has been designated with the invented Yucatec word *tzolkin*,[4] but contemporary K'iche' speakers say this calendar has more accurate translations. One rendition is the Rajalb'al Q'ij, the "counting of days," or "of counting"; the other, and more common, is Chol Q'ij, "to loosen," "to order," "to untangle" (Shol Q'ij), or "between days." The first translation carries within it numerous shades of meaning: an enumeration, a calculation, taking into account, or an ascription of the days. The second rendering, Chol Q'ij, "to untangle," invokes the model of the Mesoamerican cosmogram and uncovers the intention of the calendric text within a larger schema.

Mesoamerican art and literature illuminate a general belief that the universe is bounded, defined, and contained by long, thin supple objects of a cord-like form. While the upper universe was conceived as a neatly woven house, the model of the underworld was a tangled, knotted wad or ball, whose loose ends connected with the openings in the surface of the earth. The interface in relation to the joining of heaven and earth implies the presence of a giant cosmic seam (Klein 1982, 1–35). Cecelia Klein has written that the sacred cords' "common function lies in their ability to connect disparate points and thus provide means of passage and communication" (2). The cycles of the sun, moon, planets, and stars were the basis of their connection between the worlds.

The connection between time and threads is present in many ancient Maya texts and cosmogonies, such as the creation account in which the creator spins time like a thread. At the beginning of a *katun*, "the rope shall descend, the cord shall descend from heaven" and a new "year bearer" will assume his burden. The idea of "year bearers" gives us an insight into how the Maya envisioned time: each day/year was a "burden" to be carried by the deity who presided over it until his leg of the relay was complete, at which time he transferred it to the next deity, and so on (León-Portilla 1988, 51). *Popol Wuj*, which reflects an underlying plot and context for human meaning, gives us a further insight into the relation of the Ajq'ij and the calendar. K'iche' writer Adrián Inés Chávez writes that there are two meanings to the word *pop*, of *Popol Wuj* (or *Popul Vuh*). One is the common understanding of the *petate*, or woven mat. The other, more refined mien, which "only learned and wise people understand," is that *pop* signifies time or event, happening, or incident (1997, xxxi). Transformed continuities of time remain. Ajq'ijab' continue to understand their burden, their spirituality, capacity, and work, to be held in sacred time.

If we pull at the rendition of the calendar as an "untangling," the role of the Ajq'ij as a "keeper of the calendar" is to "untangle the cords," to help a person understand his or her destiny within sacred time and space. When a client comes to an Ajq'ij and needs a consultation or a cleansing because he or she is confused, sick, or entangled in problems, the client "has a *SoQ'ij*" (untangling of days), because he or she is *soloniq* (all messed up in life). The person asking advice is "trying to clear his day"; the Ajq'ij will "do a *solonik* (a cleansing) on that person. That is why we can say that the role of the Ajq'ij is to "untangle cords," to illuminate the meaning of one's day, that is, one's destiny, one's capacity and potentials according to the sacred calendar. Further, Ajq'ijab' often carry the "burden of the days," the accompanying suffering and responsibility of the spiritual.

Ajq'ijab' say that as humans, "We carry the calendar in our bodies." That is, the numbers and day signs are embodied, twenty in the digits of the human body, thirteen in the major joints (Figure 5.2). Indeed, in many Mayan languages the word for *person* is the same as the word for "twenty." Doña Marta, of Cantel, explains,

> The word *hun winak* signifies a person with twenty fingers and toes. In K'iche' the word for *person* and the word for *twenty* is the same; the number twenty is also a sign of completion. Where does the number 20 come from? It comes from the human body: ten fingers, ten toes, that is twenty digits in all.

"The number 13," Doña Marta continues as she points out the major joints, beginning at her neck, then counting down from left side of her body returning to her right shoulder, "corresponds to the great movements of the human body: the neck, the shoulders, elbows, the wrist, the hip joints, knees, and ankles.

"The ancestors did this great study of the human body," she concludes, "and came up with the numbers 13 and 20. Each of the twenty days and every one of the thirteen numbers form the human body."

When I ask further about the calendar in the human body, Doña Marta shows me a photocopy showing a nude man, surrounded by the twenty day signs, each one connected by a line to a part of the body. She explains, "This was a diagram from the Nahuas in Mexico," whom we both knew shared the Mesoamerican calendar and a similar worldview with the Maya. I would later identify it as plate lxxiii of the *Códice Vaticano Latino 3738*, where the interpreter of the codex explains the pre-Hispanic concepts of the relationship of the twenty symbols and their relationship to disease and curing (Seler 1963, 207) (Figure 5.2).

Martha Macri, of the University of California at Davis, suggests that the counting scheme of thirteen numbers and twenty day names is based on various segments of the lunar cycle and corresponds to numerical glyphs:

> In addition to associating 20 with the 20 digits of the human body, the Classic Period Maya directly substituted glyphs for the moon with the number twenty . . . the lunar significance of 20 is that it is the number of days from the first visible crescent to the third quarter of the lunar cycles. That is, 20 is the number of days during which the moon is visible in the evening sky. (2005, 284)

She suggests that astronomy was common knowledge at first, but from 250 to 850 CE, it became relegated to the priestly class. In time, common people lost an understanding of the relationship of the thirteen numbers and twenty day names to celestial events. What is left are interpretations of the embodiment of numbers.

The question of the origin and composition of this 260-day calendar is still a puzzle. One suggestion offered by Zelia Nuttal in 1928, and more recently by Malström, is that at the latitude of 14.8\o, the latitude of Ixapa, Guatemala, and Copán, Honduras, 260 is the number of days between the zenithal sun's southward and northward passage (1997, 4). However, Mesoamerican scholars have sharply criticized this idea. The most compelling criticism is that there are no calendar inscriptions from Ixapa (Vail 1997, 72). Others favor the explanation that 260 days approximates the length of human gestation; in this view, the genesis of the 260-day calendar is attributed to the use of the lunar cycle for determining the length of human gestation (measured by the K'iche' of highland Guatemala in terms of nine twenty-nine-day lunations, or 260 days) (Vail 1997, 72).

Astronomical explanations are speculative, so we search for support also from archaeological, ethnohistorical, and ethnographic evidence. Not-

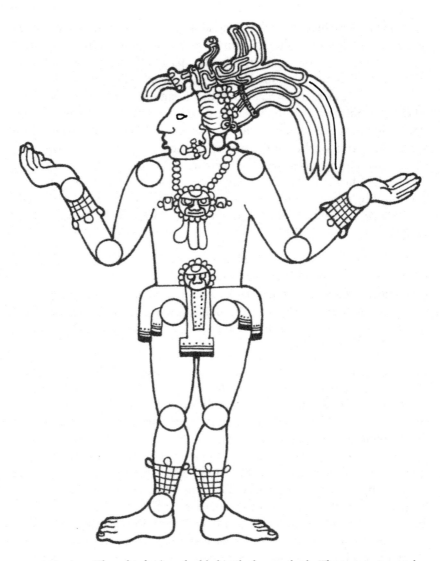

FIGURE 5.2. The calendar is embedded in the human body. The twenty toes and fingers parallel the twenty days; the thirteen major joints mark the thirteen numbers. Drawing by René Humberto López Cotí.

ing that the phenomenon of the waxing moon has held significance for peoples throughout history, as it is universally and directly observable, Martha Macri suggests that these counting schemes of thirteen and twenty testify to the importance of the period of the waxing moon in Mesoamerica. She proposes that the Mesoamerican calendrical cycles of thirteen numbers, twenty day names, and repeating cycles of nine and seven are based on various segments of the lunar cycle. She writes,

> Over 2500 years ago, some Mesoamerican culture (perhaps several) observed and incorporated into their worldview a lunar cycle that was composed of three segments: a 13-day waxing period, a 7-day waning period from the full moon to the third quarter moon, and a 9-day period from the third quarter through the period of invisibility. Some group—perhaps a single person, almost certainly speakers of a Mayan language—then took each of these three segments and created several independent repeating cycles. This group then had enough political power and cultural energy to set in motion the eventual spread of at least certain aspects of this new scheme to peoples throughout Mesoamerica.
>
> The segments of the lunar cycle that they identified correspond to the trecena (the repeating count of 13 days), the twenty Mesoamerican day names (consisting of the trecena plus 7 more days), a count of nine (known from the Aztecs as the Nine Lords of the Night), and a recently identified count of seven. (2005, 279)

The proposal that the average number of days from the first visible crescent to the full moon is thirteen, which may account for the sacredness of thirteen to the Maya as well as to other cultures, is an important and significant contribution. Researchers have remarked on the relationship between the head variants and Maya day signs, but Macri further posits that the set of glyph head variants, unique to the ancient Maya, represent their numbers 1 through 13, and originally marked the waxing moon.

> The glyphs are distinct, however, only up to the number 13. The number 13 sometimes has a unique sign, but it may, like the numbers 14–19, be composed of the head for the smaller number (3–9) with the addition of a skeletal jaw. The head variant for 10 is the skull, so these composite signs are actually based on a decimal system—as are the numbers 13–19 in Mayan languages. (280)

Between 250 and 850 CE, this calendar system was appropriated, institutionalized, and politicized to construct and justify a comprehensive and hierarchical social organization of classes based on power and wealth. Rulers and familial lineages identified themselves with Ajaw and began to engrave Ajaw's image and important calendric dates on their staffs, stelae, tombs, and temples. They distanced themselves from the rest of the community and established themselves as a hierarchy, justifying their human political power on earth as they governed the flow of prescribed tribute, knowledge, and power.

To investigate the legacy of the political control and use of the calendars after 1200 CE, ethnohistoric evidence in the K'iche' central highlands is helpful. Utatlán, a large K'iche' highland town comprised of a confederacy of three original peoples, the Nima Quiches, who migrated from the Toltec stock in Mexico from 1225 to 1240, then subdued, incorporated, and gained ascendancy over the Tamubs and the Ilocabs, positioned itself as the most important politico-religious center in pre-Conquest Guatemala from 1400 to 1524 (Carmack 1988, 3–7). Research demonstrates that both nobles and vassals utilized the solar and sacred calendars in Utatlán.

The solar calendar was geared to the production of maize; its strong calendrical associations with ecological relationships formed the basis of agricultural life. Carmack writes that it "was almost a blueprint of how the Quichés viewed the relationship between agriculture and other features in the environment" (1988, 84). He explains that in Utatlán, "solar and 'sacred calendars' used by the lords to schedule wars, public works, marriages, and rituals were also used by the vassals to perform agricultural labor and conduct lineage affairs" (210); he further notes that both town and rural peoples of this community followed the 260-day calendar (210). This indicates that use of these calendars continued, though with different political usages and interpretations. During the colonial period the Church became thoroughly entrenched in the K'iche' communities, so that the religious practices, including calendars, took on appropriated, syncretic forms. In the first third of the twentieth century, liberalism promoted capitalism, Latinization, and modern culture, which contributed to the erosion of the use of the calendar (Carmack 1988, 348).

CHARTING CALENDRIC APPROPRIATIONS

J. Eric Thompson asserts that "the Maya calendar of today is a pitiful survival," with only its bare structure remaining and all the "embellishments" gone (1954, 90). This view suggests that the ancient ways are in effect dead, with merely a shadow, a simulacrum, remaining. Ruth Bunzel, on the other hand, writing about Chichicastenango in the 1930s, says, "This 'book of the days' is used as it was employed in the times of the ancient Maya and Aztecs, for divination, witchcraft, and establishing time for all the religious ceremonies" (334). Her view suggests more of a continuity between antiquity and the contemporary expression of the keeping of the calendar. In my recent ethnographic work, I have found, as did Barbara Tedlock in her important work *Time and the Highland Maya* (1982), that many K'iche', Kanjob'al, Mam, and Kaqchikel people in the highlands persisted in observing the calendar for ritual and discernment, often within family or clandestine confidences, for centuries. From this perspective, what has changed over time is less the use of the calendar than it is the public avowal of that use. Now, some Maya utilize the calendar publicly as a mapping of human identity and capacities, a marker for ritual practices, and for social, political, and economic activities.

In this use of the calendar, objects become "the focus of contemplative memory, and hence a generator of self" (Harvey 1990, 292). The Chol Q'ij, with its associated twenty day names and thirteen numbers, is central to present-day Ajq'ijab' study. In the contemporary reassessment of these days and numbers, traditionalists engage with these texts, which were constructed and produced in a particular way, and conveyed a particular understanding of the world. Today, the calendar provides a cartogram and rhythm which Ajq'ijab' utilize in ritual and interpretive practice. The twenty days and thirteen numbers are a referential field for discernment and advice: the days are read in the *tz'ite'* bean sortilege and in dream interpretation, and discerned in the ceremonial fire and in "the lightning in the blood," which is the symbolic alignment of time in their bodies during a consultation (B. Tedlock 1982, 132–147, 152–179).

The meaning-making dimension is abundantly clear from the history of interpretation, which shows how the same text can be understood in many different ways, according to the prevailing codes that have been brought to bear on it. As Wolfgang Iser writes, "Every literary text inevitably contains a selection from a variety of social, cultural, and literary systems that exist as referential fields outside the text" (4). The same text can make "sense" in a variety of historical situations.

It should be clarified that in the highlands, the calendar traditionally had day names; there is no evidence of visual images for the days in that geographic region. In the lowlands and in the Peten, the names on an icon are distinct from the visual image on the glyph. Since the early 1980s, Maya have reappropriated the visual representation with the day glyph. To complicate the process, many Maya have reappropriated the interpretations by way of Western scholars, not from their traditional elders.[5] Other indigenous religious specialists, elders, scholars, and community workers not only study written texts with local and transnational specialists (Schele and Grube 1996), but also engage with "ways of knowing and methods of study of the ancestors" to perceive, clarify, and interpret the meaning of texts. In these generative processes—intuitional, ritual, dialogic, and rational—potentials for new meanings emerge.

In its ancient manifestation, the calendar, the object of understanding to which Thompson and Bunzel refer, conveyed particular interpretations of the world; contemporary Ajq'ijab' continue anew to translate the calendar as a potential for discerning meaning. María del Carmen Tuy explains,

> Our ancestors said and reminded us that each person comes into the world with a character, a vocation, a capacity according to his or her day. The personality is resonant with the day of the birth of the person. A person has certain work; a person born on a particular day has a specialty, but also has limitations. All days are good; they are special and important for us. Each of us is a specialist in something. We love the person, cherish and respect the person as she or he reveals the day.

Contemporary Ajq'ijab' interpret the lexicon of the calendar as a psychological schema, which can also be understood as a literary text, a referential field, or a patterning of elements. "We have our own psychological system, it is the calendar," explains Roberto Poz. As a super-sign, the calendar contains the basic elements of life and maps a given world. These signs can create an open system of transformation and generation. As a dynamic icon of twenty day names and the numbers 1–13, it unfolds a whole network of possible combinations. When the Ajq'ij engages with the horizon of the text, s/he decodes and exploits the generative multiplicity of meaning, thus illuminating its rich aesthetic potential.

The creation of meaning emerges in accordance with the calendar system. In a consultation, the Ajq'ij identifies the concordant day name and number for the particular client or problem. In this act of selection, s/he turns the days into objects for observation. The Ajq'ij focuses on, interprets, and extends the qualities and capacities of the day name, in an attunement with the movements in their bodies, as if playing with filaments of light. This enacted discourse reveals the perception and attitude adopted by the Ajq'ij to a given world. There are multiple interpretations around an image, and Ajq'ijab' interpret the day name in different renderings. In the act of combining the day name with the designated number, the Ajq'ij brings into clearer focus the potentialities and forces at hand. For example, Roberto interprets the day Hun No'j, or One Wisdom.

> A person born on the day No'j (Wisdom) is intellectual, mentally active, astute, practical, and progressive. She or he has the capacity to

understand and interpret things and good ideas, to investigate and to lecture. A person born on No'j has strong convictions and many talents and is responsible. On the other hand, this person can be angry, resentful, and unreasonable. This person, born on Hun No'j, can order, can be a governor. He or she is very intelligent, has a facility for dialogue and leadership. On the other side, this person may also have health problems and get angry for small things. The challenge in life for the person born on No'j is to maintain his or her own life with a plan; his or her solution is to be more flexible and patient with his- or herself and with others.

Hun No'j also orders communal and ceremonial life. Roberto continues:

> It's a good day to ask the Heart of Heaven and of the Earth for all that we need in life. Wisdom is of God, but for us, we ask Heart of Heaven and Heart of Earth for wisdom so we will act in appropriate ways. On this day, our ceremonies are to ask for a unity of ideas, to ask for a good road for society, and to ask for understanding, wisdom, and knowledge.

In the relational process, the client considers, engages with, and usually accepts the advice of the Ajq'ij. This act of accepting one's day can be generative and transformational. As the client hears the interpretation, there is the urge to make it meaningful so that he or she may bring the experience back to what is familiar, to sound out the meaningfulness of the interpretation. "This drive is both natural and unavoidable," writes Iser (1993, 18) about the relational process.

The person appropriates the image he/she hears into his/her body-image. The individual, then, anchors her- or himself, and the problems and decisions s/he must engage with, within a larger schema of life, to balance his/her life. Its potential is that a person can relate his/her life to a reality that is larger than the self. It is an act of "boundary-crossing" from self-absorption to a generative matrix of the calendar text, which recognizes the basic creative and destructive elements of life. Here I emphasize that this activity must have some practical use, some purpose.

The individual may begin to interpret and understand problems, misfortunes, good luck, relationships, and decisions within the matrix of the calendar. Individuals utilize the calendar as a referential field to interpret why things are the way they are. Listen to these narratives.

> It's because of my day that I cannot stay in the house. My day is E and E is the road. My day, my destiny, my luck takes me to many people

outside of my village. My work is in Chimaltenango, Guatemala City, and sometimes in San Francisco, California. It is the force, the strength, of my day.

MARÍA DEL CARMEN TUY, AJQ'IJ, EDUCATOR,
COMMUNITY WORKER

In my case, I am the rock [Tijax: the obsidian blade] that suffers heat and cold. What does this mean? I understand that I have had much suffering in my life, many struggles, too. But also that this is the way to purify my life, to understand the suffering of humanity so I can share my life with humanity.

CALIXTA CABRIEL, AJQ'IJ, SOCIAL WORKER

I was born in the city of Quetzaltenango June 23, 1958. My birthday is Kieb Tz'ikin, which means two birds, one that sees the past and the other that sees the future. According to the grandparents, this sign indicates an enterprising person, one who creates paths and faces challenges.

NORMA QUIXTÁN CHOJOJ, GOVERNOR OF QUETZALTENANGO

Two years ago the store burned in the Democracia market. It was a cross, a suffering, but one carries suffering under the sign of one's birth. I am 13 K'at, 8 E, and 3 Ajpu'.

MARÍA ANTONIETA COFULUM, AJQ'IJ,
MERCHANT IN QUETZALTENANGO

María del Carmen relates a person's work to his/her configuration:

I gave a lecture to students who were involved in human rights. Many people in that group had the day Tijax in the configuration of their birth dates. I realized many people in this work had the days: Tijax, Tz'i, Keme' influencing them. I told them, "You have to go forward, you have to go ahead with this work. But take these forces into account as you work. They will support and influence you."

But that is not all, Martín explains. "There is within the day also a way to balance yourself. There is a way to purify yourself so you can live more harmoniously and peacefully." In some cases, a traditionalist may undertake particular activities, such as the initiation of a business, payment of debts, travel, or specific ritual practices on particular days of the sacred calendar. That is, as the individual reinterprets his or her life within this schema, new possibilities, resources, and options emerge. As they orient their lives through the interplay of the twenty day-name and thirteen number combinations, their interpretations collect meaning, depth, and breadth, much like the unfolding of a spiral.

Within this system, there is also a danger, an interpretation of fate: "That's just the way things are." For example, one Ajq'ij will not travel on the day Imox (crazy) because she fears some type of accident. Roberto interprets it differently: "You just have to be careful and take precautions if you travel on that day."

UNBUNDLING THE DAY NAMES: A LEXICON

Other ethnographers have presented work on Maya day names;[6] here, I am interested in how Ajq'ijab' interpret the sacred calendar as a psychological/spiritual map, in ways that assist others to chart their identities, capacities, and decisions. Further, I want to investigate the underlying order and relations which form contemporary Maya psychology and discernment.

The calendar reveals a dynamic, cyclical, textual world. "The twenty days represent the elements of life. Each element has its place, each has its moment: the calendar gives expression to each element," explains Miguel Matias. Each day is a bundle of meaning; the numbers from 1 to 13 render the tone or power of that element. The combination of a particular day name and a particular number designates the quality of that day. Roberto explains,

> For us K'iche', each day possesses a special character, determined by two elements: the number and the day sign. Each of the day names refers to a phase of the life, an attribute, or a religious concept. These twenty days express all the basic forces of creation and destruction, the bad and the good of what is operating in the world, in society, and in the heart of humanity.

In interpreting the meaning of specific days thematically, the intention is to unlock the manifoldness of Maya day interpretations, to unbundle day meanings. While one's day of birth is held most significant, it should be noted that to Ajq'ijab' there are two other important days that influence each human's life: the luck day of the past and the protection day of the future. It is necessary to determine and to point out the influence of

FIGURE 5.3. Twenty day signs of Chol Q'ij.

the interplay of these three days, as I will show later in this chapter. First, I present to you a lexicon of day names, elicited from several Ajq'ijab', particularly Roberto Poz and María del Carmen Tuy, and other texts (Figure 5.3).

> *B'atz'* (thread, monkey)—signifies the thread, the placenta, the count thread of time. It is a day referring to spin, as in spinning thread, or rolling or winding up, to ask. This day marks our origin, a continuation with the past. It was this energy that orientated the first wise ones to form humanity and it is the ultimate end of the universe. It is a good day to begin or initiate any activity.

> *E* (the road, destiny, tooth)—signifies the good road, the straight road, the long road, destiny; the nerves in the human body. It is the day marking the development of history.

Aj (the cornstalk, the reed, the young ear of corn)—signifies the home, the family. In *Popol Wuj*, Junajpu and Xb'alanke each plant an ear of corn in the center of their grandmother's patio before they depart to play ball in Xib'alb'a, the underworld. They leave these instructions with their grandmother: "Each of us will plant an ear of corn. We'll plant them in the center of our house. When the corn dries up, this will be a sign of our death: 'Perhaps they died,' you'll say, when it dries up. And when the sprouting comes, 'Perhaps they live,' you'll say, our dear grandmother and mother" (D. Tedlock 1985, 133). Aj, then, is related to the home, to the family; it is the sign of triumphing over all forms of illness, even death; it is a symbol of resurrection.

I'x (strength, jaguar, tiger, sacred appeal of the earth)—symbolizes vigor, the creative forces of the universe. It is a day of feminine energy. It also represents the Maya altar, the place of the sacred power of the earth; it is the day of the mountains and the plains.

Tz'ikin (fortune, bird, eagle, wisdom, and knowledge)—the day who sees all things from up above, who mediates between God and humans. This characteristic represents space, the air, the light, the clouds, the cold, the warmth of the Heart of Heaven and Heart of Earth that has put itself in our service. It is a day to cry for, to ask for money, success.

Ajmaq (vulture or owl, pardon, the dead ancestors)—a symbol of moral forces, a day to remember our dead ancestors, to ask pardon for our sins before the sky, before Ajaw, before the earth, before the ancestors. Those who have gone before guide the present and help us so the best will come in our future.

No'j (wisdom, creativity, intelligence)—relates to the earth's movement, to motion or movement, the result of applied force, as an earthquake. It signifies intelligence, wisdom and understanding, and creativity, which are of Ajaw.

Tijax (obsidian knife, suffering, pain)—signifies suffering. The glyph is the flint knife or the sharpened obsidian knife, the emblem of the gods of the sacrifices. This day is a reminder of how the first parents struggled with themselves through danger, suffering, and pain. It is the day of healers.

Kawoq (lawsuit, difficulties, problems, bad luck)—signifies lightning and thunder, concomitants of the electrical storm, celestial dragons; also the rain. On the earth there are problems, but as our first grandparents demonstrated, they were able to conquer the obstacles and to accomplish their work for humanity. It is a day for judges, lawyers, and those who intercede for health or an end to problems.

Ajpu' (deer hunter, sun, hero)—the glyph sign for Ajpu' is Ajaw, which represents the radiant sun, a manifestation of *kinh* (day). It is not only a divine face, but also the root of time. Further, it is a flower. In *Popol Wuj*, Ajpu' is one of the hero twins who passed through death in Xib'alb'a, but revived and was transformed into the sun. So this day represents a triumph over problems and difficulties.

Imox (craziness, lake, water lizard)—the sign, a fish-like animal, a crocodile, signifies the material beginning of existence or life in the Earth or in the individual, the occult forces in the universe. It can also indicate one who becomes possessed or crazy, one who tends too much to details in life. It is a day to humble oneself before Mam, the Earth Lord.

Iq' (air, wind, Tepeu)—like the secret breath of life, this day carries a mystic spirituality and intelligence. It's the day of the winds of the altars that fill us with life.

Aq'ab'al (dawn, obscurity, harmony)—symbol of the first rays of dawn, the closing of the darkness, literally the aurora, the guardian of all creation. The sunrise appears over the mountains and shatters the night's obscurity and confusion. It is a day of peace and happiness.

K'an (snake, Q'ukumatz, Plumed Serpent)—symbolizes the force of the universe, the warmth of the Plumed Serpent, which appears on the horizon and communicates between the earth and the sky; a manifestation of the Heart of the Sky, Heart of the Earth. It is the mystery of the coiling in creation. The sign of the Creator, the Founder, it also is the duality of good and bad. The day is justice. K'an is the vision of the Maya people.

K'at (the net to guard the corn, a womb; also heat, fire, fervor). It is a sensitive day because it can roast one; it also symbolizes the fire. It is a special day to entangle, snare, or wind something, but also a day to untangle, unsnare, or unwind something. It's a day to look for companions to form a group.

Keme' (death)—the termination of something, of life, of obscurity, of death. It is a symbol of day and night with lot of roads, nervousness, sicknesses, a day to ask pardon.

Kiej (deer, pillars of the four cardinal points)—as the four cardinal points, pillars sustain the dynamic relationship between the earth and the sky; it is the day of solid foundations, a day of authority and honesty.

K'anil (seed; the four colors of corn in Mesoamerica)—this day is the seed, the germ, the origin of the life, of plants and of animals. K'anil is the guardian of all kinds of seeds and ye..st. It is the special day to ask for seeds, to have an abundant harvest, to begin a project.

Toj (offering, to pay, suffering, pain)—this day symbolizes suffering due to sin, so it is the day indicated to offer, to pay, to give, to ask for strength, for justice.

T'zi' (dog, raccoon)—the dog, as a symbol of disequilibrium, disorients wisdom, can bring destruction. This day is the day to dig for the good, for example, to investigate laws, to bring order and justice. It is day of authority, friendliness, intelligence.

INTERPRETING NUMBERS 1–13

A day sign never appears separately, acting alone. The numbers 1–13 further influence the interpretation of the day's capacity. Bunzel, in Chichicastenango, and Tedlock, in Momostenango, noted that the low numbers—1, 2, 3, are "gentle" while the high numbers—11, 12, 13—are "violent." The middle numbers—7, 8, 9—are "indifferent"; as Tedlock writes, "these days of measured strength" are used for "the regularly recurring ceremonies to ensure tranquil life" (Bunzel 1981, 283; B. Tedlock 1982, 107–108). While I concur with their general interpretations, I would note that Ajq'ijab' have further rendered the numbers, not in a linear model, but one that mirrors a metaphoric worldview.[7]

Batz Lem writes that for the ancestors, the quality of Ajaw, the fundamental principle of time, is to be mother and father, a duality. Everything around this pair, mother and father, is respected and reverenced. For this reason the double of two, four, is another characteristic of Ajaw. This doubling is manifested in the four cardinal points, the first four women and men, the four colors, the two pairs of twins in *Popol Wuj*, the four time/burden carriers (1996, 33). Eight is the number of the first parents: eight were created. Thus, the number 2 and its multiples are balancing, stabilizing agents.

María del Carmen elaborates: "Each day journeys from 1 to 13. Odd-numbered days are chaotic and creative; even-numbered days are more favorable because they are balanced. Every number has its significance, but the most important are 4 and 13."

The number 4 is very significant because it represents a multiple of the dualities: night and day, cold and hot, day and night. It represents the four cardinal points. It represents the four forces: heart of sky, heart of earth, heart of air and heart of water. Number 8 is very positive because it is the double of four. The number 13 is powerful, very powerful, but it has to be presented in a ceremony to become positive.

Numbers 1 and 7 are very important for our Maya calendar. Why? Let me explain. The Chol Q'ij doesn't have a beginning or an end. It doesn't begin with 1, but with 8, or *wajxaqib'*, that is, with the mathematical plan, $1 + 7 = 8$. The number 1 is *hun, ajpu'*; the number 7 is *keme'*, or death, the final number. Number 8 represents the total, the beginning and the end, the unity of time.

USE OF THE CALENDAR FOR PERSONAL MAPPING

Three day signs inform a person's life: the past, the birth, the protection for the future. By drawing relationships to a day nine days before and to a day nine days after one's birth date, Ajq'ijab' enlarge and deepen the interpretation of one's capacity and work. María del Carmen explains the following configuration:

Tz'i	Tijax	Keme'
(past)	(birthdate)	(future)

Tijax, the birth date, is the obsidian blade. Parents, who know the day sign, can help the child, help his/her ability. My grandmother said of me, "This child has a lot of work to do." So they knew from the beginning because of my sign that I had a lot to do. Tijax is a strong, a valiant person. This child has strength. This child has no fear of animals, snakes, nor is he or she afraid of the dark. A person born on Tijax will also suffer much. But this person doesn't suffer just to suffer, but for something in the future. As an adult, she will come to a capacity, and will attend others in their problems, as a leader. Tijax doesn't speak much, but has a noble heart and is sensitive to others. The face doesn't show the person's feelings, but the feelings are very deep toward other people.

But in this configuration, there is another day, nine days forward, which influences Tijax. That is Keme' (death). Death you take as a culmination of a work; death is a transition. Keme' influences the personality. Persons of Keme' aren't afraid to do very difficult work, such as working with drug addicts, the imprisoned, or murderers. They have this capacity to work with them. They can do work that is emotionally difficult, such as working with people who have AIDS. They have the wisdom, the courage to pursue human rights. They are not attracted to criminals because they have this internal force which protects them. When they ask or pray for help, the response is almost always positive. They help others with their force, but they have to know themselves.

There is also another day, nine days backward, which influences Tijax. It is Tz'i' [authority, dog]. From the day Tz'i' comes the force to be a leader who sends, who directs, who has to say what you have to do. The person born on Tz'i' is valiant, powerful, and an authority. But there are other details.

In conversation with Roberto, I found there is more to this triple chrono-paradigm than meets the untrained eye. This model is an intricate, mythic, and mathematical blueprint. The following story will elucidate this for you.

One evening, I asked Roberto, "Where do you get your information in your consultations?" He matter-of-factly responded, "From the Plumed Serpent."

I thought, what could he mean? Yes, I knew from archaeological studies that the Plumed Serpent was the energy-primal force anthropomorphized as Quetzalcoatl to the Aztec, as Q'ukumatz to the Maya. So I thought perhaps he was referring to the highly developed intuitive way of knowing that he felt as energy rippling through his body.

Rather, the answer lay in a calculated, mathematical plan.

"The Ajq'ij has a great responsibility in the community," explains Roberto. "For example, someone comes and says, 'I have a problem.' I ask for his or her name, the day of birth, then I take up this book, *Fija del Destino del Hombre y la Mujer*. Let's say his name is Manuel and he was born on June 17, 1972. I relate June 17, 1972, on the Gregorian calendar with its corresponding date on the Maya calendar. Manuel's birthday on the 260-day calendar is 1 Aq'ab'al.

"Now I pass to a more specific interpretation. What does it signify? *Aq'ab'al* means 'the dawning'."

"But two other days are important: his conception and the day (luck) in front of him. This person is born on 1 Aq'ab'al, so I count back nine to 6 Tz'ikin and count forward nine to 9 B'atz."

"I am going to show you a formula to specify the person." Roberto pulls out a paper and begins counting out days and drawing a blueprint. "It's really a schema of nine Maya symbols, on a sequence of 7."

From 6 Tz'ikin he counts seven backward to 13 Toj, and then forward seven to 12 Imox. From 9 B'atz, he counts seven forward to 2 No'j, and then seven backward to 3 K'an. From 1 Aq'ab'al he counts seven backward to 8 No'j, and seven forward to 8 Toj.

13 Toj	6 Tz'ikin	12 Imox
8 No'j	1 Aq'ab'al	8 Toj
3 K'an	9 B'atz	2 No'j

He pauses, examines the pattern, then elaborates: "As I read it, this configuration specifies that the person consistently has problems. A person with this constellation is emotional, intellectual, and dynamic. He likes economic situations; he acts quickly and punctually. But he has to give his life for what is spiritual because he continually gets sick. Sure. He has a specialty to be a spiritual guide. It is the strong spiritual power in him moving him to receive his *vara*. He has to give his life for what is spiritual. That's what this advice would be. This person has a specification to be an Ajq'ij.

"This constellation tells us how to understand this person, the way he expresses himself, his characteristics. This person is not conflictive, but very powerful. Through this consultation, we are giving the person a schema for his life. There is an order here for his life. Every nine months, on 13 Toj, this person must give an offering. Every twenty-eight days he must take time to reflect deeply and widely, and make an offering. Here it is on 13 Toj for sacrifice; 6 Tz'ikin for success; and 8 No'j for wisdom. After that comes 12 Imox, 1 Aq'ab'al, 3 K'an, 7 Toj, 9 B'atz, and it ends in 2 No'j. Following this blueprint, making offerings, paying on the right days will make this person happy. We are sure this is a direct form, one direct form within the cosmos to live in harmony, and to remember, to give back to the cosmos. You see," he explains, tracing the zigzag lines through the blueprint, "in each of our day constellations, there is the Plumed Serpent" (Figure 5.4).

"The three days: one's birth date, the day of the past, and the day of the future, influence one the most. The other six days are helpers. Note that two days—Toj and No'j—are repeated. These are the guardians. And if you look at the diagram from 13 Toj to 2 No'j, it is twenty-nine days and one hour, which makes the lunar month. It is within this map that you find your vocation, your partner, your social organization. You see, embedded in the calendar is the Plumed Serpent. The calendar is one of its manifestations."

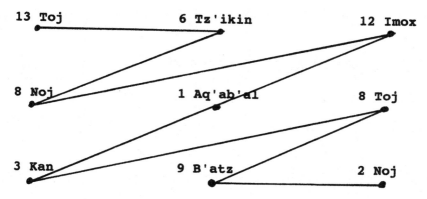

FIGURE 5.4. Calendar formula to "specify the person" shared by Roberto Poz. The Plumed Serpent is embedded in the constellation of one's day signs.

Because the calendar matrix is rooted in a cosmic system, it provides the underpinning for respect for and acceptance of oneself and others. María del Carmen explains,

We have to accept ourselves as we are. When I look at the calendar, then I can understand myself as I am and others as they are. I cannot criticize another person because every person carries abilities and weaknesses. In our communities we accept others in a very natural way. Parents know this child will be a businessperson or this girl will be a good healer. Only parents know it; but we don't talk about it. It is just part of life. In this way we respect it because we know each one has a work on earth. So we have to serve and respect the elders because they have to complete their work. This is mutual respect and support.

Every person is a specialist in what they need to do. As you know your day and your capacities, you live out of that potential. You perfect yourself and your service to humanity. Then when we leave this life, we will have left this life satisfied that we have completed our work.

Finally, there is one other set of relationships between the days which Ajq'ijab' utilize to advise others on social relationships: the quadrant cosmogram. Roberto details how in the calendar cartogram the days are mathematically related to the four directions, and more importantly, how he interprets their significance as a psychological and functional schema. He points out that the twenty days are mapped in four groups of five each; the combined days complement one another and have similarities. "They operate as teams," he explains. "People on the same teams make very good

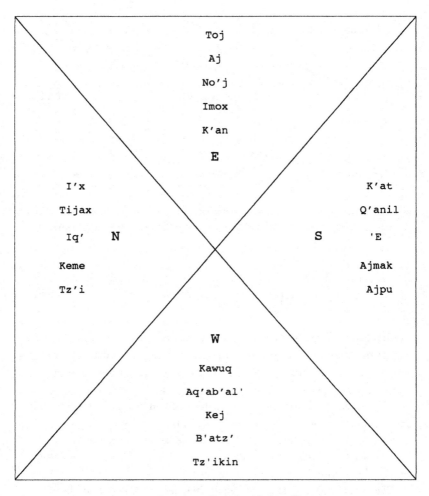

FIGURE 5.5. Day signs aligned with four directions.

friends, spouses, and even working relationships. Within this schema you find your partners or the best organizations to work with. This is a reason why some members in the family get along, and others do not."

He drew out the chart aligned with the directions (Figure 5.5).

As we have seen, Ajq'ijab' continue to project meaning into the cycles of time. They find in the Chol Q'ij not only a living embodiment of ancient wisdom and discernment, but also a complex and comprehensive cartogram through which they can understand and orient their lives.

Processes of transnational capitalism and globalization homogenize time, with sound bites and linear constructions of Western measures, yet the Maya calendar endures as the heart of the wisdom of the Maya people (León Chic 1999). Chol Q'ij contests these processes, providing a much larger and deeper mathematical and metaphorical cosmological schema, far richer than can be demonstrated here. Utilizing the calendar, Ajq'ijab' interpret lives in cycles of time, in folds of darkness and light. As people utilize the calendar, individuals and groups create a new temporal field, one endowed with spiritual qualities. It provides a text within which a people can order their lives and endure problems and crisis in life with wisdom, humility, patience, and good humor. Guatemalan author Walburga Alvarado writes, "The calendar is a spiritual force that has continued and united the Maya people in a social environment of tremendous political disarticulation, dispersion and destruction" (1997, 2). This dynamic matrix, rooted in ancient Mesoamerican observations of lunar cycles, endures as a source of personal discernment, social organization, and political memory.

CHAPTER 6

Ceremony
The Fire Speaks

One afternoon I follow Catarina through the earthen patio into the large dark adobe room of her parents' home in Zunil. A wooden bed in one corner, an altar in the opposite, and a weaving loom set centered against the back wall.

"Here, for you, Doña Juana," Catarina says as she pulls a low three-legged stool for me to sit on, facing the loom.

"Where are you going to sit, Catarina?"

"Right here," she answers, tucking strands of her dark hair under the woven cinta *(hair wrap) twisted round her head in Zunil style as she stands in front of the loom. Catarina kicks off her sandals. I notice a large callus on each ankle, skin thickened from hours kneeling as she weaves cloth and grinds maize. She kneels down, folds her legs under herself, fastening the backstrap of her loom behind her back, and selects threads, one by one, from the basket to begin the rhythm of weaving.*

"Are you living with your parents now?" I ask, knowing that her husband had left for the States two years ago.

"Yes, it's better than living with my in-laws," she laughs. "His parents gave us a little plot of land, and my husband sent some money, so we are beginning to build a house. It's small, but it will be ours. In January, I will go and live there by myself, to get accustomed to living alone. I'm afraid of living alone in the house. It's pretty sad to live alone," she nods.

Minutes later, three little boys, her nephews, dart into the room, chasing each other. They come to a full stop in front of her. In K'iche' they insist they need money for Fritos and Chiclets. She tugs at a small coin purse tucked in her waistband, gives them a few quetzales, and waves them out of the room.

"These boys just bother all the time!" she says, shaking her head. Catarina pulls the shuttle down tight over the weft, snapping it tight, but after three motions, stops. "I can't weave and talk. Let's just talk. I get my ideas and designs mixed up. I need silence to concentrate on my designs."

"It's like writing," I comment. "I need to concentrate."

She looks at me, her dark eyes exchanging a confidence. "It's just the same about God. I have to pay attention to how God speaks to us."

I listen, and then say, "Catarina, I want to ask you something. Roberto told me once that an Ajq'ij's life is 'to enter the mystery.' How do you understand that?"

"It's just like weaving," she says. "You have to be quiet and pay attention. God speaks to us in the fire, in our dreams, with the beans, and in our bodies. That's how God speaks to us."

Catarina grew up in a family where she learned ancestral knowledge systems. While young indigenous women and men in Guatemala, today more than ever before, have access to high school and university studies which are Western in mode, people also continually seek to understand ancestral ways and consult with elders to recuperate them. "Many people of Maya blood are encountering the way and the method of the studies of the ancestors," writes José Mucía Batz Lem (1996, 6).

Lem, as you can see in the paragraph below, used the method of study of the ancestors. This is how he describes the process:

> The answer didn't come speedily nor intensely, but the question had its answer slowly. The ancestors answered my petition. In the midst of conversations, in the search in the sacred fire, I encountered the first answers, the first explanations and I marveled as a child. What they gave me encouraged me to continue excavating until I encountered with greatest clarity—the understanding of the wisdom of the ancestors. (7)

People in the highlands have developed particular ways of knowing in recognizing signs tied to and interpreted through the calendar matrix: in dreams and visions, in the passing of eye and hand over the *tz'ite'* beans, in interpreting muscular contractions of "the lightning in the blood," and in reading signs in nature. The cosmos, the earth, the fire, the wind, the sea, and the human body all comprise texts to perceive, but more accurately, to engage with and translate. Ajq'ijab' attend to the movement of energy and perceive signals both inside the human body and outside, in nature, mapped and interpreted in the calendar matrix. In fact, at the root of these mystical states are psychobiological techniques—mappings and perceptions which they understand are means of recognizing the language of the "incomprehensible Ground of Being" (Rahner 1968).

These ways of knowing flow from epistemologies that are distinct from Western knowledge and that offer alternative perspectives and intuitions based on their own locally developed practices. They reflect the profound sense of relatedness rooted in the perception of a shared spiritual reality in all creation. Through a close interaction with the physical world around them, Ajq'ijab' translate the activity, the phenomena revealed in the physical world, into a language that sustains and supports human life. "It is a theology of experience," explains Tomás García. "If one takes care of the earth, the earth takes care of us. The earth, then, is the direct contact." For example, Ajq'ijab' say that their prayers speak: "We [the prayers] go in your presence in the candles, in the wall, in the great roads, in the planets." They pray with a vision of God present and intimate in nature. García continues, "All in nature is real and living; the love of God is in all."

POSITION OF HUMANS IN THE UNIVERSE

This "theology of experience" is grounded in the understanding of human positioning and activity in the universe within distinct epistemological constructs of time and space. To make what Daniel Matul calls the "model for life" transparent, I draw from a conversation with him in which he points to the "root metaphor" of the quatrefoil, but now multiplied and enlarged to a three-dimensional cubic matrix (Figure 6.1). He first details the horizontal and then vertical connotations of this geometric paradigm, amplifying its multivalent spatial significance.

> The cubic model encompasses the cardinal points, the solstices and equinoxes. It is our model for life. Further, what is above is also below. In our cosmovision, we see three worlds: the physical, the spiritual, and the cosmic. The spiritual is that which unites the material level with the cosmic level. That is where the Ajq'ijab' stand, positioned between the material and the cosmic, to intercede between the two planes.

He illustrates how the cubic model also encompasses time.

> Within this model are the thirteen numbers [the four directions on three levels and the center point from where the Ajq'ij stands] and the twenty days—our sacred calendar. So the Ajq'ij is within both sacred

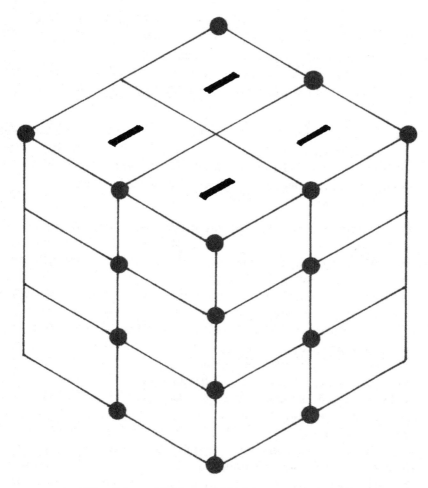

FIGURE 6.1. The cubic model, "the model for life" encompassing space and time.
Drawing by René Humberto López Cotí.

space and sacred time, the calendar. Also, wherever the Ajq'ij stands, he or she is between the four points of the cosmos level and the four points of the material level: $(4 + 4 = 8)$; eight is the number of completion because it is the sum of 1 (the beginning) and 7 (the death). That's why our Maya calendar begins with 8 B'atz' and why the cubic model is the matrix of Maya cosmovision. (Interview with author, July 2003)

This cruciform cubic model positions the Ajq'ij in sacred time-space. In ritual, the Ajq'ij evokes B'itol Tz'akol. Here, grounded in affection, s/he is connected to "the center in which we trust," which is experienced, dialoged with, and interpreted through this model of life. In the natural, material world, which in K'iche' is "a place of much happiness and energy," humans can come to a deep and wide knowing through dialogic activity. Here I tie their experience into Bakhtin's sense of dialogue as human activity.

> Life by its very nature is dialogic. . . . In this dialogue a person participates wholly and throughout his life; with his eyes, lips, hands, soul, spirit, with his whole body and deeds. He invests his entire self in discourse, and this discourse enters into the dialogic fabric of human life, into the world symposium. (1984, 293)

In their spiritual work—dialogic activity with "the Owner of us all"—Ajq'ijab' engage with the sacred in physical phenomena. The fundamental part of Maya spirituality is what they hear, feel, listen to, sense in their bodies. "Ajq'ijab' develop distinct ways of knowing," explains Roberto Poz. "Some Ajq'ijab' look in the water. I do not. I perceive it in this way, in the movements in the body. My body is order. I know how to reflect with it, to receive its messages." Here he refers to the human body "conceived as a microcosm filled with movements that reflect the past and future events of the macrocosm" (B. Tedlock 1982, 139).

The human body as text in ancient Mesoamerica is well documented in Alfredo Lopez Austin's (1988) *The Human Body and Ideology: Concepts of the Ancient Nahuas*. And Jill Leslie McKeever Furst's *The Natural History of the Soul in Ancient Mexico* describes the Mexica's beliefs about the soul and the divinatory system in human physiology and bodily sensation, with particular attention to joints, blood, and breath. She focuses on how this Native American group "turned, not to theological pronouncements and speculations to verify their ideas, but to experience—to what can be seen, touched, heard, and in some cases, even smelled" (1997, 2–3). For contemporary interpretations, I refer you to *Time and the Highland Maya*, where Barbara Tedlock discusses the dialectical methods of the internal reading of the blood and of sortilege, or how understanding is achieved by the "mixing, grabbing and arranging of piles of *tz'ite* seeds, the counting and interpreting of the 260-day divinatory calendar, and the jumping and speaking of the diviner's blood" (153).

While an underlying knowledge system is shared in various methodologies, forms differ from region to region, and from individual to individual. What has become clear in my ethnographic research is that Ajq'ijab' know and use various methods of understanding—reading the fire; reading the *tz'ite'* beans, water, or crystals; and (particularly women) listening to the movements in their bodies. These techniques help carry and support a respectful, sacred relationship with the natural world.

THE SIGN OF THE FIRE

In 1985, after I participated in "the giving thanks to the mountain" ceremony, I asked Roberto Poz, "Why is fire the central element of Mayan ritual?" He answered:

There are four elements: air, water, earth, and fire. The air gets polluted. The water, too, while it cleanses, is often full of impurities because of all the places it travels and the ways people use it. The earth is important to the Maya, but the fire, the fire is the conduit of humans to the Creator and of the Creator to humans. It is the place of speaking with God. The flames purify. The flames and smoke carry our prayer, our intercessions, our language, to God. The fire also is the language through which God speaks to us.

I initially understood that in Maya ceremonies fire is the element through which the Ajq'ij intercedes and communicates to the Creator. Over time, I came to see that fire was a center of communication in which Ajq'ijab' perceived facts and information. It became clear to me that the ceremonial fire is the aesthetic hearth of Maya logical and metaphysical art, a source of understanding, support, and spiritual discernment. Further, ritual involving fire strengthens, balances, and invigorates the community. I learned that the fire transmits life. As Vilma Poz says, "It takes from us, and it gives to us. It takes away the negative, and gives us, fills us. The little we can give it are aromatic things, but it gives us life." Years later, I came to understand this prayer:

Oh Ajaw!
Oh, you, sacred fire, purifying fire.
You who sleep in the *pom* [incense]
who rise up in brilliant flames above the altar
You are the heart of the sacrifice
the daring flight of the prayer
the hidden spark in all things
You are in the glorious soul of the Sun.

PRAYER OF KOMON TOHIL

The legacy and ceremonial nature of fire throughout Mesoamerica is documented in codices and precolonial stories. Fire drilling was done between the completion phrase of one cycle of activity and the beginning of another. The "drilling of fire," or "making fire" ceremony accompanied the inauguration of new rulers and corresponded to fifty-two-year New Fire ceremonies (Kelley 1976, 144) (Figure 6.2). For the Mexica, the ease or difficulty of its ignition predicted the positive/negative character of the future (Furst 1997, 68). The fact that fire glyphs appear in the Maya inscriptions in years which are the equivalents of the Mixtec-Toltec new-fire ceremonies implies a basic unity in Mesoamerica. At Chich'en Itza, *Kak,* the "fire" glyph, recurs repeatedly in inscriptions and is associated with the "drill" glyph, the context which Kelley identifies as "fire ceremonialism" (150). The ancient Mexica believed that the deities ignited a fire in the chest (analogous to making fire with a drill) when the child dropped in the uterus, breathing the *tonalli* (soul, or "sign under which one is born") into the child (Furst 1997, 64–67). Among the Aztec, one's prestige was perceived as an inner fire, and sorcerers of the eighteenth century were sometimes said to turn into fire in their dreams, flying to both known and imaginary places, during which journeys they would interact with other beings (Lopez Austin 1988, 370).

In *Popol Wuj,* the first humans—"the great wise ones, the great thinkers, penitents and sacrificers"—unwrapped their *copal* (incense), and "there was triumph in their hearts when they unwrapped it." They incensed the direction of the rising sun, "crying sweetly as they shook their burning *copal,* the precious *copal*" (D. Tedlock 1985, 181). "What they brought and burned before Tohil was not great. All they burned before their gods was resin, just bits of pitchy bark, along with marigolds" (185). In the last scene of *Popol Wuj,* Jaguar Quitze leaves a bundle of flames, a sign of his being. "The bundle became precious to those who remained, and they burned offerings before this memorial to their fathers" (198).

Today, the ceremony before the fire is a way to express affection, thanks, and intercession as well as a process of understanding. The design of the ritual space, the base of the fire, is the image-space of the ancient world. The Ajq'ij constructs an ephemeral map built up of natural aromatic materials. Sugar is drizzled first in a circle, then in a straight line from the East to the West, from the North to the South, designating the fourfold markings. Flowers and candles, or sometimes colored soda bottles, red, black, white, and yellow, are set at their appointed solstice locations, the green and blue in the center. The practitioner then places the *copal* discs, spiraling round and round, sunwise until they fill the circle. Laurel leaves or

A   B

C

FIGURE 6.2. Drilling of fire. A and B: Mexica (central-Mexican glyphs for the *xiuhmolpilli*, or 52-year period). Two examples of the stick drill used to kindle the sacred fire. C: God Q from Dresden 6b as in Kelley (1982, 146).

rosemary sprigs encompass the circle. The ritual site becomes a microcosm, a landscape, patterned of quatrefoil spatial designs, colors, and images, a text, a "window" leading to the world *behind* the text. Tomás García explains,

> These four cardinal points, these four sides are our totality. It's the perfection of humanity, but it is not enough. The fifth point is development, to improve oneself, and it has the colors of blue and green. The perfection begins here. Why? We are called to develop for something more. We stand at the nexus of the mother earth which is green, and the father sky which is blue. We put them together, they cannot be separated. In ceremonies, we put them together, they cannot be separated. It is one vision, together, to create a reality. It is not only casual, but a definite, intentional meeting.

The prepared ritual space now designates a territory, set apart in geography and time. In this arena, participants will through ritual performance cross boundaries of time and enter a liminal space. As Catherine Bell writes, "Beliefs, creeds, symbols and myth emerge as forms of mental content or conceptual blueprints; they direct, inspire, or promote activity" (1992, 19). The Ajq'ijab' evoke the sacred through language as they name the Creators, the land and seas, the ancestors. Each of the 260 days is remembered, and before the fire the Ajq'ijab' intercede and dialogue with the Owner of us all. Offerings are made to restore the balance of that which has been lost. If the purpose of the ceremony is grave, the sacrifice of an animal is required, usually a hen or rooster, or mourning doves. Animals chosen for sacrifice are treated with affection and respect as Ajq'ijab' speak to them, asking for pardon in anticipation of their sacrifice. The animal's neck is twisted, the heart pulled out and held before the fire while still beating. The heart is offered in deep supplication, then tossed in. The remainder of the body follows. Ajq'ijab', through their concentration, deepest emotions, and faith, sounded in the rhythm of words and the repetitive feeding of the fire, humbly beseech the sacred to hear and acknowledge them, to accept their offerings. Then with careful attention to the flames, they tend the fire, casting *pom*, seeds, flowered water, and alcohol to evoke a response; in the fire's flames, they discern the reply.

For most Native American peoples, ceremonial actions occur in circling or spiraling motions. Before the Ajq'ij, the fire shoots up and up, flames burst through gaps in *copal*, crackling and swelling in external forms. Attention is given here to the traveling and spiraling of the flames. As each day of the twenty days is named, and numbered one to thirteen,

Ajq'ijab' continuously make aromatic offerings and tend to the language, the signals in the fire. They watch where on the four points—the East, West, North, or South—the flames circle, how high or low, how fast or slow the flames travel while that day is named, numbered, and fed. Doña Marta elaborates:

> If the fire speaks in the East, it is triumph; if on the West, it can't be helped. Two flames in the East, it's good. If the fire throws two flames in the West, it is very good. If two on the right, there is sin before God; if two in the left, one is pardoned. If it circles up, counterclockwise, it is received. If it dances and is tied, there is no solution.

Generally there is agreement that if the fire moves in the direction of the sun, it is a good prognosis; if it moves clockwise, something adverse may happen. Further, the meaning depends upon how fast the flame moves and whether it swirls upward, sparks, or crawls along the ground. During the ceremony, Ajq'ijab' may consult with one another as they observe the flames and tend to corresponding signals in their bodies.

Pablo, of Panajachel, concurs as he explains the work of María, his wife.

> The people come to ask help. María lights candles for particular problems, for one's work, one's business. While people are confessing, she is working. Two candles are lit. She takes them to the place of the ceremony. They confess again. If their petition is received well or not, the place of the flame will indicate if this person believes or not. The fire travels, the sun is in the middle. If the person's belief in God is strong, the fire is in the center. Then, all this person asks, it will be given. If one doesn't believe, and brings the materials "only to try, to see," this lack of faith cuts the power. If one comes with faith, one leaves with a change. If the fire circles on the west, it means there is a serious problem. It could indicate death. So take care, more offerings are needed so God helps. If it circles "under the air," that is, in the North, it means an illness, fevers, headaches, illness. So the person has to confess, and ask for help.

Among various regions, people work with the fire differently. "Not all of us work it the same way," explains Vilma Poz. "The Mames, for example, use incense and candles more. They work more with the smoke and the light."

I remember one afternoon when Berta, her mother, her sister Violeta, and I were doing a ceremony near Zunil. "The fire is happy, content," Berta said as she pointed to it. "Look how it jumps and dances!" Flames were shooting high and strong, comforting to me as I heard Berta talking

FIGURE 6.3. Women Ajq'ijab' purify and strengthen their *varas* and crosses in the fire.

to, cajoling, begging the fire to intercede for safe journeys, good things, peace in our family, wisdom in my work, and a safe return home. At the end, the fire spurted a spark, which snapped and jumped. "Ah, the fire wants you to know it is happy with all you brought to offer. It was the gift to make her happy!" Then her little sister, Violeta, smiled at the fire and exclaimed, her eyes dancing, "It's like a necklace of jewels!" (See Figures 6.3 and 6.4.)

DISCERNMENT, WAYS OF KNOWING

As a writer, a woman with a Catholic background, trained in cultural and historical studies of spirituality, I am faced with the question, how do I interpret these ways of knowing? I understand that Ajq'ijab' differ from Western thinkers and healers. They navigate within cultural and psychological constructions in which they inhabit and experience their bodies and perceptions of life from an intuitive attuning to life. I think to be attuned to the language of the universe is "an increasing coordination" toward the world of another text. As Trix, who draws a parallel with the tuning of a musical instrument for jazz, notes, "Attunement thus refers to a 'diminishing of difference,' or positively, 'an increasing coordination'"

(1993, 19). Ajq'ijab' translate a perception of spiritual reality through language. They articulate diverse experiences of knowing (reading water or crystals, movements in the body, the *tz'ite'* beans, etc.). What they hold in common is a profound understanding of the great equilibrium of nature. Ajq'ijab' coordinate, name, and translate their perception of manifestations of the sacred, of energy, to order human life. This is the spiritual and religious tradition of a community.

My discussion with Fr. Victoriano Castillo González on Maya ceremonies and discernment resonates with what I sensed. He explains,

> In the mentality of the Maya, the whole world is sacramental so it is not only in the fire that God will reveal. In their ceremonies, all elements are sacramental; and there is a reality behind these elements. We utilize these elements to interpret the will of God. Who puts the meaning in it? It is the community which is celebrating.
>
> So what is the role of the fire? The fire is not the intermediary, but the face of God, visible in the moment that I have to interpret. That is, it is not the fire that is communicating. It is not the *tz'ite'* that is communicating. No, it is God communicating to me. And there I think is the force of Maya spirituality.

FIGURE 6.4. Roberto interprets the message of the fire.

FIGURE 6.5. Images of the fire glyph were evident in early Mesoamerican writings (Kelley 1982, 149).

He continues:

> Yet, the will of God does not depend upon external signs to give me a message. God is not limited to these forms. God is bigger, bigger, than that.

What emerges in conversations with participants in ceremonies is that these rituals strengthen, support, and order life. Lima Soto writes, "The ceremony represents and converts you in harmony with nature, with the universe, with the Creator, with humanity" (1995, 55). He continues,

> In the ceremony you handle distinct elements: fire, water, music, dance, color, and lots of aromatic materials. It is a part of nature and transforms you in a fiesta, in happiness for the community. The ceremony is an acknowledgement of every element of nature, of life, of creation of our own body: bones, flesh, arteries, all of our feelings. This is the feeling, the reason for the ceremony. If we do it with surrender, with devotion and honesty, there are many good things for us. We also invoke the ceremonies when there are conflicts, pain, or overwhelming problems. This is good. The ceremony is a communal moment when we reaffirm our identity, when we consolidate one common force that unites us, that organizes us, that makes us proud of our values, customs and traditions. This is where we are parents and grandparents. Those who are not among us physically are both remembered and involved. It is when the children and the young are strengthened in education and live in what is proper. (55–56)

FIGURE 6.6: Ajq'ijab' pray at Ab'aj Takalik; here the men are purifying their *vara* (sacred bundles) before the fire.

With roots that extend thousands of years back, Maya's interaction with the fire continues to sustain Maya community into the future (Figures 6.5 and 6.6). We hear, in the following contemporary prayer, a confident dialogue with B'itol Tz'akol and with Maya ancestors. In couplet form, the community intercedes for the present human community, for future generations, and for the dawning of a time not yet come to light.

Oh, you, B'itol Tz'akol!
Look at us! Listen to us!
Do not leave us, do not abandon us.
Oh Ajaw, who are in the heaven and in the earth,
Heart of sky, Heart of earth!
Give us our descendants, our successors,
while the sun walks and gives clarity
that dawns, that brings the Aurora!
Give us many good roads, plain roads!
That your people have peace, much peace and are happy;
and give us good life and a useful existence!

Oh you, Kakulja, Chipi kakulja,
Raxa kakulja Chipi-Nanauk, Raxa-Nanauak,
Voc Jun Ajpu,
Tepeu Gukumatz'
Alom Q'ajalom,
Ixpiyakok Ixmukane',
Grandmother of the sun, Grandmother of the light!
That you dawn and bring the Aurora!

KOMON TOHIL PRAYER GUIDE

Part 4

THINKING, CONTEMPLATING,

AND ACTING INTO THE FUTURE

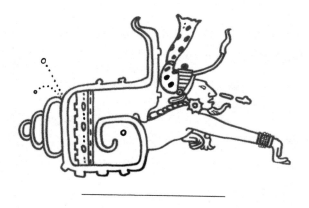

CHAPTER 7

The Ancient Things Received from Our Parents Are Not Lost

Many minds are engaged in building our future, thinking about it, and recreating it. The idea is to use the powerful symbols of the past to reconstruct the present and build the future, as we retrace the footprints of our ancestors on the ancient bridge that links the past to the present. From those building blocks we want to create the Mayan culture of the future.

VICTOR MONTEJO, "THE MULTIPLICITY OF MAYAN VOICES"

In Quetzaltenango, hosts of the fiesta invite guests, one by one, to dance the *son*. Hosts and dozens of guests position themselves across the room, forming two complementary rows. Women face women on the right, men face men on the left. Each side bows and greets each other, then slowly dances forward toward the opposite side in the deeply felt rhythms of *sones* tapped on the marimba. Women, their full skirts pulled slightly out, gently sway in unison as they inch, three steps forward, two steps back, toward the other side; men, their hands grasped behind their backs, parallel this motion. Only the gentle swishing sounds of feet lifting, as the two rows slowly come together, greet one another with warm smiles, then recede back in the same gentle strokes across the floor. This ebb and flow of dancers, coming together then parting, is repeated until four cycles are completed, about forty-five minutes. Of this very formal social dance, typical in Quetzaltenango, Roberto Poz says,

When dancing the *son*, all enter the rhythm very solemnly. No one speaks. You feel the rhythm with your being. In the rhythm, you enter silence. You enter the most primordial space of the Heart of the Sky and the Heart of the Earth. The *son* is very ceremonial. It narrates. In this way, we narrate with our bodies. In the ceremonies we narrate all we do. You express something very profound in the *son*. You give yourself at this moment to the Creator.

This ancient silent dance reverberates and mirrors the harmony and balance underlying Maya cosmovision. Maya spiritual and ceremonial traditions, at the beginning of the twenty-first century, are positioned in processes of globalization: international migration, a sharply rising cost of living, the plague of common crime, and human rights abuses in Guatemala. The public emergence and reaffirmation of Maya spiritual traditions, facilitated in part by a people's right of self-determination and the 1995 Agreement on Identity and Rights of Indigenous Peoples' emphasis on human rights, brings to the forefront indigenous spiritual traditions and religious rights. Maya spirituality, a vital and vibrant practice, is now formally recognized as one of the religious faiths practiced in the multiethnic, multicultural, and multilingual Guatemala. Its public revitalization highlights the strongly visible religious diversity in Guatemala.

To Catholic, mainline Protestant, and evangelical religions this reclamation poses new dynamics, challenges, and potentials. Interreligious dialogue, whether focusing on understanding one another's traditions or on the role of religion in the construction of peace, could promote human rights and build a more vibrant, complex, and comprehensive Guatemalan society. For example, in Santa María Chiquimula, projects of reconciliation and enculturation have healed centuries of discord. The reclamation and reaffirmation of elders' teaching on cultural, linguistic, and religious lifeways has supported, invigorated, and unified the community (Molesky-Poz 2004). Further, these institutions may find that for many people, their faith is bolstered by a creative fluidity across traditions.

At the state level, this reclamation is also challenging the legal and political framework for religious freedom. While the Guatemalan constitution provides for freedom of religion, and the Guatemalan government generally respects this right in practice, the government has not implemented the 1995 Agreement on Identity and Rights of Indigenous Peoples. The Agreement calls for Congress to pass legislation to amend the Constitution to "recognize, respect, and protect the distinct forms of spirituality practiced by the Maya, Garifuna, and Xinca" groups. For the most part, government involvement has been superficial. Legislation could support

FIGURE 7.1. Before the fire, this child of the future generation is strengthened and learns the ways of her ancestors.

indigenous spiritual rights and be the underpinning for progressive projects of land and sacred site co-management, indigenous linguistic recuperation, and the development of inclusive and inculturated educational curriculums based on human rights and cultural inheritances.

Among practitioners of Maya spirituality there are internal concerns, several mentioned in Chapter 3. Some Ajq'ijab' misuse their position for personal power, economic gain, or political position, due in part to poor preparation. Other zealous Ajq'ijab' dogmatize teachings and assume authoritarian roles. This counters what is inherent in the Mayan system: the individual interpretation of religious phenomena. At certain public events, Ajq'ijab' have created a "show," undermining the nature of Mayan rituals. One woman Ajq'ij explained, "A lot of Ajq'ijab are getting sick. A lot are abusing their power." Many are initiated too young to bear the responsibility of this inheritance.

There is one more aspect which deserves our attention, the danger of the institutionalization of Maya spirituality. The danger is that the schema could be locked into fundamentalist interpretations and imposed upon society, as in the case of the Maya in earlier periods. However, with the social and cultural transformations of the past few decades, particularly the diversity of religious institutions in Guatemala, this is a remote possibility.

FIGURE 7.2. Community in Zunil prays around the fire at a Wajxaqib' B'atz ceremony.

The tendency of Maya spirituality is not "to make converts," but to be available to help individuals live more peaceful and harmonious lives. For example, Doña Catarina, of Santa María Chiquimula, shared, "A group of evangelicals came from another village to ask me if they were wrong in being evangelicals. I told them that they should stay in their way if they have peace with God."

As Don Martín Chacach said that morning in Antigua, "This rebirth of Maya culture, spirituality, and intellectuality is bound to the will of the people. It is a dynamic process and has a life, like the life of a people." In efforts to live and maintain this spirituality, an Ajq'ij is what M. M. Bakhtin defines as the *answerable* person, "one who is thinking theoretically, contemplating aesthetically, and acting ethically" from one's horizon of being. Their ritual practice is what Bakhtin would call *aesthetic activity*. It "collects the world scattered in meaning and condenses it into a finished and self-contained image" (1990, 191). He expands,

> Aesthetic activity finds an emotional equivalent for what is transient in the world (for its past and present, for its present-on-hand being), an emotional equivalent that gives life to this transient being and safeguards it; that is, it finds an axiological position from which the transient in the world acquires the axiological weight of an event, acquires validity and

stable determinateness. The aesthetic act gives birth to being on a new axiological plane of the world: a new human being is born and a new axiological context—a new plane of thinking about the human world. (191)

This aesthetic activity sustains those for whom it gives life, some privately, some publicly and communally. José, a fifty-year-old carpenter and grandfather in Zunil, explains that when he went to Florida in December 2000 to visit his twenty-three-year-old son, many people in the village had told him that since he had a visa to travel in the United States, he should "stay and get some extra money." He said, "But I couldn't. This is my life. Here is my work, going to the mountains, praying in the sacred places, working in my ceremony. Here I am harmony with the Creator. Here in these places I communicate with Ajaw. This is my work, here in these places."

On Wajxaqib' B'atz, May 28, 2004, the Great Confederation of the Councils of the Principal Mayan Ajq'ijab' of Guatemala gathered in the city of Chimaltenango. Before the sacred fire, Ajq'ijab' declared their concerns about the international adoptions of Maya children who are sent in an illicit and inhumane way out of the country; the rise of teenage pregnancies; the increase in the assassination of women in Guatemala; the invasions and torture occurring in the Middle East. They recommended constitutional policies to protect their entrance into sacred sites, to protect the right of indigenous ways of life, to implement educational programs in their maternal languages. In these cases, the words of *Popol Wuj* resonate: "This is when they remembered the instruction of their fathers. The ancient things received from their parents were not lost" (D. Tedlock 1985, 203).

In working with Ajq'ijab', I have uncovered a rich difference in perceiving and experiencing the sacred, as well as its practical implications. I respect this richness not only as difference, but through dialogic activity, I have come to a deep respect for its wisdom. It has provoked me to ask how these ways of knowledge might, in turn, teach us to become more fully human. It has generated an attentiveness to our relatedness to the earth, with other creatures, and tied to the cycles of creation. Creation as a whole is sacramental. I understand María del Carmen Tuy's words.

Mayan spirituality is not exclusively for ourselves. As Maya we have to look after others. How is this done? By helping people understand our current reality. There is a lot of technology and modernization. And this is good; it is not bad. But we have to help people become more human and sensitive so they have feelings, a felt love, and to develop a relationship with all their surroundings. They must understand that everything around us has life. If we don't teach through spirituality to keep and maintain everything around us in harmony, we will then perish. This is our way to contribute to humanity. It is a message of living in peace and harmony with all that surrounds us.

This present renewal contributes to the self-determination of indigenous people. Its ancient roots, now continuities transformed, sustain a people and support the multiple ways of being Maya, of being human.

Notes

INTRODUCTION

1. The term *Maaya* is a Yucateco word that describes the language spoken by indigenous people in Yucatan, Mexico. Western scholars have ascribed the name *Maya* to indigenous people who live in the region which spans across southern-eastern Mexico, the Yucatan peninsula, Guatemala, Belize, and parts of Honduras and El Salvador, and whose over twenty-three languages may be rooted in the tonal Yucateco language (Sharer 1994). This region has been designated *Maya Mundo* by a confederation of the five governments previously mentioned. While indigenous peoples in the highlands have identified themselves with their geographical and linguistic communities, since the late 1980s many have assumed the term *Maya* for projects of self-determination, cultural resurgence, and social construction (Warren 1998). The dynamics of the term *Maya* as an adoption for cultural identity can create a sense of pan-Maya identity and empowerment for many who embrace the word, but the idea has also been used as an overgeneralized identity for the purpose of commercial or scholarly endeavors.

2. John Templeton fellows discussed the paradigm of Emergence at the Reductionism and Emergence Conference, sponsored by the Center for Theology and the Natural Sciences, the Vatican Observatory, and the University of San Francisco (USF), held at USF, October 7–11, 2003.

CHAPTER 1

1. George Ellis presented this paradigm, the Five Levels of Emergence, at the Reductionism and Emergence Conference at the University of San Francisco, October 7–11, 2003.

2. For overview of religion in Guatemala, see T. Steigenga's (1999) "Guatemala," in *Religious Freedom and Evangelization in Latin America: The Challenge of Religious Pluralism*, 150–174.

3. *Pop Wuj* and *Popol Wuj* will be used interchangeably in this text. *Pop Wuj* will be used when K'iche' speakers are quoted since this identification is more commonly used among the K'iche'. Sam Colop, K'iche' linguist and columnist, explains that *Popol Wuj* is more correct because the suffix -*ol* gives the term a sacred connotation (personal communication, 2005; see also Carmack 1981; D. Tedlock 1985).

CHAPTER 2

1. "There are wonderful things lying around," explained Judith Thorn. "We just don't know why they are remainders. We cannot rewrite history every time we speak. It is occluded. We don't want then to know. But it is removed into a metaphoric form: art, pottery, and clotting, in the case of the Maya. Remainders are revisiting the past,

examining shards as if they were precious." Judith Thorn, phone conversation with author, July 6, 1997. Special recognition to Judith Thorn for the concepts of ritual space as a *map, landscape,* and *center* (unpublished paper).

2. Whereas the backstrap loom has most often been used by women to weave cotton cloth for private use, the treadle loom is typically used by men to produce both wool and cotton fabric commercially.

CHAPTER 3

1. Dennis Tedlock (1985) writes, "*Chuchqajaw* is composed of *chuch,* "mother," and *qajaw,* "father," but pronounced as a single word. It carries the sense of parent without any reduction of the difference between motherhood and fatherhood. It further refers to the first four human males, the male heads of present-day lineages" (349).

2. Walburga Rupflin Alvarado (1997) discusses Maya priests in Chapter 3 of her *El Tzolkin Es Más Que un Calendario.* Benjamin N. Colby and Lore M. Colby (1981) record three types of traditional religious specialists in Nebaj, in the Ixil region of the highlands (46), in their ethnographic work *The Daykeeper: The Life and Discourse of an Ixil Diviner.* Barbara Tedlock (1982) identifies the Maya practitioner as a "daykeeper" in her ethnographic work of Momostenango, *Time and the Highland Maya.* Robert S. Carlsen (1997b), in *The War for the Heart and Soul of a Highland Maya Town,* identifies people who practice *costumbre* in Santiago, Atitlán, as the "Working People." Working People, Carlsen writes, participate in the grueling rituals which followers of the Old Ways *(costumbres)* believe are absolutely essential for the continuity of the world's vital cycles of existence (171, n. 6). In my ethnographic work, I found many Maya reject the terms *shaman* and *priest,* indicating that these concepts are Eurocentric and do not express the reality of their experience.

3. Special recognition and gratitude to Judith Thorn for her discussion of the journey of the self and birth of consciousness, framed by Bakhtin's work, in her *The Lived Horizon of My Being* (1996).

4. In recent years, Guatemalan Ladino women and men as well as persons from El Salvador, North America, and Europe have also prepared under a trained Ajq'ij and been initiated as Ajq'ijab'. For example in 1997 on 8 B'atz', twenty non-Maya were initiated at the San Francisco de Alto altar in Totonicapán.

5. See Barbara Tedlock (1982), "Shamanic Priests and Priestly Shamans," Chapter 3 of *Time and the Highland Maya,* 46–85, for an overview of ethnographic work on spiritual leaders in southern Mexico and the Guatemalan highlands.

6. Shamanism as a category of Western academic study began in late seventeenth-century ethnographic accounts among the Tungus—a central Siberian tribe which can be found from the arctic region to the Chinese frontier—and extends to contemporary studies. See John A. Grim's (1983) Chapters 1 and 2, "Introduction" and "Siberian Shamanism," in *The Shaman,* for a comprehensive overview and criticism of shamanic studies and interpretive methodologies.

7. See Grim (1983).

8. The "capacity" is a kind of soul, called "lightning" *(coyopa),* which enables a person to receive messages from the external world, both natural and supernatural, within his or her own body (B. Tedlock 1982, 53; see her Chapter 6, on the diverse manifestations of this capacity).

9. B. Tedlock (1982, 53–58) describes the recruitment of the "divine election" through birth, illness, and dreams, followed by marriage to a spirit spouse at the initiation of Momostenango daykeepers.

10. Carol Gilligan (1982) shows that many girls and women reach moral decisions in a different way than do boys and men.

11. The statement "You have to work" refers to making offerings, paying, petitioning, giving thanks.

12. *Brujo* is Spanish for "witch," a pejorative term from Spanish colonialism, which considered indigenous religious traditions pagan and diabolic.

13. While some individuals identify this experience as a "call," others negate the term *call*, saying, "This is not what it is. It is about our day, our obligation."

14. Bakhtin writes: "A *worldview* organizes and unifies the performed acts; it imparts unity to a life's act-performing directedness to meaning—the unity of a life's answerability, the unity of its going beyond itself, of surmounting itself. . . . A *worldview* organizes and unifies man's *horizon*" (1990, 205).

15. See B. Tedlock (1982, Chapter 5).

16. Victor Lem also explained that people in their formation learn to use energy. "People also abuse energies, use bad, negative works. There are people who enter to work at this level, who do negative things. Many years ago in Alta Verz Paz many operated at this level. Also in Samaya, in the southern region, Ajitz [those who work with obscure or dark forces] work at this level and they are very powerful." Interview by author, May 25, 1997, Quetzaltenango.

17. Wajxaqib' B'atz' (8 Thread or 8 Monkey) is the day which commemorates the creation of humans. It is the day marked as the day of origins, of remembering creation, and of honoring artists, weavers, and creators.

18. Karen Bassie-Sweet (1991, 176–180) notes that the quadripartite world model appears in Postclassic ceremonies, where the ritual space was defined by the Chac imitators placed at the cardinal points (see Tozzer 1966, 160). The space around highland towns, such as Zinacantan, is defined by four sacred mountains (Vogt 1969, 602). While visiting San Juan Chamula in Chiapas in June 1997, I saw visitors from a neighboring village first pilgrimage with incense and music to the four corners of San Juan Chamula before they stopped to talk with Chamulans in the village center. According to B. Tedlock (1982, 82), "this sacred circuit is called both the 'sowing and the planting' *(awexibal tichal)* of the town and the 'stabilization' *(chac'alic)* of the town."

19. Maya dance.

20. Maya musical instruments: *chirimía*—wooden flute; *tambor*—drum; *chinchin*—gourd rattles.

21. *Huipil*—Maya woven overblouse; *corte*—woven skirt, either wrapped around or gathered at the waist.

CHAPTER 4

1. The root of this tradition may be linked to the zenith passage of the sun on May 2, though the specific celestial connection has been forgotten in the processes of colonialism, in this case, with the replacement of the feast, the Day of the Cross. Barbara Tedlock (1992a) writes that in Momostenango, stars are used to herald the time of year for ritual and agricultural purposes. The most important are the winter and summer solstice sun-

rise and sunset positions, called the *xolkat b'e*, "change of path or road." The zenith passages of the sun annually occur on May 2 during the sun's northward movement, and August 11, its southward return. The sunrise and sunset positions on both zenith passages are referred to as *jalb'al*, "place of change," indicating a change of paths.

2. Walker (1993) reviewed some three hundred sacred sites in the Northwest, Southwest, Eastern Woodlands, Subarctic, and Arctic regions of North America. She noticed that all Native groups tend to hold sacred the boundaries between cultural and geological zones. All groups possess a body of beliefs concerning the appropriate sacred times and rituals to be performed at such sites. She writes, "Sacred sites serve to identify fundamental symbols and patterns of American indigenous culture. They also project an image of the social order and lend concreteness to the less visible systems of human relationships. They create an organization. These sacred, symbolic systems, when superimposed on geography, give it significance and intelligibility. The more central a place is in the religious life of a group, the more numerous the symbolic representation it will possess. Sacred sites create a conceptual and emotional parallelism between the objective order of the universe, the realm of the spirits, and the constructs of human culture" (111).

3. Second Maya Congress, August 6, 1997, Guatemala City.

4. Scholarship devoted to the definition and description of sacred places has developed in three directions over the last thirty years, notes Belden C. Lane (2001, 42–61). Each comes to the question of interpreting the intimately personal (and transcendent) experience of place from very different philosophical and methodological starting points. The *ontological approach*, exemplified by historians of religion such as Mircea Eliade, sets sacred place apart from everything profane; it is a place of hierophany. The *cultural approach* insists that every human attribution of sacrality is always a social construction. The *phenomenological perspective* stresses listening to the place itself, recognizing its unique topography and material character as suggesting affordances or offerings of their own.

5. Grube (1996, 3) discusses crosses and the Maya who lived in the eastern part of the Yucatan peninsula, now known as the Mexican state of Quintana Roo. He writes, "The point where the two bars of the cross meet is called *uyòol*, a word that means both 'his spiritual center' and 'his doorway.' This is the place where the cross has its *pixan*, its soul."

6. Grube (1996, 7) relates a similar story, quoting Don Cecelio Can, keeper of the books, scribe, and talented narrator. "All crosses, whether large or small are brothers. *Tuláaklo'*. They are born in the sky, and long ago, when the *mehen p'úuzob*, the small hunchbacks still lived on earth, they descended from sky to earth, using the *kuxa' su'm*, the living rope, to descend to their respective places. The *kuxa'n su'm* has been cut by the Spaniards, yes, but it still is alive, it only rests in the cenotes, in the caves, and under the ballcourt of Chich'en Itza. Even though the *kuxa'n su'm* does not lead to the sky any more, it still connects all the crosses with each, right there where the *óol* of the cross is."

7. Walker (1993) discusses the role of dreams and visions among Amerindian peoples, noting that the Judeo-Christian tradition tends to create its own sacred space and times arbitrarily by special ritual of sacralization, [whereas] American Indians attempt to discover 'access points' or 'portals' to the sacred that are often impossible to know before dreams or visions reveal them" (104).

8. For interpretations of solstital directions, see Girard (1962), Tichy (1981) and Villa Rojas (1968); of the sun's path, see Coggins (1980) and Stross (1991); see also Bricker (1983). For architectural structures as chronographic markers and ceremonial centers, see Miller (1999), J. Carlson (1976), Krupp (1997), Baudez (1996). For directions in codices see León-Portilla (1988). For associated color glyphs and directions, see Bricker (1983), Kelley (1976), Roys (1965), and Stross (1991). For quadripartite ordering of Maya world, see Mathews and Garber (2004).

9. See D. Tedlock, *Popul Vuh* (1985); Montejo, *El Kanil* (1984).

CHAPTER 5

1. Daniel G. Brinton (1893, 5) writes that the same calendar system was in use "among the Nahuas of the Valley of Mexico and other tribes of the same linguistic family resident in Tlascallan and Mextitlan, in Soconusco, Guatemala and Nicaragua; that it prevailed among the Mixtecs and Zapotecs; and that of the numerous Mayan tribes, it was familiar to the Mayas proper of Yucatan, the Tzentals, and Zotzils of Chiapas, the Quichés and Cakchiquels of Guatemala, and to their ancestors, the builders of . . . Copan and Palenque."

2. For studies of the 260-day calendar, see the following: Daniel G. Brinton (1893) collects month and day names of the Maya stock and "subjects them to an etymological analysis and comparison with their correspondents in the Zapotec and Nahuatl tongues, and endeavors to read the symbolic significance of the Calendar as a mythical record and method of divination" (4). Ruth Bunzel (1981, 332–343) discusses the meaning of the days from her ethnographic work in Chichicastenango in the 1930s. Barbara Tedlock (1982) discusses the earliest records of calendar day signs, geographical locations in both Maya lowland and highland, and the preservation and utilization of the calendar in various linguistic regions; on pp. 107–131, she discusses the significance of the individual days and use of the sacred calendar in the town of Momostenango. Walburga Rupflin Alvarado (1997, 73–160) provides contemporary interpretations of the days from ethnographic work with several Ajq'ijab'. Eduardo León Chic (1999) provides contemporary interpretations of the sacred calendar and its uses from his ethnographic work among forty elder Chuchqajaw in Santa María Chiquimula, his native village. See B. Tedlock (1982, 89–104) for more extensive ethnographic chronicling.

3. The basic unit is the day: *kin,* or *q'ij.* Periods of time were counted by periods of twenty days (the *uinak*), periods of 360 days (the *tun*), twenty-year periods of 360 days (the *katun*), and 400-year periods (the *baktun*); 800 made a *pictun,* and 160,000 made a *calabtun*—this counting continues on, in multiples of twenty, toward infinity. Its basic unit was a 360-day year, which the Maya called a *tun,* or "stone," because they marked the end of each of these years by setting a stone in the ground (Schele and Freidel 1990, 81).

4. B. Tedlock (1982, 219) notes the genealogy of the word *tzolkin.* "William Gates, in his 'Review of *Archaeology of the Cayo District,* by J. Eric S. Thompson,' takes credit for inventing the word *tzolkin* in 1921; and he modeled it after the Quiché Maya *ch' ol k' ij,* meaning 'arranging' or 'ordering the days,' as a way of getting away from the use of the Aztec term."

5. See David Humiston Kelley (1976, 3–8) for a history of decipherment.

6. Barbara Tedlock's (1982) Chapter 5, "The Day Lords," presents an interpretation of the mnemonics, rituals, divinatory meanings, and character of each of the twenty day names, as taught and practiced in Momostenango. Bunzel (1981, 332–343) also lists characteristics of the day names and number symbols from her work in Chichicastenango in the 1930s. Walburga Alvarado (1997) presents contemporary interpretations from ethnographic highland sources.

7. Calixta Gabriel Xiquín (1999, 125–126) describes number signification from a Kaqchikel perspective in her thesis on the social function of spiritual Kaqchikel Maya spiritual guides in San José Poaquil.

Bibliography

Alvarado, Walburga Rupflin. 1997. *El Tzolkin Es Más Que un Calendario*. 2nd ed. Guatemala City: CEDIM.

Amlin, Patricia. 1987. *Popul Vuh: Creation Story of the Maya-Quiche*. Berkeley and Los Angeles: University of California.

Arias, Arturo. 1990. Changing Indian Identity: Guatemala's Violent Transition to Modernity. In *Guatemalan Indians and the State, 1942–1988*. Ed. Carol Smith. Austin: University of Texas Press, 230–257.

Asad, Talal. 1986. The Concept of Cultural Translation in British Social Anthropology. In *Writing Culture: The Poetics and Politics of Ethnography*. Ed. James Clifford and George E. Marcus. Berkeley and Los Angeles: University of California Press, 141–164.

Ashmore, Wendy, and A. Bernard Knapp. 1999. Archaeological Landscapes: Constructed, Conceptualized, Ideational. In *Archaeologies of Landscape: Contemporary Perspectives*. Ed. Wendy Ashmore and A. Bernard Knapp. Oxford: Blackwell, 1–30.

Bakhtin, Mikhail. 1984. Toward a Reworking of the Dostoevsky Book. Appendix 2 in *Problems of Dostoevsky's Poetics*. Ed. and trans. Caryl Emerson. Minneapolis: University of Minneapolis Press.

Bakhtin, Mikhail. 1990. *Art and Answerability*. Ed. Michael Holquist and Vadim Liapunov. Trans. Vadim Liapunov. Austin: University of Texas Press.

———. 1993. *Toward a Philosophy of the Act*. Ed. Vadim Liapunov and Michael Holquist. Trans. Vadim Liapunov. Austin: University of Texas Press.

Bassie-Sweet, Karen. 1991. *From the Mouth of the Dark Cave*. Norman: University of Oklahoma Press.

———. 1996. *At the Edge of the World*. Norman: University of Oklahoma Press.

Bastos, Santiago, and Manuela Camus. 2003. *Entre el Mecapal y el Cielo: Desarrollo del Movemiento Maya en Guatemala*. Guatemala City: FLACSO.

Batz Lem, José Mucía. 1996. *"NIK": Filosofía de los Números Maya*. Guatemala City: SAQB'E.

———. 1997. *Jun Raqän [Maya Cosmovision and Numbers]*. Guatemala City: SAQB'E.

Baudez, Claude F. 1996. The Cross Group at Palenque. In *Eighth Palenque Round Table, 1993*. Ed. Martha J. Macri and Jan McHargue. San Francisco: Pre-Columbian Art Research Institute, 121–127.

Becom, Jeffrey, and Sally Jean Aberg. 1997. *Maya Color: The Painted Villages of Mesoamerica*. New York: Abbeville Press.

Bell, Catherine. 1992. *Ritual Theory, Ritual Practice*. New York: Oxford University Press.

Benson, E. P. 1976. Ritual Cloth and Palenque Kings. In *The Art Iconography and Dynastic History of Palenque*. Part 3. Ed. M. G. Robertson. Pebble Beach, CA: Robert Louis Stevenson School, 45–58.

Bolz, Norbert, and Willem Van Reijen. 1995. *Walter Benjamin*. Trans. Laimdota Mazzarins. Atlantic Heights, NJ: Humanities Press.

Boyarin, Jonathan. 1994. Space, Time, and the Politics of Memory. In *Remapping Memory: The Politics of TimeSpace*. Ed. Jonathan Boyarin. Minneapolis: University of Minnesota, 1–38.

Brady, James E., and Wendy Ashmore. 2000. Mountains, Caves, Water: Ideational Landscapes of the Ancient Maya. In *Archaeologies of Landscape: Contemporary Perspectives*. Ed. Wendy Ashmore and A. Bernard Knapp. New York: Blackwell, 124–145.

Breckenridge, Carol, and Arjun Appadurai. 1989. On Moving Targets. *Public Culture* 2.1 (Fall): i–iv.

Bricker, Victoria. 1981. *The Indian Christ, The Indian King: The Historical Substrate of Maya Myth and Ritual*. Austin: University of Texas Press.

———. 1983. Directional Glyphs in Maya Inscriptions and Codices. *American Antiquity* 48: 347–353.

Brinton, Daniel G. 1893. *The Native Calendar of Central America and Mexico: A Study in Linguistics and Symbolism*. Philadelphia: MacCalla & Company.

Bunzel, Ruth. 1981. *Chichicastenango*. Guatemala City: Jose de Pineda Ibarra.

Cabrera, Edgar. 1995. *El Calendario Maya: Su Origen y su Filosofía*. San José, Costa Rica: La Liga Maya.

Carlsen, Robert S. 1993. "Discontinuous Warps: Textile Production and Ethnicity in Contemporary Highland Guatemala." In *Crafts in the World Market: The Impact of Global Exchange on Middle American Artisans*. Ed. June Nash. Albany: State University of New York Press.

———. 1997a. The Unraveling of Peace in Santiago Atitlan. *Report on Guatemala* 18.4 (Winter): 8–12.

———. 1997b. *The War for the Heart and Soul of a Highland Maya Town*. Austin: University of Texas Press.

Carlson, Eric D. 1995. "From Mystery to Mystery." In *Cosmic Beginnings and Human Ends*. Chicago and La Salle, IL: Open Court.

Carlson, John B. 1976. A Geomantic Model for the Interpretation of Mesoamerican Sites: An Essay in Cross-Cultural Comparison. In *Mesoamerican Sites and World-Views*. Ed. Elizabeth P. Benson. Conference at Dumbarton Oaks, October 16–17. Washington, DC: Dumbarton Oaks Research Library and Collections, 143–215.

Carmack, Robert M. 1988. The Story of Santa Cruz Quiche. In *Harvest of Violence*. Norman: University of Oklahoma Press.

———. 1998. *The Quiche' Maya of Utatlán: The Evolution of a Highland Guatemala Kingdom*. Norman: University of Oklahoma Press.

Certeau, Michel de. 1988. *Practice of Everyday Life*. Trans. Tom Conley. Berkeley and Los Angeles: University of California Press.

Chávez, Adrián I. Trans. 1997. *Pop-Wuj: Poema Mito-Histórico Ki-che*. Quetzaltenango, Guatemala: La Liga Maya.

Choy, Alberto. Esquit, and Víctor Gálvaz Borrell. 1997. *The Mayan Movement Today: Issues of Indigenous Culture and Development in Guatemala*. Guatemala City: Editorial Serviprensa.

Christenson, Allen J. 2001. *Arts and Society in a Highland Maya Community: The Altarpiece of Santiago Atitlán*. Austin: University of Texas Press.

Codex Féjerváry-Mayer. 1972. Ed. C. Burland. Graz, Austria: Akademische Druckund Verlagsanstalt-Graz.

Codex Madrid, Codex Tro-cortesianus. 1967. Graz, Austria: Akademische Druckund Verlagsanstalt-Graz.

Coggins, Clemency. 1980. The Shape of Time: Some Political Implications of a Four-Part Figure. *American Antiquity* 45: 727–739.

Cojtí Cuxil, Demetrio. 1997a. *Ri Maya'Moloj pa Iximulew: El Movimiento Maya en Guatemala.* Guatemala City: Editorial Cholsamaj.

———. 1997b. The Politics of Maya Revindications. In *Maya Cultural Activism in Guatemala.* Ed. Edward F. Fischer and R. McKenna Brown. Austin: University of Texas Press, 19–50.

Colby, Benjamin N., and Lore M. Colby. 1981. *The Daykeeper: The Life and Discourse of an Ixil Diviner.* Cambridge: Harvard University Press.

Cook, Garrett W. 2000. *Renewing the Maya World: Expressive Culture in a Highland Town.* Austin: University of Texas Press.

Cook Garrett W., and John W. Fox. 1994. Sacred Journeys and Segmentary Polities in Mayan Culture. Paper presented at Maya Hieroglyphic Workshop, University of Texas, Austin. March.

Davis, Sheldon H. 1988. Introduction: Sowing the Seeds of Violence. In *Harvest of Violence.* Ed. Robert M. Carmack. Norman: University of Oklahoma Press, 3–36.

Deloria, Jr., Vine. 1999. *For This Land: Writings on Religion in America.* New York: Routledge.

De Paz, Antonio. 1993. *The Mayan Calendar: The Infinite Path of Time.* Guatemala City: Gran Jaguar 2.

Earle, Duncan. 1995. Maya Religion, Mayanist Ideologies and Forms of Conquest. Paper prepared for the Latin American Studies Association, Washington, DC.

Edmonson, M. 1988. *The Book of the Year: Middle American Calendrical Systems.* Salt Lake City: University of Utah Press.

Fahsen, Federico. 1987. A Glyph for Self-Sacrifice in Several Maya Inscriptions. In *Research Report on Ancient Maya Writing, 11.* Washington, DC: Center for Maya Research.

Falla, Ricardo. 2001. *Quiché Rebelde: Religious Conversion, Politics, and Ethnic Identity in Guatemala.* Austin: University of Texas Press.

Farris, Nancy M. 1984. *Maya Society under Colonial Rule: The Collective Enterprise of Survival.* Princeton: Princeton University Press.

Fischer, Edward F. 1996. Induced Culture Change as a Strategy for Socioeconomic Development: The Pan-Maya Movement in Guatemala. In *Maya Cultural Activism in Guatemala.* Ed. Edward F. Fischer and R. McKenna Brown. Austin: University of Texas Press, 51–73.

Fischer, Edward F., and R. McKenna Brown. 1996. *Maya Cultural Activism in Guatemala.* Austin: University of Texas Press.

FLACSO and Comisión Organizadora de un Encuentro. 1994. *Cronología de un Encuentro con la Sabiduría Milenaria de ABYA YALA / América en Iximche and Tikal.* Paper prepared for the Facultad Latinoamericana de Ciencia Sociales Programa, March 9\ 22, 1994, Guatemala City.

Foucault, Michel. 1985. Nietzche, Geneaology, History. In *The Foucault Reader.* Ed. Paul Rabinow. New York: Pantheon.

Freidel, David, Linda Schele, and Joy Parker. 1993. *Maya Cosmos: Three Thousand Years on the Shaman's Path*. New York: Quill.

Furst, Jill Leslie. 1997. *The Natural History of the Soul in Ancient Mexico*. New Haven, CT: Yale University Press.

Gabriel Xiquín, Calixta. 1999. Rejqalem Kisamaj Ri K'Exelom chuqa' ri Ajq'ija. MA thesis, Universidad Rafael Landivar.

Garrard-Burnett, Virginia. 1998. *Protestantism in Guatemala: Living in the New Jerusalem*. Austin: University of Texas Press.

Gilligan, Carol. 1982. *In a Different Voice: Psychological Theory and Women's Development*. Cambridge: Harvard University Press.

Girard, Rafael. 1962. *Los Mayas Eternos*. Mexico City: Antigua Librería Robredo.

El Gobierno de la República de Guatemala y La Unidad Revolucionaria Nacional Guatemalteca. 1995. *Acuerdo sobre Identidad y Derechos de los Pueblos Indígenas*. Guatemala City: Saqb'ichil-Copmagua.

Goldin, Liliana R., and Brent Metz. 1997. Invisible Converts to Protestantism in Highland Guatemala. In *Crosscurrents in Indigenous Spirituality: Interface of Maya Catholic Protestant Worldviews*. Ed. Guillermo Cook. New York: E. J. Brill, 325–338.

González, Victoriano Castillo, S.J. 1998. *Ri Loq'Alaj K'utb'al. [Sacramental Rites in the Language and Worldview of the Maya]*. Santa María Chiquimula, Totoniapán: IK'laja.

Gossen, Gary H. 1974. *Chamulas in the World of the Sun: Time and Space in a Maya Oral Tradition*. Cambridge: Harvard University Press.

———. 1988. *Symbol and Meaning beyond the Closed Community: Essays in Mesoamerican Ideas*. 2nd ed. Albany: Institute for Mesoamerican Studies.

Graham, Ian. 1977. *Corpus of Maya Hieroglyphic Inscriptions*. Vol. 3. Part I. Yaxchilan. With Eric von Euw. Cambridge: Peabody Museum of Archaeology and Ethnology, Harvard University.

Grim, John A. 1983. *The Shaman: Patterns of Religious Healing among the Ojibway Indians*. Norman: University of Oklahoma.

Grube, Nikolia. 1996. Crosses in Exile. Paper represented at the Maya Meetings, University of Texas, March 7.

Handy, Jim. 1984. *Gift of the Devil*. Boston: South End Press.

Harvey, David. 1990. *The Condition of Postmodernity*. Cambridge and Oxford: Blackwell.

Historical Clarification Committee (CEH). 1999. Guatemala City: Memory of Silence.

Info Maya. 2002. Red Mesoamericana de Información. Accessed November 9, 2002.

Iser, Wolfgang. 1993. *The Fictive and the Imaginary: Charting Literary Anthropology*. Baltimore: Johns Hopkins University Press.

Katz, Steven T. 1978. Language, Epistemology and Mysticism. In *Mysticism and Philosophical Analysis*. Ed. Steven T. Katz. New York: Oxford University Press, 22–74.

Kelley, David Humiston. 1976. *Deciphering the Maya Script*. Austin: University of Texas Press.

Klein, Cecelia F. 1982. Woven Heaven, Tangled Earth: A Weaver's Paradigm of the Mesoamerican Cosmos. In *Ethnoastronomy and Archaeo-astronomy in the American Tropics*. Vol. 385. Ed. Anthony F. Aveni and Gary Urton. New York: New York Academy of Sciences, 1–35.

Komon Tohil. 1997. *Majib'al re xulkulem [Ceremonial Prayer Guide]*. Pamphlet. Quetzaltenango, Guatemala.

Krupp, E. C. 1997. *Skywatchers, Shamans and Kings: Astronomy and Archaeology of Power*. New York: Wiley.

La Farge, Oliver. 1994. *La Costumbre en Santa Eulalia*. Rancho Palos Verdes, CA: Yax Te' Foundation.

La Farge, Oliver, and Douglas Byers. 1993. *The Year Bearer's People*. New Orleans: Tulane University Press.

———. 1997. *El Pueblo del Cargador del Año*. Rancho Palos Verdes, CA: Yax Te' Foundation.

Lane, Belden C. 2001. *Landscapes of the Sacred: Geography and Narrative in American Spirituality*. Baltimore: John Hopkins University Press.

Las Casas, Bartolomé de. 1993. *The Devastation of the Indies: A Brief Account*. Trans. Herman Briffault. Baltimore: Johns Hopkins University Press.

León Chic, Eduardo. 1996. *Ri Ojer Taz Tzij Pa Tz'olojche: Antiguas Historias K'iche's de Santa María Chiquimula*. Quetzaltenango, Guatemala: Instituto Guatemalteco Educación Radiofónica.

———. 1999. *El Corazón de la Sabiduría del Pueblo Maya* or *Uk'u'xal Ranima' ri Qano'jib'al [The Heart of the Wisdom of the Maya People]*. Iximulew: CEDIM.

León-Portilla, Miguel. 1988. *Time and Reality in the Thought of the Maya*. Norman: University of Oklahoma Press.

Lima Soto, Ricardo E. 1995. Fundamentos de la Cosmovisión Maya. In *Aproximación a la Cosmovisión Maya*. Ed. Ricardo E. Lima Soto. Guatemala City: Universidad Rafael Landivar, 17–92.

Lopez Austin, Alfredo. 1988. *The Human Body and Ideology: Concepts of the Ancient Nahuas*. Trans. Thelma Ortiz de Montellano and Bernard Ortiz de Montellano. Salt Lake City: University of Utah Press.

Lopez Mejia, Alma, Audelino Sac Coyoc, Byron Guzmán Chan, Daniel Tucuy, Rolando Aguilar Orozco, Clara Mariela Limatuj Ixcot, and Rigoberto Quemé Chay. 1994. Fundamentos de la Educación Maya. Paper presented at the First Congress of Maya Education in Guatemala. Quetzaltenango, Guatemala, August.

Love, Bruce. 1994. *The Paris Codex: Handbook for a Maya Priest*. Austin: University of Texas Press.

Lovell, George W. 1992. *Conquest and Survival in Colonial Guatemala: A Historical Geography of the Cuchumatán Highlands, 1500–1821*. Kingston: McGill-Queen's University Press.

Macleod, Morna. 1998. *Poder Local: Reflexiones sobre Guatemala*. Guatemala City: Cholsamaj-OXFAM.

MacLeod, Murdo. 1973. *Spanish Central America: A Socioeconomic History, 1520–1720*. Berkeley and Los Angeles: University of California Press.

Macri, Martha. 2005. A Lunar Origin for the Mesoamerican Calendars of 20, 13, 9 and 7 Days. In *Current Studies in Archaeoastronomy: Conversations across Time and Space*. Selected Papers from the Fifth Oxford International Conference at Santa Fe, 1996. Ed. John W. Fountain and Rolf M. Sinclair. Durham, NC: Carolina Academic Press, 275–288.

———. Day Names. 2001. In *Oxford Encyclopedia of Mesoamerican Cultures*. Ed. David Carrasco. Oxford: Oxford University Press, 314–318.

Malkki, Liisa. 1992. National Geographic: The Rooting of Peoples and the Territorialization of National Identity among Scholars and Refugees. *Cultural Anthropology* 7.1: 24–43.

Malström, Vincent H. 1997. *Cycles of the Sun, Mysteries of the Moon: The Calendar in Mesoamerican Civilization*. Austin: University of Texas Press.

Marcus, George E., and Michael M. J. Fischer. 1986. *Anthropology as Cultural Critique*. Chicago: University of Chicago Press.

Mathews, Jennifer P., and James F. Garber. 2004. Models of Cosmic Order. In *Ancient Mesoamerica*. Vol. 15. Cambridge: Cambridge University Press, 49–59.

Matul, Daniel. 1989. "Estamos Vivos: Reafirmación de la Cultura Maya." *Nueva Sociedad* 99 (January/February): 147–157.

———. 1991. *Meditaciones en la Bondad del Universo: Religiones del Mundo ante las Amenazas a la Vida de la Terra*. Costa Rica: Liga Maya Internacional.

———. 1994. *Somos un Solo Corazón: Cultural Maya Contemporánea*. San José, Costa Rica: Liga Maya Internacional. Internacional.

McAnany, Patricia A. 1995. *Living with the Ancestors: Kinship and Kingship in Ancient Maya Society*. Austin: University of Texas Press.

Menchú, Rigoberta. 1984. *I, Rigoberta Menchú: An Indian Woman in Guatemala*. Ed. Elisabeth Burgos-Debray. Trans. Ann Wright. London: Verso.

Mendoza, Mario Recancoj and Francisco Recancoj Mendoza. 2002. *Pedagogía Maya*. Mixco, Guatemala: Editorial Saqil Tzil.

Meyer, Jean. 1989. *Historia de los Cristianos en América Latina, Siglos XIX y XX*. Mexico City: Vuelta.

Milbrath, Susan. 1999. *Star Gods of the Maya*. Austin: University of Texas Press.

Miller, Mary Ellen. 1999. *Maya Art and Architecture*. London: Thames and Hudson.

Miller, Mary Ellen, and Karl Taube. 1993. *The Gods and Symbols of Ancient Mexico and the Maya: An Illustrated Dictionary of Mesoamerican Religion*. London: Thames and Hudson Ltd.

Minh-Ha, Trinh T. 1991. *When the Moon Waxes Red: Representation, Gender and Cultural Politics*. New York and London: Routledge.

Molesky-Poz, Jean. 1999. A New Cycle of Light: The Public Emergence of Maya Spirituality in Guatemala. PhD diss., Graduate Theological Union.

———. 2004. The Dawning of Something Ancient, Yet New: Reconciliation and Inculturation at Santa María Chiquimula in the Guatemalan Highlands. In *Christianity and Native Cultures: Perspectives from Different Regions of the World*. Ed. Cyriac K. Pullapilly, Bernard J. Donahoe, David Stefancic, and William Svelmore. Notre Dame, IN: Cross Cultural Publications, 519–535.

Monroy, Agustín Estrada, and Carlos Rivers Sandoval. 2001. *El Despertar del Jaguar*. Guatemala City: Editorial UNIPRES.

Montejo, Victor. 1984. *El Kanil: Man of Lightning*. Trans. Wallace Kaufman. Carrboro, NC: Signal Books.

———. 2002. The Multiplicity of Mayan Voices. In *Indigenous Movements, Self-Representation, and the State in Latin America*. Ed. Kay B. Warren and Jean E. Jackson. Austin: University of Texas Press, 123–148.

Morris, Phillip. 1987. *Living Maya*. New York: Harry H. Abrams Inc.

Morson, Gary Saul, and Caryl Emerson. 1990. *Mikhail Bakhtin: Creation of a Prosaics*. Stanford: Stanford University Press.

Oakes, Maude. 1951. *The Two Crosses of Todos Santos: Survival of Maya Religious Ritual.* Princeton: Princeton University Press.

Oss, Adrian C. van. 1986. *Catholic Colonialism: A Parish History of Guatemala, 1524–1821.* London: Cambridge University Press.

Otzoy, Irma. 1996. *Maya' b'anikl Maya' atzyaqb'al. [Maya Identity and Maya Clothing].* Guatemala City: Editorial Cholsamaj.

Penon, Casanova. *Distant Voices, Distance Thunder.* Lincoln, NE: Native American Public Broadcasting, 1990.

Perera, Victor. 1993. *Unfinished Conquest.* Berkeley and Los Angeles: University of California Press.

Proskouriakoff, Tatiana. 1973. The Hand-Grasping-Fish and Associated Glyphs on Classic Maya Monuments. In *Mesoamerican Writing System.* Conference at Dumbarton Oaks, October 30–31, 1971. Ed. Elizabeth P. Benson. Washington, DC: Dumbarton Oaks Research Library and Collection, 165–173.

———. 1993. *Maya History.* Ed. Rosemary A. Joyce. Austin: University of Texas Press.

Rahner, Karl. 1968. *Spirit in the World.* New York: Herder & Herder.

Recinos, Adrian. 1957. *Crónicas Indígenas de Guatemala.* Guatemala City: Editorial Universitaria.

Recovery of Historical Memory Project (REHMI). 1999. *Guatemala: Nunca Mas!* New York: Orbis Press.

Ricard, Robert. 1966. *The Spiritual Conquest of Mexico: An Essay on the Apostolate and the Evangelizing Methods of the Mendicant Orders in New Spain, 1523–1527.* Berkeley and Los Angeles: University of California Press.

Rivera, Otto. 1994. Cronología de un Encuentro con la Sabiduría a Milenaria de ABYA YALA /América en Orme Final. Guatemala City. Unpublished paper.

Rowe, Ann Pollard. 1981. *A Century of Change in Guatemalan Textiles.* New York: The Center for Inter-American Relations.

Roys, Ralph L. 1965. *Ritual of the Bacabs.* Norman: University of Oklahoma Press.

———. 1967. *The Book of Chilam Balam of Chumayel.* Norman: University of Oklahoma Press.

Sandoval, Marte Trejo. 1992. *Las Ciudades del Cielo [The Cities of the Sky].* 2nd ed. Mexico City: Círculo Cuadrado.

Sanford, Victoria. 2003. *Buried Secrets: Truth and Human Rights in Guatemala.* New York: Palgrave Macmillan.

Schele, Linda. 1982. *Maya Glyphs: The Verbs.* Austin: University of Texas Press.

Schele, Linda, and David Freidel. 1990. *A Forest of Kings: The Untold Story of the Ancient Maya.* New York: William Morrow.

Schele, Linda, and Nikolai Grube. 1996. The Workshop for Maya on Hieroglyphic Writing. In *Maya Cultural Activism in Guatemala.* Ed. Edward F. Fischer and R. McKenna Brown. Austin: University of Texas Press, 131–140.

Schele, Linda, and Mary Ellen Miller. 1986. *The Blood of Kings: Dynasty and Ritual in Maya Art.* Fort Worth: Kimball Art Museum; New York: Braziller.

Schneiders, Sandra. 1990. Spirituality in the Academy. In *Modern Christian Spirituality: Methodological and Historical Essays.* Ed. Bradley Hanson. Atlanta: Scholars Press.

Secaira, Estuardo. 2004. A Fruitful Dialogue between Local Protected Area Manager and Spiritual Guides: The Case of Chicabal Volcano and Lagoon in the

Western Highlands of Guatemala. Paper presented at the World Park Congress, September 12.

Seler, Eduard. 1963. *Commentarios al Códice Borgia*. Vol. 1. Codice Vaticano Latino 3738, ixxii. Mexico City: Fondo de Cultura Económica.

Sexton, James D. Trans. and Ed. 1992. *Mayan Folktales: Folklore from Lake Atitlán, Guatemala*. New York: Anchor Books.

Sharer, R. J. *The Ancient Maya*. 1983. 5th ed. Stanford: Stanford University Press.

Smith, Carol A. 1990. *Guatemalan Indians and the State, 1540–1988*. Austin: University of Texas Press.

———. 1991. Maya Nationalism. *NACLA Report on the Americas* 23.3: 29–33.

Stanzione, Vincent. 2000. *Rituals of Sacrifice*. Illustrated and Published by author. Guatemala City.

Steigenga, Timothy J. 1994. Protestantism, the State and Society in Guatemala. In *Coming of Age: Protestantism in Contemporary Latin America*. Ed. Daniel R. Miller. Washington, DC: University Press of America, 143–172.

Stoll, David. 1988. Evangelicals, Guerrillas, and the Army: The Ixil Triangle under Rios Montt. In *Harvest of Violence*. Ed. Robert Carmack. Norman: University of Oklahoma Press, 90–119.

———. 1999. Guatemala. In *Religious Freedom and Evangelization in Latin America: The Challenge of Religious Pluralism*. Ed. Paul E. Sigmund. New York: Orbis.

Stross, Brian. 1985. Color Symbolism of a Maya Glyph: The Kan Cross. *Journal of Mayan Linguistics* 5.1 :73–112.

———. 1991. Classic Maya Directional Glyphs. *Journal of Linguistic Anthropology* 1: 97–114.

Tate, Carolyn E. 1992. *Yaxchilan: The Design of a Maya Ceremonial City*. Austin: University of Texas Press.

Tedlock, Barbara. 1982. *Time and the Highland Maya*. Albuquerque: University of New Mexico Press.

———. 1992a. The Road of Light: Theory and Practice of Mayan Sky Watching. In *The Sky in Mayan Literature*. Ed. Anthony F. Aveni. New York: Oxford University Press.

———. 1992b. The Role of Dreams and Visionary Narratives in Mayan Cultural Survival. *Ethos* 20.4: 453–476.

Tedlock, Dennis. 1985. *Popul Vuh: The Definitive Edition of the Mayan Book of the Dawn of Life and the Glories of Gods and Kings*. New York: Simon & Schuster.

Thompson, J. Eric S. 1954. *The Rise and Fall of Maya Civilization*. Norman: University of Oklahoma Press.

———. 1970. *Maya History and Religion*. Norman: University of Oklahoma Press.

Thorn, Judith. 1996. *The Lived Horizon of My Being: The Substantiation of the Self and the Discourse of Resistance in Rigoberta Menchú, M. M. Bakhtin and Victor Montejo*. Tempe: Arizona State University.

Tichy, Franz. 1981. Order and Relationship of Space and Time in Mesoamerica: Myth or Reality. In *Mesoamerican Sites and World-Views*. Conference at Dumbarton Oaks, October 16–17. Ed. Elizabeth P. Benson. Washington, DC: Dumbarton Oaks Research Library and Collections, 217–245.

TIMACH. 2002. *Ukab' Umolib' Chikixol Ajnao'j puwi' Pop Wuj: Memorias del \.. Congreso*. Quetzaltenango, Guatemala: Timach.

Tozzer, Alfred. 1966. Landa's Relación de las Cosas de Yucatán: A Translation. Papers of the Peabody Museum of American Archaeology and Ethnology. Vol. 28. Harvard University.

Trix, Frances. 1993. *Spiritual Discourse: Learning with an Islamic Master*. Philadelphia: University of Pennsylvania Press.

Tyler, Stephen. 1986. Post-Modern Ethnography: From Document of the Occult to Occult Document. In *Writing Culture: The Poetics and Politics of Ethnography*. Ed. James Clifford and George E. Marcus. Berkeley: University of California Press, 122–141.

U.S. State Department, Bureau of Democracy, Human Rights, and Labor. 2003. *International Religious Freedom Report of 2003*. http://www.state.gov/g/drl/rls/irf/2002/14046.htm.

Vail, Gabrielle. 1997. Review of *Cycles of the Sun, Mysteries of the Moon: The Calendar in Mesoamerican Civilization*, by Vincent H. Malmström. *Australian Archaeology* 45: 72.

Villa Rojas, Alfonso. 1968. Los Conceptos de Espacio y Tiempo entre los Grupos Mayances Contemporáneos. In *Tiempo y Realidad en el Pensamiento Maya*. Ed. Miguel León-Portilla. Instituto de Investigaciones Históricas. Universidad Nacional Autónoma de México, 119–167.

Villacorta, C. J. Antonio, and Carlos A. Villacorta R. 1976. *Codices Mayas*. 2nd ed. Guatemala City: Tipografía Nacional.

Vogt, Evon Z. 1969. *Zinacantan: A Maya Community in the Highlands of Chiapas*. Cambridge: Harvard University Press.

———. 1981. Some Aspects of the Sacred Geography of Highland Chiapas. In *Mesoamerican Sites and World-Views*. Conference at Dumbarton Oaks, October 16–17. Ed. Elizabeth P. Benson. Washington, DC: Dumbarton Oaks Research Library and Collections, 119–142.

Walker, Deward E., Jr. 1991. Protection of American Indian Sacred Geography. In *Handbook of American Indian Freedom*. Ed. Christopher Vecsey. New York: Crossroad, 100–115.

Wallace, Anthony F. C. 1956. Revitalization Movements. In *American Anthropologist* 58: 264–281.

Warren, Kay. 1978. *Symbolism of Subordination: Indian Identity in a Guatemalan Town*. Austin: University of Texas Press.

———. 1998. *Indigenous Movements and Their Critics: Pan-Maya Activism in Guatemala*. Princeton: Princeton University Press.

Watanabe, John. 1992. *Maya Saints and Souls in a Changing World*. Austin: University of Texas Press.

Weil, Simone. 1952. *The Need for Roots*. New York: G. P. Putnam's Sons.

Wilson, Richard. 1995. *Maya Resurgence in Guatemala: Q'eqchi' Experiences*. Norman: University of Oklahoma Press.

Zapeta Galamez, Estuardo. 1998. The Mayan Intellectual Movement and Sovereignty in Guatemala: After the Peace Accords. Paper presented at the Indigenous Intellectual Sovereignties: A Hemispheric Convocation. University of California at Davis.

Zetina, Miguel A. Méndez Zetina. 2001. En Busca de la Geografía Sagrada. *Prensa Libre* (July): 2.

Index

Activism: linguistic, 15–16, 26–27; Maya movement, 11–13, 25–27, 29–33; Maya political and cultural, 25–33; religious, 16, 27–28, 172–173, 175
Aesthetical self-activity, 3, 4, 64–65, 174–175; and problem of the soul, 8, 64; and ritual, 174. *See also* Bakhtin
Aesthetics, 64. *See also* Bakhtin
Agreement on Identity and Rights of Indigenous Peoples, 172
Ajaw (Owner of the Earth, Earth Lord), 96, 97, 98; as addressed in ritual, 45–47, 119; and altars, 111; communication sites with, 118; duality as quality of, 45, 46–47, 148; feeding, 98, 104–107; figures of, 127, 130–131; as fire, 159; in glyphs, 130–131; lineage identification with, 137–138; Mam as, 98, 113; in numbers, 147; offerings to, 106; and origin of cosmos, 46–47; prayer to, 119–120, 159, 167–168; as principle of time, 128, 130–132; qualities of, 45–47, 147; on *rajaw juyub* (mountain owner), 97. *See also* B'itol, Tz'akol; Heart of Sky, Heart of Earth
Ajitz, 62–63; work of, 115
Aj Itz del Pueblo, 26
Ajnawal mesa, 64
Ajq'ij, definition of, 62, 132
Ajq'ijab' (plural of Ajq'ij), xi, 65–90; acceptance of obligation, 73–74; aesthetic and ethical lives, 4, 67; answerability, 74, 76, 79; birth date of, 67; calendar in their bodies, 134; capacities of, 66, 79, 84–85, 155–156, 178n8; and ceremonial practice, 53, 157–158, 162–163; commitment of, 64; definition of, 62, 133, 134; dialogues with, 6; dialogue with a place, 117; in dias-

pora, 16; and discernment, 155–156; inauthenticity of, 88–90, 173; initiation as, 76–79; interpret the calendar, 140, 181n2; interpret their lives, 36; as "keepers of the days," 128; Ladino, European, and North American, 65, 178n4; and memory, 83; misappropriation by, 88–90, 173; obligation to the Creator, 74; positioned in sacred time-space, 156–157; preparation to become, 74–83; reading the calendar, 134, 162; reading the fire, 116, 162–163; research on, 178n2; responsibility of, 83–86, 134; repression, persecution, and murder of, 18, 21–22, 32; and ritual, 157–158; and sacred places, 111–115, 118; studying ancient texts, 38; "time to receive" their obligation, 67–73; "untangling the cords," 134; ways of knowing, 155–156, 158, 159, 162–164, 165–167; work of, 133, 164–165
Altars, 22–25; and answers given, 82, 107, 114; and capacities of, 113; and Catholic Church, 108; ceremonies and altars, 109; and crosses, 112; design and construction of, 160–162; and dreams, 79–80; dual energies of, 114–115; in homes, 22–25; mountains, 32, 111; quatrefoil cartography of, 119
Alvarado, Walburga Rupflin, 76, 153, 178n2, 181n2, 182n6
Amlin, Patricia, 53
Ancestors: advice of, 34, 47, 102; and calendar, 128, 132; and ceremony, 13, 166; clothing of, 49–50; and cosmology, 102; dialogue with, 167–168; inherited capacity of, 73; intercessory role of, 43–44; and memory, 13, 29; practice,

Ceremony, xi–xviii, 13, 29, 53–54; clothing of, 49–50; and communal identity, 166, 167; communication through ceremony, 75, 160; on Day of the Cross, 119–120; and energy, 75; "Giving Thanks to the Mountain," xi–xviii; and harmony, 166; purpose of, 166; of reconciliation, 21; on *Wajxaqib' Batz*, 76, 175. *See also* Fire; Ritual practice

Ceremonial dance, 171–172

Certeau, Michael, 111

Chacach, Martín, 11–13, 174

Chacach Tzoy, Bascilio, Fr., 43–44, 98–102

Chávez, Adrián Inéz, 26, 30, 134

Chikab'al, Lake, 38, 116; as ceremonial site, 126; ceremony at, 94–96, 119–120; management of, 126

Chilam Balam, sacred sites in, 110

Chol'Qij: AjQ'ijab use of, 13, 62, 140; basis of Maya cosmovision, 41, 44; and contemporary woven textiles, 13, 50–52; day signs, 143–147; day signs and numbers, 134, 139, 143; definition of, 132, 133; discernment with, 128–129, 132, 139, 153; as "field of vision," 67; foundational to spirituality, 128, 132, 153; as heart of the wisdom of the Maya, 128, 152, 153; in the human body, 134, 135, 139; and human gestation, 135; and identity, 140–143, 153; interpretation of, 128, 139–143; and lunar cycles, 135–138, 153; mathematical and metaphoric, 127; matrix, 8, 132; name, 181n4; numbers, 143, 147–148; as "ordering the days," 133, 134, 181n4; origin of, 135–138; as psychological system, 140–143; in ritual, 139; as spiritual force, 153; training of *Ajq'ijab'* and calendar, 75; use of, 128, 132, 138–139, 143–144, 153; use of in highlands, 128, 181n1; in woven textiles, 48–53. *See also* Calendar; Discernment

Chomb'al juyub'tay'j, 97

Choy, Alberto Esquít, and Víctor Gálvaz Borrell, 25, 27, 28, 30

Christenson, Allen J., 2

Chuchqajaw, 62, 178n1, 181n2

Clothing: accessibility to use, 53; cultural creative and political resistance, 48, 52; and cultural identity, 50–51; day signs in, 13, 50, 51; description of, 48, 179n21; *huipil*, 13, 48–52, 53, 58, 120, 179n21; and identity, 48–49, 50, 53; and Lady Xoc, 49–51; linked to ceremony, 52; and right to use indigenous clothing through Peace Accords, 52; on *sutib'al su't*, 76; transmission of cosmovision, 49–51, 58; woven, 13, 48–51, 178n2

Codices: calendar computations, 121, 129, 135; Dresden, 38, 39, 161; Madrid, 103

Cofulum, María Antonieta, 68, 85, 97, 142

Coggins, Clemency, 181n8

Cojtí Cuxil, Demetrio, 25, 30, 31

Colby, Benjamin N., and Lore M. Colby, 178n2

Colonialism, Spanish, xvii; imposition of Spanish, 1, 16–17

Cooke, Garrett W., and John W. Fox, 122

Coordinator of Organizations of the Maya People of Guatemala (COPMAGUA), 31

Cosmology: and ritual practice, 102, 179n1; as sacred, 102; and sacred places, 109–110; and structure of the universe, 121–122, 156–157; and three-dimensional universe, 110, 156–157. *See also* Astronomy; Solstital directions

Cosmovision: Bakhtin on, 179n14; as intuitive connection with universe, 74; Maya, 4, 34–35, 53–54, 59, 67, 100, 172; model of universe, 110, 133, 156–158; as philosophy, 41, 42–44, 100, 107; reclamation of, 32; and spirituality, 34–36; underpinning of, 100; in woven textiles, 48–53, 58

"Counting of days," 133. *See also Chol Q'ij*

Cotí, Aura Marina, 34, 85, 114–115

Cross, Maya: and altars, 112; as center of communication, 180nn5,6; in contemporary designs, 120; as doorway,

110, 180n5; foliated, 118; in human body, 120; as ideational image-space, 126; origin of, 121; as symbol of *Ajq'ij*'s life, 80; as tree connecting worlds, 110; used in ceremony, 119

Crosses, as brothers, 180n6

Cubic matrix, 156–158

Cultural activism, Maya, 25–28, 30–31

Davis, Sheldon, 18, 27

Daykeepers. *See* Aj'qijab'

Day of birth: *of Ajq'iajb'*, 69; calendar interpretation of, 143–148; configured with other day signs, 148–152; and quadrant mapping, 151–152

Day of the Cross, 93–96, 119–120, 179n1

Day signs (names): aligned with four directions, 151–152; appropriation of, 139; in clothing, 13, 50, 51; interpretation of, 140, 143–147, 181n2; as object of understanding, 139; process of discerning, 141–143; qualities and capacities of, 140, 182n6. *See also Chol Q'ij*; Discernment; Numbers

Deloria, Vine, Jr., 107, 117–118

Dialogic activity, 7

Diaspora, and Maya spirituality, 13, 16, 29, 57

Discernment, 69; calendar and, 139, 140, 143, 147–148, 152, 155–156; and day signs, 141–143; and fire, 162–166. *See also Chol Q'ij*; Dreams; Fire; *Tz'ite'* (beans); Ways of knowing

Discovering Dominga, 42

Dreams: and calendar interpretation, 132; role of, 180n7; as ways of knowing, 60, 66, 69, 72, 79–80, 81

Duality: energies at sacred sites, 114–115; as quality of *Ajaw*, 45, 46–47, 147

Earle, Duncan, 1, 2, 89

Ecosophia, 107

Education, International Congresses on *Popol Wuj*, 27

El Kanil, 86–88

Ellis, George, on Emergence, 14–16

Emergence: definitions of, 14–16; and

historical context, 13–14, 16–33; and identity, 16; of Maya cosmovision, xvii; of Maya spiritual traditions, xviii, 2, 7, 11–13, 19–22; paradigm of, 3

Encantos, 111

Escalante, Carlos, 88–89

Ethnography, 4, 7

Fahsen, Ricardo, 104

Faith, 74; as key to Maya existence, 90

Falla, Ricardo, 1, 18, 62

Farris, Nancy M., 2, 17

Father Sky, Mother Earth. *See B'itol*, *Tz'akol*

Fire: calendar in the fire, 162–163; centrality of, 8; ceremonial, 13, 38, 39, 47, 57, 59, 101, 173, 175; as conduit, 159; consult the, 69; and dialogic activity, 74, 75, 159; and discernment, 159; "drilling of fire," 160; feeding the fire, xvi, 76, 98, 99, 162; field of, 72–73; glyphs, 160–161; as hearth, 159; legacy in Mesoamerica, 8, 160; reading signals in, 75, 82, 107, 155, 162–163, 164; role of the fire, 75, 159, 165; sustains community, 167, 173

First Congress of Maya Education, 15, 30, 47

Fischer, Edward F., and R. McKenna Brown, 26, 30

Foucault, Michel, 14

Four directions, 181n8. *See also* Quadrant Image Space; Quatrefoil

Friedel, David, Linda Schele, and Joy Parker, 2, 103, 109

Furst, Jill Leslie, 158, 160

Gabriel Xiquin, Calixta, 3–4, 42, 44, 57–62, 68, 72, 82, 182n7

García, Fr. Tomás, 67, 84, 85–86, 156, 162

Garrard-Burnett, Virginia, 17, 19

Gender: and *Ajq'ijab'*, women, 20–21, 32, 69, 179n10; homosexual, 65; and interpretations of, 69, 81–82

Gilligan, Carol, 179n10

Girard, Rafael, 181n8

Glyphs: of Ajaw, 130–131; appropriation

of, 139; of blood letting, 103–104; of
fire, 166; of fire ceremonialism, 160;
of fire drilling, 160–161; of fish-in-
hand, 103; and lunar cycle, 135; numbers and head variants, 137; of offerings, 96, 103; of self-sacrifice, 101,
103–104
Golden, Liliana R., and Brent Metz, 19
González, Victoriano Castillo, S.J., 21,
44, 90, 132, 164–166
Gossen, Gary, 2, 107
Grim, John A., 178nn6,7
Grube, Nikolia, 139, 180nn5,6

Handy, Jim, 17, 27
Hart, Tom, 112, 114–115, 117
Harvey, David, 139
Heart of Sky, Heart of Earth, xiv, 40, 45;
and *Ajq'ijab'*, 54; as origin of crea-
tion, 46–47
Historical Clarification Committee, 31–32
Huipil, 13, 48–52, 53, 58, 120, 179n21
Human body, as text, 134–135, 136, 158
Human Rights, 29–30, 31–32, 52, 172–173

Indigenous peoples, on self-
determination, 171, 174, 176
Instruments, musical, 77, 179n20
Iser, Wolfgang, 139, 141
Ixcot, Edgar Rolando, 20, 66, 89

Junajpu and *Xb'alanke*, xiv; as models
for human activity, 46–47, 83; as
sources of light, 88, 89

Katz, Steven T., 6, 36
Kelley, David Humiston, 103, 160, 161,
166, 181n8
Klein, Cecelia F., 133
Kojb'al, 111
Kojonik (faith), 45, 74
Komom Tohil, 4, 38–39, 53, 64, 167–168
Krupp, E. C., 121, 181n8

Lady Xoc, 49–51
La Farge, Oliver, 2
La Farge, Oliver, and Douglas Byers, 103

Lane, Belden, 96, 111, 180n4
Language: distinctive human capacity
for, 40–41; on *K'iche'*, 7
Legal rights, 3, 29–31
Lem, Victor, 71, 85, 179n16
León Chic, Eduardo, 43, 106, 106, 153,
181n2
León Portilla, Miguel, 129, 131, 133, 181n8
"Lightning in the blood," 4, 75, 116,
178n8. *See also* Discernment
Lima Soto, Ricardo, 33, 40, 164, 166
Lopez Austin, Alfred, 158, 160
Lovell, George, 1, 17, 102
Lunar cycle and *Chol Q'ij*, 136–137

Macleod, Morna, 126
MacLeod, Murdo, 17
Macri, Martha, 130, 135–7
Malkki, Liisa, 60
Malström, Vincent H., 135
Marcus, George E., and Michael M. J.
Fischer, 7
Mathews, Jennifer P., and James F. Gar-
ber, 181n8
Matul, Daniel: on cosmovision, 35, 37,
40–41, 96–98; on *ecosophia*, 107; on
Popol Wuj, 98; on quatrefoil, 156–158
Maya, root of the word, 177n1 (Intro)
Maya strategies of resistance, 2, 22, 25
Medellín, 18, 27
Memory, narratives of, 37–38
Menchú Tum, Rigoberta, 30, 34, 37
Mendoza, Mario Recancoj, and Fran-
cisco Recancoj Mendoza, 96
Meyer, Jean, 17
Miguel, Matías Miguel, 13, 72, 81–82, 132;
on calendar, 143
Miller, Mary Ellen, 181n8
Miller, Mary Ellen, and Taube, Karl, 109
Minh-Ha, Trinh, 7
Models and metaphors: of cubic, 156–
157; of Plumed Serpent, 151; of the
sacred, 45–46; on time as, 130–131
Molesky-Poz, Jean, xi–xviii, 2, 22
Momostenango daykeepers, 65
Montejo, Victor, 27, 30, 35, 86–88, 111,
171, 181n9

122; in cubic model of life, 156–157; as ideational logic, 120–121; as model for life, 120; as organizing Mesoamerican image-space, 120, 122, 126; origin of, 121; and *Popol Wuj*, 120; as text for entering Maya space and time, 122, 126; and Utatlán, 122; in Zunil, 122, 125. *See also* Maya cross; Quatrefoil

Quatrefoil: altars at Santa María Chiquimula, 112; as altar space, 24, 119; and cartography, 8; and codices, 121; as embodiment of time and space, 120; in icons, 120; in Postclassic ceremonies, 179n18; in ritual space, 13, 120, 162; as structure of the cosmos, 121; in Zunil, 122–123. *See also* Quadrant image space

Quixtán, Norma, 15, 25, 28, 142

Rabjalb'al Q'ij, 75, 133. *See also Chol Q'ij*

Rahner, Karl, 35, 156

Rajaw juyub (mountain owner), 97. *See also Ajaw*

Recinos, Adrian, 122

Reciprocity: culture of, 42–43; legacy of, 102–107; relations and rituals of, 96–107, 108. *See also* Offerings

Reclamation of ancestral spirituality, 2, 8, 11–13, 20–22, 172, 174; after civil war, 29–31

Recovery of Historical Memory Project (REHMI), 31

Revitalization: religious, 12–13, 18, 25–26, 38. *See also* Activism; Emergence

Ricard, Robert, 17

Ritual circuits, 77, 179n18

Ritual practice: as aesthetic activity, 174; ancient practice, 102–104; as cornerstones of spirituality, 44–45, 74, 79, 96, 97; and cosmology, 102, 179n1; feeding the earth, 97–102; quatrefoil in, 162; time and place of, 103. *See also* Ceremony; Fire

Ritual space, 160–162, 179n18. *See also* Ceremony

Ritual speech, 40–42, 45–46, 107, 167–168

Roys, Ralph L., 181n8

Sac Coy, Audelino, 82

Sacred places, 96; as centers of communication, 107, 111–112, 118; dialogue with, 116–117; energies of, 114–115; geological formations of, 96, 109, 112–113; and guardian spirit (*nawal*), 111, 113, 115; how to approach, 113; and identity, 110, 118; and indigenous peoples, 180n2; management of, 126; as natural maps, 118; as networks, 112; and Peace Accords, 123–126; as portals, 110; right of entry to, 123; scholarship on, 180n4; selection of ritual sites, 115–117, 180n7; as sites of communication with ancestors, 118; spiritual functions of, 113, 115–116; and stories, 111; three vertical layers of, 110

Sacrifice, as strategy for acknowledging the Earth Lord, 104. *See also* Offerings

Salanic Poz, Lesbia, 3, 48–49, 94–95

Santa María Chiquimula: altars and cemetery, 43, 112; on calendar use, 181n2; on Catholic Action in, 18; on *chuchqajaw* in, 62; on offerings, 43–44, 106, 107; reconciliation in, 21; stories from, 43, 116; 172, 174; on strength of faith, 90

Schele, Linda, and David Freidel, 110, 129

Schele, Linda, and Nikolia Grube, 139

Schneiders, Sandra, 45

Secaira, Estuardo, 126

Seler, Edward, 135

Sexton, James D., 111

Shamanism, 65–66, 178n6. *See also Ajq'ij; Ajq'ijab'*

Solstital directions, 102, 121–122, 156–157, 181n8

Son (formal dance), 171

Spanish colonialism, 1, 16

Spirituality: *Chol Q'ij* as base of, 127–129; as communication, 47–48; contemporary forms of, 2, 139; on faith, 74;

and the fire, 159–168; as fundamental dimension of humanity, 45; and harmony, 166, 174, 176; hidden or disguised, 20–25; and identity, 16, 25; interpretation of, 45, 47–48; as intuitive understanding, 47–48; as legacy, 47; Maya ancestral, 4, 6, 8, 11, 13, 16, 19–20, 22, 34–36, 59, 83; obligations of, 69; principles of, 44, 47; progression in, 80–83; purification, 81–82; as resilient, 25, 153; as resource for living, 33, 175–176; right to practice, 172–173; and survival, 33, 90, 153, 175–176

Stanzione, Vincent, 97, 98, 113

Steigenga, Timothy J., 17, 19, 177n2

Strategies of resistance in colonial period, 2

Stross, Brian, 181n8

Sutib'al su't (ceremonial headscarf), 76

Tedlock, Barbara, 65–66, 139, 147, 158, 178nn2,5, 179nn9,15,18, 181nn2,4

Tedlock, Dennis, xvii, xviii, 2, 38, 178n2, 181n9. See also Popul Wuj

Temple-pyramids, 38

Thompson, J. Eric S., 102–103, 104, 129, 138, 140, 181n4

Thorn, Judith, 42, 73, 74, 79, 177–178n1, 178n3

Tichy, Franz, 181n8

Time: Ajaw as fundamental principle of, 128, 130–132; in calendars, 129–130; connection between time and threads, 133–134; primacy of time among Maya, 129–130; sacredness of, 128, 131–132. See also Chol Q'ij

Tozzer, Alfred, 129, 179n18

Transformed continuities, 96, 176; on ceremony as, 53–54; on Chol Q'ij as, 128–140; on clothing as, 48–53; on fire as, 38, 159–162. See also Ceremony; Cosmovision; Offerings; Reciprocity; Sacred Places

Trix, Frances, 164

Tuy, María del Carmen: on Ajq'ij, 62, 66, 68, 84; on the calendar, 141–142, 144, 148–149; on human capacity and calendar, 67, 75, 140, 151; on initiation, 76; Maya spirituality, 175; on number interpretation, 147–148

Twins. See Junajpu; Xb'alanke

Tyler, Stephen, 7

Tz'ite' (beans), 9, 13, 75–76, 79; consulting, 69

Tzolkin, 133, 181n4. See also Chol Q'ij

Unfinalizability, 79, 80

Uk'ux (heart, owner, nawal), 111

Utatlán: as political and religious center, 122; use of calendar, 138

Vail, Gabrielle, 135

Vara (ritual bundle), xiii, 76, 80, 98. See also Bundles, sacred

Villa Rojas, Alfonso, 181n8

Vogt, Evon Z., 109, 110, 179n18

Wajxaqib' B'atz, 76, 174, 175, 179n17

Walker, Deward E., 118, 180nn2,7

Wallace, Anthony F. C., 27

War, civil, 28–29, 31–32, 57, 59; Historical Clarification Commission (CEH), 31–32; massacre, 42; Nunca Mas, 31; widows, effect on, 53

Warren, Kay, 18, 27, 30

Watanabe, John, 17, 18, 27

Ways of knowing, 35, 40, 113, 155–156, 158–159, 162–165. See also Chol Q'ij; Discernment; Fire

Weil, Simone, 61

Wilson, Richard, 17, 18, 27

Women: as Aj'qijab', 20–21, 32, 69, 81, 179n10; Centro de la Mujer Belejeb' B'atz, 15; on clothing and identity, 48–49; interpretations of preparation, 81–82

World model: three dimensional, 110; tree or cross, 110

Worldview. See Cosmovision

Zapeta Galamez, Estuardo, 30

Zetina, Miguel A. Méndez Zetina, 109–110

Zunil, xi; *Ajqijab'* in, xi, 4, 20, 22–23, 38–39, 45, 50, 53–54, 70–71, 94, 113–114, 175; altars in, 113–114, 122–125; caves, 110, 113–114; center of village, 124–125; ceremony in, xi–xviii, 14, 53–54, 113, 122–123, 124, 174; *cortes* and day signs, 50, 51; faith interpreted, 45; quatrefoil mapping of altars in, 122–123, 125; on sacrifice in early twentieth century, 105–106. *See also Komon Tohil;* Poz Perez, Roberto

CPSIA information can be obtained
at www.ICGtesting.com
Printed in the USA
FSOW04n1332030417
32662FS